# PORSCHE 911

SINCE **1997**

First published in August 2008

A catalogue record for this book is available from the British Library

ISBN 978 1 84425 525 2

Library of Congress control no. 2008922592

Published by Haynes Publishing,
Sparkford, Yeovil, Somerset BA22 7JJ, UK.
Tel: 01963 442030 Fax: 01963 440001
Int. tel: +44 1963 442030
Int. fax: +44 1963 440001
E-mail: sales@haynes.co.uk
Website: www.haynes.co.uk

Haynes North America Inc., 861 Lawrence Drive,
Newbury Park, California 91320, USA

Design by Richard Parsons. Layout by Camway Creative Limited

Printed and bound in Britain by J. H. Haynes & Co. Ltd,
Sparkford, Yeovil, Somerset BA22 7JJ

# AUTOCAR
## COLLECTION
# PORSCHE 911
## SINCE **1997**

**Haynes Publishing**

# CONTENTS

*Autocar* Collection: Porsche 911 since 1997

The best words, photos and data from the world's oldest car magazine

# INTRODUCTION

**Chas Hallett**
Editor, *Autocar*

Porsche's remarkable 911, born in 1963 and greater now than ever, has a very special significance to *Autocar*, simply because, as the world's oldest motoring magazine, we've tested every single model going. Opinions vary about just how many separate versions that is – the answer seems to be well over two dozen, depending how you count – but there's no argument about the car's enduring desirability, or its unique position in the sports car firmament.

The car has been a rule-breaker all its life. Descended from the Porsche 356 (which itself was derived directly from the ubiquitous VW Beetle), the 911 was born in an era when quite a number of car designers thought it acceptable to mount a car's engine behind the rear axle, as a way of delivering vastly better cabin space. Without considerable development (and a certain amount of driver ability) this layout could lead to instability and disaster: even the early 911s earned a reputation for tail-happiness.

Indeed, in the mid-'70s one of Porsche's bosses even brought forward a plan to phase out the rear-engined 911 in favour of more conventional front-engined models like the 924 and 928. However, owner-power prevailed, and it was the conventional models that fell by the wayside, leaving the 911 to be honed, refined and sharpened. This book's unique collection of features and road tests tells the story of the water-cooled 911s with a from-the-coalface authenticity no history book can match. It underscores the courage of the 911's creators in retaining their unconventional approach, and celebrates their relentless pursuit of perfection.

This last quality – extreme robustness – is another property that distinguishes the Porsche 911 from the rest of the world's performance cars. Even 30-year-old models can be used day-to-day, don't have to cost the earth, and retain every shred of the desirability they were built with. Perhaps, one day, you'll buy your own Porsche 911. Sitting down with this book is a great way to start.

# FIRE STARTER

911 GTI This is the car Porsche built to blow the McLaren F1 away. At Le Mans this year it succeeded, emphatically. Steve Sutcliffe drives the car that has changed GT racing forever

Hockenheim is deserted when we arrive. Spooky quiet, like a ghost town, abandoned. Except for a lone transporter at the far end of the paddock, surfer-style graphics emblazoned on its enormous flanks, a huddle of people mulling around the back doors as it precariously gives birth to its exotic contents.

As the 911 emerges and is rolled silently into an allotted garage, a team of computer men appear from somewhere and begin firing up their equipment in the corner. Thierry Boutsen, the bloke responsible for much of this car's development, along today to show us what and what not to do with a 600bhp works racing Porsche, seems rather less concerned about the techno than he is about the track surface. "Eet's a little dusty today," he announces, nonchalantly, and then clambers aboard.

Even before it is ignited, numerous laptops and electronic gauges are plugged into the sides and ends of the GTI. Seconds later they are removed and, before anyone has had time fully to register the significance of the unfolding event, Boutsen has engaged first, dropped the clutch and, in a cacophony of whistles, whooshes and tell-tale gear whine, exited the pit lane in a hail of noisy drama.

Most folk would take it easy for a lap before nailing it on cold slicks on a parky morning with six times as much power as your average warm hatch spraying out through the rear wheels. Not Boutsen. We stand on the pit wall and listen, transfixed, as the GTI's 3.2-litre, water-cooled, twin-turbo flat six is run out to its 8900rpm maximum somewhere out of sight on the back half of the circuit. Between the wastegate chatters that punctuate the barks of acceleration, the exhaust note hardens and ricochets off Hockenheim's empty auditorium, cackles and cracks of exhaust gunfire telling us clearly when he's backing off or feathering. Which isn't often.

And then finally he reappears, a little shimmy of opposite lock through the right-hander that leads back on to the start-finish straight, an outside rear

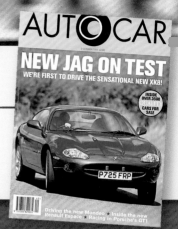

**ABOVE** The cockpit of the GTI bears no relation to the road car, although the driver's seat does slide on runners!

**OPPOSITE** The works GTIs stage a formation finish at Le Mans to beat the pursuing McLaren FIs. The works team almost won the race outright, but was narrowly beaten by the TWR Porsche WSC95 prototype; teamwork plays a big part at Le Mans. The car of Wendlinger/ Dalmas/Goodyear takes on fuel during a night-time pit stop.

Michelin momentarily thudding along the kerbing, like Schumacher on a qualifier.

It's only when the GTI blares right past our noses in fifth gear at 150mph, before shedding two gears in no more than a few feet, while simultaneously spitting flames a good five feet long, that we realise the full seriousness of the situation. Because today we are not just here to watch. Unless Boutsen does something completely out of character in the next few minutes, I'm up next. And believe me, this is well beyond anything I've previously been fortunate enough to drive.

The GTI is the million-dollar car Porsche has developed in order to regain its dominance of sports car racing. And, having already cleaned up in its class at Le Mans this year and blitzed both the other BPR rounds it has contested at Brands and Spa, it's clear this is no half-hearted effort. So much so that many have levelled criticism at Porsche for spoiling GT racing with this works-backed racing car.

The rules say that there must be a road car from which the race car is derived. Which means the paddock usually consists of cars such as the McLaren FI, Porsche 911, Lotus Esprit and Ferrari F40.

Porsche, however, sees it differently. It makes no bones about the GTI being a racing car first, not a road car. But, in order to stay within the rules, it has, like all the sharpest innovators, bent them to suit its requirements by also announcing that a road version will eventually be built and sold in just as big a number as the McLaren FI. Nothing in the rules, you see, says the road car needs to come first. All you have to do is prove that one exists – which Porsche already has – after which it matters not when the road car appears.

Next year Porsche will build 15 racing GTIs for private customers, then the road cars, after which GT racing won't be the same again. Which is either progress or an act outside the spirit of the rules, depending largely on your point of view.

Right now, I'm disinterested in any such bitching. As

## 'THE ENTIRE STRUCTURE VIBRATES AND FIZZES WHEN THE ENGINE EXPLODES INTO LIFE'

all race drivers do, Boutsen gives the engine one last wap of revs as he trundles back into the pits. Then he cuts it and rolls serenely to a halt beside me.

He climbs out and gestures for me to get in. Though my hands are shaking slightly, I make a fine job of looking composed. Until I walk forward and half trip on one of my boot laces, which, in the rush of anticipation, I've plain forgotten to do up.

All sorts of thoughts spiral through my mind as I walk towards the open door of the GT1. Apart from the fact that it looks more like something returned from a not entirely incident-free reccie over the Gulf than it does a racing car, I am also acutely aware of the privilege of the occasion. This is the first of only three 911 GT1s in existence, the car Stuck & co did all the endurance development work on at Paul Ricard. In years to come, it will become a legend, worth even more than the millions it is now.

I fumble the carbon fibre door and am astonished at how light it is. It feels as if I'm manipulating a chunk of air around via a handle; yet somehow it still feels brittle, strong, engineered. Totally Porsche.

Once ensconced in the deep bucket seat, which I'm equally puzzled to discover is on adjustable runners, just like the road car, I take a moment to drink in the cabin and its multitudinous switches, buttons, cooling ducts, gauges and levers.

The driving position isn't remotely like that of a regular 911's. Bare metal pedals are conventionally laid out and perfectly-positioned. And at the end of a complicated linkage that appears from behind my right elbow is a tall baton of carbon fibre, just inches away from the wheel rim.

I prod the brake pedal: rock hard. I dip the clutch and am startled to find it as light as an ordinary 911's. To at least look as if I know what I'm doing, I clack the gear lever around its precise gate: there are six in there somewhere, although today I doubt I'll go anywhere near the last two.

I ask Boutsen to talk me through the controls before I venture on to the circuit. But after a while he loses me. It's like being told traffic directions: you go hazy after the third T-junction. I take in that this car has ABS with two sensitivity settings, one for wet, one for dry. Even though it's dry I go for the wet setting. Just in case.

I prod the little red button on the surprisingly big, suede-rimmed Momo steering wheel and wait, tensed, for the flat six to erupt. Nothing happens. I press it again and realise I'm actually flicking through the menu on the Stack display. A man wearing a bright red

Porsche coat leans in, wiggles the gear lever to make sure it's in neutral, then twists a switch on the dash, right where a regular 911's key goes.

The entire structure vibrates and fizzes when the engine explodes into life and settles on a busy 3000rpm idle. I stab the throttle a couple of times. Instantly, the revs soar, the bar graph on the electronic tacho confirming the spontaneous reaction in a scatter of 500rpm chunks.

Given that this engine is turbocharged, I hadn't expected it to feel so immediate, so similar in sound and response to the Judd V8 of the F3000 car I drove a couple of years back. It has that same metallic, thrashy, mechanical quality to it that only full-blown racing engines seem to possess.

"Seven thousand," the man in the red jacket shouts into my helmet as he gives one final yank on my shoulder straps. "No more, not this morning." I give him a reassuring nod, snick the gear lever into first, dial in around 4500rpm and ease the clutch out.

Around two-thirds of the way up there is a solid, definitive biting point, so I give it a few more revs and away we go, rumbling down the pit lane without a stall in the bag.

The ride is rock hard and the front end bounces and thumps over the bumps at the end of the pit lane. As I turn the wheel to drive out on to the circuit for real, I can't believe how light the steering is. I weave around from side to side, not to do anything as pretentious as dial heat into the tyres, but to get used to the feel of the steering.

By the time I reach the first corner, a sharp right-hander, I'm already more than a little confused: the engine doesn't feel turbocharged at all, delivering great jolts of thrust the instant I open it up above 4000rpm. But it's the steering that really throws me: it seems too light in my inexperienced hands. The only way to detect a slide at the front, it seems, is via a change of scenery, which I find about as reassuring as a slap in the face.

## 'THE ACCELERATION IS SO SAVAGE THAT I'M ALMOST HYPNOTISED BY IT'

For a lap I just wander around, feeling out the brakes, seeing what happens when I stand on them (it stops so fast I almost stall), arranging the electric mirrors so I can see out of the back. Then, just before re-entering the view of my peers, I open it up. Properly. In second. And the force, even though I'm braced to accept a 600bhp per tonne wallop in the neck, is incredible.

At 3500rpm the rushes and whooshes of the twin KKK turbos start to dominate the engine's operations, acceleration already swelling at a fierce rate. At 4000rpm it is developing sufficient shove to make me think seriously about backing off. But it's from here to 7000rpm that the GT1 enters the twilight zone, an area of performance which, unless you're genuinely used to it, is frankly uncomfortable to begin with. The acceleration is so savage I'm almost hypnotised by it for a couple of seconds before realising I've gone way beyond the theoretical 7000rpm limit requested of me. In fourth gear. In this million-dollar car.

So, rather than get further carried away, inevitably towards the undergrowth, I try to calm down and take stock of this extraordinary vehicle. Leaning on it a little harder through the long right-hander after the pit straight in fourth at about 90mph, I begin to feel a little more confident about squeezing on the power early, feeling the 14in wide slicks chew into the tarmac, dipping into the incredible cornering forces that this monster so effortlessly generates. This is like no road or racing car I've ever experienced: it's delicately balanced, but at the same time brutally planted to the ground, pushed into the floor by some immense, unseen hand.

In the end, the bouncing front end and the lightness of the steering, let alone the fact that it has more performance than any other car I've driven, conspire to intimidate me too deeply. I can't bring myself to throw it around as I might a regular 911. I'm glad to bring it and myself back to the pits in one piece after six laps, to be honest.

I'm over four seconds slower than Boutsen, who doesn't mind the bouncing – "You learn to drive through it". He agrees that the steering weight isn't great to begin with, but points out that it is a joy after 24 hours. Yet I'm unusually unconcerned about being so slow in comparison. I knew in my heart this would be primarily a privilege and that ultimately I wouldn't be able to get near this car.

Right now, I kind of know how the rest of the BPR GT grid is feeling.

**ABOVE** Boutsen behind the wheel at Le Mans, where he finished second sharing the car with team-mates Hans Stuck and Bob Wollek.

**OPPOSITE** Essentially a 911 front end mated to a Group C Porsche 962 rear end, the GT1 is the million-dollar car Porsche built to re-establish itself at the top of GT racing. Is it against the spirit of the rules? Porsche says nice guys never win.

# DEFENDER OF THE FAITH

**911 CARRERA** Porsche's all-new 911 replacement has a daunting task: to match the unique appeal of its predecessor. But drive it and all doubts will be laid to rest, says Peter Robinson

Doubts surge as Porsche's new Carrera pulls up outside our hotel on the old Solitude GP circuit. It's my first chance to see it undisguised and I'm shocked. Dismayed, even.

In profile it looks stretched – pulled at both ends to exaggerate the overhangs and lengthened in the centre section of the body. It is still unmistakably a 911, but the new Carrera is also noticeably bigger. The tautly compact proportions of the old car have been replaced by a shape that, for all its smooth-flanked modernity, looks somehow different, somehow wrong.

But spare a thought for Porsche: the challenge and opportunity of the first clean-sheet redesign of motoring's great icon in 34 years, without the stylists being trapped into a retro look. And yet, from deep inside the Weissach design centre, the compulsion to retain that classic shape while incorporating contemporary crash protection, increased interior space, better aerodynamics, greater performance and superior handling.

Even so, after taking in the exterior with its Boxster nose and headlights, the high, slightly bloated rear bumper and flat rear fenders, and the kicked-in look of the lower door area, it's only when you sit in the car that the transformation really hits home. In effect, Porsche has jumped three generations of interior. The design reach from 1963 to 1997 has been taken in one vast leap. It's as if Ferrari had gone directly from the 250GT to the 550 Maranello.

The first thing you notice is that while the doors close easily, they don't think with the solidity of the old car. Shared with the Boxster, they have frameless

windows which are automatically lowered 20mm or so when a door is opened or closed, and no quarter vent windows for added strength.

To the obvious benefit of roadholding and handling, the new body shell is 45 per cent stiffer in torsional rigidity and 50 per cent stronger in static bending. But you certainly wouldn't know it from the sound of the closing doors.

It's the perception of greater space in the new car's cockpit that brings home how old-fashioned the 911 had become. Compared to the 993, the new 996 Carrera is, well, normal. No longer does the fuel tank infringe into the passenger footwell, you don't rub shoulders with the passenger, and the windscreen (now sloped at 60deg versus 55deg) isn't at your nose. But look around and many traditional 911 cues linger: the rounded headlining, the gentle downward slope of the side windows, the tiny, individual fold-down rear child seats, the tacho dominating the instruments and the ignition on the dash between, steering column and door.

But on the whole, change abounds. The fuel filler is on the right and unlocks via the central locking and not a specific latch on the dash, the seatbelts get height adjustment, door airbags are optional for the first time and flimsy, removable cupholders slot into holes on the air vents. They look like an afterthought, but it's a neat trick to keep the drink cool or hot. Five large circular dials have been reduced in size (though the count remains) so that all can be read through the steering wheel. Essentially, it's pure Boxster with small half-circular dials for volts and oil pressure tacked on either side, plus a more conventional typeface for the dials, and the hood above the instruments enclosed.

The centre console is identical to the Boxster, with the same shiny black push-button controls and disappointingly cheap plastic surrounds for the outer air vents. And there's no glovebox – just pockets in the doors, a console bin and tray below the sound system.

You sit high – higher than expected, though the

## QUICK FACTS

| Model | 911 Carrera |
|---|---|
| Price | £62,795 (est) |
| 0–62mph | 5.1sec |
| Top speed | 174mph |
| Economy | 28.0mpg |

# FEATURE

## 10 SEPTEMBER 1997

Volume 213

No 10 | 5246

AUTOCAR

FIRST 27 FOR NEW CARS

30 EXTRA PAGES

Porsche's New 911

New V8 Jaguar

Now it's for real!

New Mini

Exclusive photos of the baby the world's been waiting for

**ABOVE** New Carrera endowed with superbly cohesive steering and handling. Sensational grip or a beautifully balanced oversteer slide? The choice is all yours.

(optional) electrically height-adjustable seats on our pre-production car prevented the cushion moving through its full range. For the first time on a 911, the steering wheel is also adjustable, even if it is only for reach. But the driving position is still brilliant, the tall buckets supportive, the pendant pedals perfectly in line with the wheel.

Now comes the real moment of truth, the event: firing up the water-cooled flat six to discover if the new 911 sounds like the old car and if the driving experience remains so utterly, wonderfully, distinctive. My heart is beating a little faster. I don't want to be disappointed.

And then I breathe easy. Despite harsh new sound regulations, the new Carrera still sounds like a Porsche. True, it's quieter and more subdued, and it doesn't have the raw-edged wail of the old air-cooled powerplant, but there is a velvety growl that swells to a spine-tingling yowl as the engine rushes from 5000rpm to the 7300rpm red line, 500rpm beyond the point where the old one had run out of breath. The Carrera powerplant doesn't have the two contrived vocal peaks of the Boxster; this engine is more serious, as befits a 300bhp, 3.4-litre quad-cam six.

In its basic configuration, the new Carrera engine owes only the 118mm bore centres to the air-cooled unit and is closely related to the 2.5-litre Boxster. But both bore and stroke are increased to take the capacity out to 3387cc, so it's 213cc smaller than the old 911 but develops more power.

Despite four valves per cylinder, four chain-driven overhead camshafts, and a variable induction system that provides three intake manifolds on each of the two cylinder heads and Porsche's Variocam variable intake valve timing, the new engine is 70mm shorter and 120mm lower than the old.

The block is pressure-cast alloy and uses what Porsche engineers call integrated dry-sump lubrication, with the oil sump separate from the crank chamber. Two water radiators are, like the Boxster, located under the front wings, though the now five-speed automatic also gets a third middle radiator to cool the transmission fluid. Service intervals have been extended to 12,000 miles or once a year.

The engine pumps out 300bhp at 6800rpm – 88bhp per litre – and 258lb ft of torque at 4700rpm. Porsche says 221lb ft is on tap from 2700rpm to 7000rpm. It's a marvellous engine, incredibly smooth and more refined than the old yet still sporting, always invigorating and alive with stronger mid-range power than the Boxster; there's not the same need to keep the crank spinning above 4000rpm. In fact, the Carrera pulls from as low as 2000rpm and never lets up, delivering a mighty, linear urge until it hits the soft electronic limiter at 7300rpm.

Thanks to a weight reduction of 50kg to 1320kg (70kg above the Boxster) and the extra grunt, Porsche claims zero to 60mph in 5.1sec, 0.3sec quicker than the old car.

Because refinement levels – not just of the engine but also suspension, tyre and wind noise – are so high, the new Carrera doesn't feel that quick. Where the Boxster always seems slightly quicker than it really is, the Carrera is awesome in its ability to accelerate to 125mph plus and stay there. We saw 165mph on one short stretch of autobahn, the 911 accelerating strongly after a snap change to sixth at just over 150mph.

The new car's stability above 125mph is vastly better than even the previous 911. The engine hood spoiler rises automatically at 75mph (25mph later than the old car) and goes down at 37mph. Porsche says lift forces have been reduced to 0.08 on the front axle and 0.05 on the rear, the difference front to rear helping stability at very high speeds.

Reducing the drag coefficient from 0.34 to 0.30 also plays a part and is one reason Porsche has been able to get away with a comparatively small 64-litre fuel tank, eight litres below the old car. The engineers claim a longer touring range because fuel consumption has been reduced by 10 per cent.

With a ride quality that transcends the ultra-low-profile tyres and firm suspension in its ability to absorb minor bumps that irritated the old car, combined with staggering agility and handling, the 911 quite simply sets a new benchmark.

At first, the refinement and spaciousness of the interior lull the driver into believing the new Carrera is more of an old-fashioned grand tourer than a sports car, for it fulfils this role to perfection. Unless you simply must have four seats, Porsche has answered the challenge of the BMW M5 and Mercedes E50 and replaced the 928 as a businessman's express for long-haul trans-European journeys.

The suspension is largely derived from the Boxster, with MacPherson struts up front and separate tie-rods and longitudinal track arms connected elastically, rather than as a rigid triangle, to allow the front wheels to respond more sensitively to small bumps. The front suspension subframe is made of aluminium alloy.

## HOW IT COMPARES

| Model | 996 | 993 | Boxster |
|---|---|---|---|
| Length (mm) | 4430 | 4245 | 4315 |
| Width (mm) | 1765 | 1735 | 1780 |
| Height (mm) | 1305 | 1300 | 1290 |
| Wheelbase (mm) | 2350 | 2270 | 2415 |
| Weight (kg) | 1320 | 1370 | 1250 |
| Distribution % | 39/61 | 37/63 | 48/52 |
| Fuel tank (litres) | 64 | 72 | 57 |
| Drag coefficient | 0.30 | 0.34 | 0.31 |
| Bhp/rpm | 300/6800 | 286/6100 | 204/6000 |
| 0–60mph (sec) | 5.1 | 5.3 | 6.7 |
| Top speed (mph) | 174 | 171 | 149 |

Steering is by a power-assisted rack and pinion system. With 3.0 turns lock to lock (the same as the Boxster), it seems lower geared than the old 911's 2.5 turns. In fact, the turning circle has been reduced by 1.1m to 10.9m, so the steering is actually even more direct.

At the rear, a combination of strut/damper units and double wishbones – mounted on cast alloy subframes that mean tyre noise isn't fed directly

**BELOW** Steering wheel adjustable, but only for reach; ignition on dash between steering column and door in traditional 911 fashion; cupholders attach to vents.

**ABOVE** The first complete redesign of one of motoring's great icons; longer, wider and now sporting smooth flanks, the new Carrera is still recognisably a 911.

Standard tyre size is now one inch bigger, with 205/50 ZR17s at the front and 255/40 ZR17s at the rear. But the 911 always looks better on bigger wheels and our test car came on the optional 225/40 ZR18 and 265/35 ZR18 rubber. Porsche being Porsche, there is also an optional sports suspension pack that brings the 18in alloys as standard, along with traction control, sports seats, harder springs and dampers, thicker anti-roll bars and a 10mm reduction in ride height.

I'd come to the conclusion that the Carrera was now a civilised coupé. I adjusted the automatic air conditioning and wondered when the navigational system – an integral part of Porsche's "communication management" pack that includes an on-board computer, mobile phone and audio system with CD changer – would go into production (early next year is the latest estimate). But then snapper Papior decided it was time to search out some twisty roads for cornering shots.

through to the cabin – support and tame any problems with the rear-mounted engine upsetting the handling balance.

Porsche brakes set the standard, which is hardly surprising when Weissach's standard test involves braking 25 times from 90 per cent of maximum speed (or 155mph) down to 60mph without inducing fade. To achieve this, Porsche fits huge ventilated discs with four-piston, one-piece alloy calipers of the type tested on race tracks in the 911 GTI and 962C. In pedal response and stopping power, nothing short of carbon brakes approach their sheer stopping ability. They also come with the Bosch ABS 5.3 anti-lock system.

Traction control turned off, I was about discover how successful Porsche had been in retaining the 911's intimacy of handling. An hour later I was convinced that the only other car that approaches this level of effortless balance and cohesion is Ferrari's 550 Maranello. Sensational grip and virtually unlimited traction are matched by steering that's close to perfect in its meaty feel, the way it weights up a touch as lateral forces rise and the agility of its turn-in, yet it isn't so sensitive that it demands constant concentration at autobahn speeds. There's no more than a hint of the traditional 911 jiggle, while the tighter

## THE 911 THAT NEVER WAS

In 1991 Porsche was planning a different future, based around the front-engined, rear-drive 989. The first four-door Porsche, it was powered by a new 4.5-litre V8 which was also intended for the 911 replacement.

Under Ulrich Bez (now charged with a new generation of Daewoo models), then head of R&D at Weissach, Porsche had already begun testing the new engine.

But in February 1992, after Bez was fired, Porsche dropped the plan for the ultra-expensive 989 and Weissach changed direction.

"The new 911 became the basis for our programme, with the Boxster as a subsidiary," says Horst Marchart, who replaced Bez.

The Boxster would reach the market first, but the two models would be developed simultaneously by the same team of people, under Bernd Kahnau, who'd previously been in charge of the 993.

Porsche planned to kill off the 968 and 928 during the four-year life of the 993, leaving a massive range of 911 models to

carry the marque until the arrival of the Boxster and, a year later, the new 996.

Marchart admits Porsche needed to sell 15,000 911s a year to survive. Remarkably, it sold 20,765 of the rear-engined classics in 1996, the 911's best sales year ever. Marchart says: "I don't believe we would have been successful with a 911 developed from the 989."

But he would say that, wouldn't he? Nevertheless, Weissach insiders admit the relationship between 989 and 911 was difficult, a sensible level of parts commonality difficult to achieve. Not so with the Boxster and 996, which share an amazing 36 per cent of their components.

Marchart admits Porsche looked at a mid-engined 911, but rejected it because "a two-plus-two, mid-engined 911 would have been another car". Much longer, even, than the 996, which has already grown 185mm in length over the 993.

turning circle brings immediate benefits in creating a perception of nimble responsiveness, despite the extra 30mm in width, 170mm in length and 80mm in wheelbase (but still 65mm shorter than the Boxster).

Working with wheel and throttle, you can place the Carrera exactly as you like. The handling and steering responses are more progressive, perfectly linear. You can hold the car in a neutral stance, feeding in enough power to delicately change its attitude inch by inch, if that is what's required to clip an apex. On the other hand, drop down a gear or two through the decisive yet fluid gearchange and it's easy to power out of a corner in a mild, predictable oversteer slide that demands no more than a rolling of the wrists. Yes, it's more fun than the old car, more satisfying and more consistent in its behaviour, despite the 61 per cent rear weight bias. It's still a true sports car.

The point is, don't pass judgement on the new 911 until you've spent varied time at the wheel, alone on a twisty road and blasting down a motorway. Only then will you grasp the extent of Porsche's achievement.

At the end of one momentous day, I stood staring at 911s old and new, and understood. All doubts were dismissed. The old 911 was great – a desirable, evocative car. But respected, loved and admired though it is, suddenly it looked and felt antiquated. And I knew the new 911 was superior in virtually every way, even how it looks, a brilliant replacement capable of playing sports car and grand tourer at a level matched only by the 550 – and that car is more than twice the price.

# SPECIFICATIONS 911 CARRERA

## DIMENSIONS

| | |
|---|---|
| Length | 4430mm |
| Width | 1765mm |
| Height | 1305mm |
| Wheelbase | 2350mm |
| Weight | 1320kg |
| Fuel Tank | 64 litres |

## ENGINE

| | |
|---|---|
| Layout | 6-cyl horizontally opposed, water cooled, 3387cc |
| Max power | 300bhp at 6800rpm |
| Specific output | 88bhp per litre |
| Power to weight | 227bhp per tonne |
| Installation | Rear, longitudinal, rwd |
| Construction | Alloy head and block |
| Valve gear | 4 valves per cyl, dohc |
| Management | DME |
| Bore/stroke | 96/78mm |
| Compression ratio | 11.3:1 |

## STEERING

**Type** Rack and pinion, power assisted
**Turns lock-to-lock** 3.0

## GEARBOX

**Type** 6-speed manual
**Ratios**/mph per 1000rpm

| | |
|---|---|
| **1st** 3.82/5.6 | **2nd** 2.20/9.8 |
| **3rd** 1.52/14.2 | **4th** 1.22/17.5 |
| **5th** 1.02/21.0 | **6th** 0.84/25.7 |

**Final drive** 3.44:1

## SUSPENSION

**Front** MacPherson struts, lower control arms, coils, anti-roll bar
**Rear** Independent, multi-link, coil springs, anti-roll bar

## BRAKES

**Front** 318mm ventilated discs
**Rear** 299mm ventilated discs
**ABS** Standard

## WHEELS AND TYRES

**Size** 7Jx17in (f), 9Jx17in (r)
**Tyres** 225/50 ZR17(f), 255/40 ZR17 (r)

## **AUTOCAR** VERDICT

Equally accomplished in sports car or GT roles, the new Carrera betters its legendary predecessor in every respect

Carrera successfully retains handling intimacy of old 911 but gains 928 levels of trans-European cruising ability; ride and high-speed stability first rate.

# PORSCHE 911

A s motoring legends go, the Porsche 911 is surely the grandaddy of them all. It has been around for more than 30 years now, yet still it sits at the sharp end of sports car evolution. It is, some might say, the car that refuses to die.

But that's not Porsche's fault. In the late '70s, Weissach produced the 928 – as a replacement for the 911. But the customers thought otherwise, and since then the 911 has easily outlasted its supposed successor. And now here we have yet another all-new incarnation.

This time, though, there's been a big change to the 911 menu. The biggest ever, truth be told. The body is longer, taller and roomier than before, while the flat six engine is now water-cooled, just like the Boxster's. The chassis and suspension design also owes a lot to the Boxster.

That the new 911 shares so many components with its cheaper cousin should not be scorned, however. It is probably the only reason it still exists. Without such commonality, Porsche might not have made it through the past decade. So the question is this: has the 911's individuality been compromised? Read on.

## QUICK FACTS

| | |
|---|---|
| **Model tested** | 911 Carrera |
| **Price** | £65,000 (est) |
| **Top speed** | 173mph |
| **30–70mph** | 3.8sec |
| **0–60mph** | 4.6sec |
| **60–0mph** | 2.7sec |
| **Economy** | 19.7mpg |
| **For** | Performance, stable handling, gearchange, quality |
| **Against** | Less character than old 911 |

### DESIGN & ENGINEERING ★★★
**Thoughtful redesign, first-rate engineering**

It's 34 years since the world first clapped eyes on a Porsche 911. Since then endless variations of the original concept have been and gone, but this is the first time Porsche has redesigned the car from the ground up.

Known internally as the 996, the new car is considerably larger than before, to allow for increased crash protection and a more spacious cockpit. The wheelbase has grown by 80mm, the overall length by 185mm and the width by 30mm.

The new body/chassis, hot galvanised, as all 911s have been for 20 years, is a practical demonstration of how various types of steel properly used can make a relatively light yet strong monocoque, here 45 per cent stiffer torsionally yet overall 50kg less heavy.

Aerodynamics have taken an equally useful leap forward. The drag coefficient has been lowered from 0.33 to 0.30, thanks to the smooth new body shape, flush-fitting glass, Bolster style headlights and a windscreen that has been raked back from 55deg to 60deg.

The most significant changes have been saved for the engine. It's still a naturally aspirated flat six design, mounted longitudinally behind the rear axle to a six-speed manual (or five-speed Tiptronic) gearbox; but there the similarities end. The 911's beloved air-cooling has been dropped in favour of water-cooling, with twin radiators mounted under the front wings. This more efficient process enables Porsche to fit a four valve-per cylinder head with twin camshafts per bank, which squeezes 14bhp more power and 6lb ft more torque from a smaller internal and external capacity. The new aluminium alloy cased engine is 70mm shorter and 120mm lower than before, with a swept volume of 3387cc rather than 3600cc. Yet it develops 296bhp at 6800rpm and 258lb ft at 4600rpm.

Porsche's Variocam valve timing and adjustable

# ROAD TEST

## 1 OCTOBER 1997

Volume 213

No 13 | 5249

**ABOVE** New 911 is longer, wider and roomier than ever.

**BELOW** Better driving position than its forebear, thanks to proper pedals.

volume inlet manifold mean the torque never drops below 221lb ft between 2700rpm and 7000rpm, while an ingenious dry sump lubrication system (with no external hoses) keeps the vital engine bearings well-oiled, even when the car is braking or cornering as hard as possible.

Like the Boxster engine, the die cast alloy cylinder blocks use the Kolbenschmidt "Lokasil" system to provide high silicon-aluminium alloy for the cylinder bore surfaces (for long life), leaving the rest of the casting in a conventional medium silicon alloy for easy machining. The main bearings are reinforced with an aluminium bearing bridge with cast-in steel bridge inserts, and each plug has its own sparking coil for extended 12,000-mile service intervals.

Suspension and sub-frames are mostly in aluminium alloy, with the same basic geometric layout as before: struts up front, five-link wishbones behind. The front suspension is designed to toe-out slightly at higher cornering rates, the rear to toe-in, in what Porsche calls an attempt to make the cars handling more forgiving. Big vented disc brakes at each wheel with four piston alloy calipers and Bosch anti-lock are responsible for keeping all that power in check.

The cabin inherits many of the Boxster's characteristics and goes some way to explaining the 36 per cent parts commonality between the two cars. At least Porsche has preserved some features, such as the circular dials and dash-mounted ignition.

## PERFORMANCE/BRAKES ★★★★★
**Fantastic performance and peerless brakes**

Anyone worried about a water-cooled 911 not having sufficient performance or character compared with the old air-cooled 3.6-litre model can bin their concerns right now. From the moment you twist the key (still mounted up on the dash to the left of the steering wheel) and that familiar whirring sound erupts from behind the shoulders, you realise that the new 3387cc flat six will do just fine in this car. Especially since it stirs up some 296bhp at 6800rpm and 251lb ft at 4700rpm, both up on before.

Yet it is not until this is taken in conjunction with the new car's 50kg lighter kerb weight that the full significance of these numbers starts to dawn. The critical statistics are the power and torque to weight ratios of 224bhp/190lb ft per tonne. The former is not as great as the Ferrari F355's, but the latter is bigger. Add this to the super-slippery new body, and you begin to understand the potential behind the latest 911.

Except that nothing can prepare you fully for the numbers that start falling out of the timing gear when the 911 squats a little, chirrups its rear tyres momentarily and then rockets up the road on a full-bore acceleration run.

To 30mph it is untouchable by any two-wheel-drive car in our experience, recording a kidney-squeezing 1.8sec. But it's the way the 911 continues to pile on the giant-felling acceleration beyond three figures that is truly astonishing.

The bald figures read 60mph in 4.6sec, 100mph in 10.5sec and a standing quarter mile of 13.0sec dead at 112mph. On its way, it gets from the urban to the legal limit in 3.8sec. And, if you can find the space and correct surroundings in which to keep your foot planted, not until a genuine 173mph registers on the clock will the new 911 actually cease accelerating. Up to 100mph it is inseparable from the Ferrari, after which it actually edges away a little between 110-160mph, only to be overhauled by the Italian thereafter (the 173mph we recorded on the F355 was taken on the banking at Millbrook, not on the autobahn where we tested the Porsche: this accounts for perhaps 5-6mph at that speed).

Unsurprisingly, considering there's not a turbocharger in sight, and that it uses a close-ratio six-speed gearbox in which even top stretches only 25.7mph out of every 1000rpm, throttle response is as sharp as it is wonderful in the new car. And as with all previous 911s, flexibility is towering. You can

# ROAD TEST 911 CARRERA

## ACCELERATION FROM REST

| True mph | seconds | speedo mph |
|---|---|---|
| 30 | 1.8 | 31 |
| 40 | 2.5 | 41 |
| 50 | 3.5 | 51 |
| 60 | 4.6 | 61 |
| 70 | 5.6 | 71 |
| 80 | 7.2 | 81 |
| 90 | 8.6 | 92 |
| 100 | 10.5 | 102 |
| 110 | 12.6 | 112 |
| 120 | 14.7 | 123 |
| 130 | 17.4 | 133 |
| 140 | 20.9 | 143 |
| 150 | 25.2 | 153 |

Standing qtr mile 13.0sec/112mph
Standing km 22.8sec/145mph
30–70mph through gears 3.8sec

## ACCELERATION IN GEAR

| MPH | 6th | 5th | 4th | 3rd | 2nd |
|---|---|---|---|---|---|
| 20–40 | - | 6.0 | 4.3 | 3.4 | 2.2 |
| 30–50 | 7.2 | 5.4 | 4.1 | 3.3 | 2.0 |
| 40–60 | 7.1 | 5.4 | 4.0 | 3.1 | 1.9 |
| 50–70 | 7.1 | 5.4 | 3.9 | 2.8 | 2.0 |
| 60–80 | 7.4 | 5.3 | 3.8 | 2.8 | - |
| 70–90 | 7.4 | 5.3 | 3.7 | 2.9 | - |
| 80–100 | 7.4 | 5.0 | 3.5 | 3.1 | - |
| 90–110 | 7.5 | 5.0 | 3.7 | - | - |
| 100–120 | 7.6 | 5.0 | 3.7 | - | - |
| 110–130 | 8.0 | 5.3 | 5.8 | - | - |
| 120–140 | 9.1 | 6.0 | - | - | - |

## MAXIMUM SPEEDS

| | | | |
|---|---|---|---|
| 6th | 173mph/9800rpm | 5th | 153/7300 |
| 4th | 128/7300 | 3rd | 104/7300 |
| 2nd | 72/7300 | 1st | 41/7300 |

## FUEL CONSUMPTION

Average/best/worst/touring
19.7/24.8/24.8/15.1mpg

| | |
|---|---|
| Urban | 19.0mpg |
| Extra urban | 23.0mpg |
| Combined | 28.0mpg |
| Tank capacity | 64 litres |
| Touring range | 349 miles |

## BRAKES

| | |
|---|---|
| 30/50/70mph | 9.6/25.7/48.6 metres |
| 60–0mph | 2.7sec |

## NOISE

Idle/max revs in 3rd 50/79dbA
30/50/70mph 61/68/72dbA

## TEST NOTES

Car you see photographed wears the big 18in wheels with 225/40 front tyres and 265/35 rears. Standard UK cars will come on 17in rims wearing 205/50s up front and 255/40 at the back.

At the 7500rpm red line in third gear the 911 produces no more noise than a Ford Ka does at 5500rpm in third.

# SPECIFICATIONS 911 CARRERA

## DIMENSIONS

Min/max front legroom 830/1090mm  Min/max front headroom 940/970mm
Min/max rear legroom 465/700mm  Interior width front/rear 340/1260mm
Boot length 420mm  Boot width/height 740/520mm  Boot volume 130litres/dm³
Front/rear tracks 1455/1500mm  Kerb weight 1320kg  Width with mirrors 1950mm

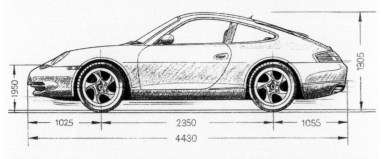

1950

1305

1025    2350    1055
4430

## ENGINE

| | |
|---|---|
| Layout | 6-cyl horizontally opposed, water cooled, 3387cc |
| Max power | 296bhp at 6800rpm |
| Max torque | 251lb ft at 4600rpm |
| Specific output | 87bhp per litre |
| Power to weight | 224bhp per tonne |
| Torque to weight | 190lb ft per tonne |
| Installation | Rear, longitudinal, rear-wheel drive |
| Construction | Alloy head and block |
| Bore/stroke | 96/78mm |
| Valve gear | 4 valves per cyl, dohc |
| Compression ratio | 10.4:1 |
| Ignition and fuel | DME engine management system intercooler |

## CHASSIS AND BODY

| | |
|---|---|
| Body | 2dr coupé, Cd 0.30 |
| Wheels | 7Jx17in (f), 9Jx17in (r) |
| Made of | Cast alloy |
| Tyres | 225/50 (f), 255/40 ZR17 (r), (optional 18in wheels and tyres fitted to test car) |
| Spare | Space saver |

## TRANSMISSION

Gearbox 6-speed manual
Ratios/mph per 1000rpm
Final drive ratio 3.95:1

| | | | |
|---|---|---|---|
| 1st | 3.82/5.6 | 2nd | 2.20/9.8 |
| 3rd | 1.52/14.2 | 4th | 1.22/17.5 |
| 5th | 1.02/21.0 | 6th | 0.84/25.7 |

## STEERING

Type Rack and pinion, power assisted
Turns lock-to-lock 3.0
Turning circle 10.6m

## SUSPENSION

Front MacPherson struts, lower control arms, coils, anti-roll bar
Rear Independent, multi-link, coils, anti-roll bar

## BRAKES

Front 318mm ventilated discs
Rear 299mm discs
Anti-lock Standard

still pull the familiar floor-it-in-top-from-800rpm trick on anyone not used to 911s and it will oblige with not even the slightest hesitation in pick up, but the real meat is delivered from 2800rpm onwards. Acceleration is served up in one long, seamless rush from here on, terminating at a 7500rpm limiter that is set purely for engine longevity, not because it has started to go off the boil by then. All in all we are talking about one of the seminal powerplants of the decade here.

You'd be hard pushed to find much fault with the new brakes, either. Porsche's always stop beautifully but this one's the best yet. Enough said.

### HANDLING & RIDE ★★★★
**More competent, not as engaging as old 911**

There is good news and bad news here. The good news is that the 996 has the most predictable handling of any 911. It is also the most effective when it comes to putting huge chunks of ground beneath its wheels in as short a time possible, and with the minimum of drama. The extra stability and body control of the new Boxster-based chassis is not to be underestimated when it comes to dispensing with difficult obstacles tackled at speed, and is way above anything the old car had to offer.

The bad news is that rather too much of the character that has distinguished the 911 as such a sharp driver's car over the years has been diluted in the process.

The steering is the most obvious culprit. Although still extremely precise and accurate on lock, it is not as richly communicative as before, offering no more than satisfactory information about the road below. Nor is it as incisive or positive as we've been used to over those first few critical degrees off-centre when turning in to corners.

Porsche knows this, naturally, and the upshot is that the 911 feels markedly more stable on the motorway than before, not to mention less tiring on any given journey, purely because the involvement factor is that much lower. At the same time, it is impossible not to lament the passing of one of the great sports car helms, even though this deliberate dulling of one of the car's most vital organs is, in many ways, a logical step in the late '90s.

Especially when you consider that, in every objective handling assessment, it is a significantly

**Cup holders that double up as air vents.**

**Big rev counter remains the dominant sight from behind the new adjustable, airbag-equipped wheel.**

**Six-speed box is light, precise, similar in feel to the Boxster's.**

superior product. According to Porsche, it is over six seconds quicker around the Nurburgring than the old car. Much of this is because the tighter rear suspension control and superior grip now on offer. It's now on Nissan Skyline terms on sheer cross-country speed.

And what makes you accept the realisation that some of the character, the feel, of the old car has been lost in achieving this extra speed and security acceptable, is that the ride is now barely recognisable compared with before. Apart from the way it smacks into deep potholes (which faze it), there is a genuine air of sophistication to this car's ride. It also generates less road noise, always a 911 weakness.

### ECONOMY ★★★
**Good for a supercar, only reasonable for a 911**

Porsche is so confident of the latest 911's economy that it felt comfortable fitting a smaller fuel tank. It claims that the range has actually increased over the previous model.

But that's not exactly how it worked out in our experience. Admittedly we drove the test car harder than usual for much of the time, but still

we couldn't get more than 24.8mpg out of it on a gentle run, which is almost exactly the same as before. Overall it returned 19.7mpg slightly worse than the 3.6 Carrera managed. That gives the new car a range of about 290 miles in the real world.

**ABOVE** Placement of controls and switches is near-perfect.

**BELOW** New 911 most comfortable version yet.

ABOVE No longer
a sports car, new 911
is now a devastatingly
effective GT.

OPPOSITE Headlight
design is just part of
commonality between
911/Boxster.

### COMFORT EQUIPMENT & SAFETY ★★★
**Tidier cabin than before, still tiny in the back**

Porsche Cars GB Ltd has yet to decide upon a
final specification for the new car, but if it all goes
to plan 911s will be better equipped than ever
before where they go on sale after the London
Motor Show. Which means the real world price will
effectively remain unchanged compared with the
outgoing model.

Although there will appear to have been a price
hike of roughly £3900 over the current model, this will
not be so once the new car's specification is taken into
account: the latest car may well come with items such
as air conditioning, leathe trim, cruise control and a top
line CD stereo as standard.

That's one way to ensure the new 911 is the
most comfortabl version yet. The other is to
stretch the interior dimensions and polish up the
refinement by cutting down on overall noise levels,
both of which Porsche has also achieved.

Trouble is, though the rear passenger
compartment is bigger according to the tape
measure, on no account is it a place in which a
normal size adult will feel comfortable. Head, leg
and hip room are still very tight, even by 2+2

standards, so inevitably you end up using the rear
seats as a supplementary stowage area to the
reasonably well sized under-bonnet boot. At least
Porsche admits as much, otherwise the seat backs
wouldn't still fold flat so that they act as a decent
load shelf.

That the 911 is significantly quieter than before
can be viewed in two ways. Porsche says some
customers have been put off the current car
because it is too loud, but if by broadening the
appeal of the model you also dilute a vital part of
its character, then, in our book, something is not
entirely correct. As far as damping out wind noise
and suspension rumble is concerned, such silencing
of the 911 is welcome, but the engine note too
has become disappointingly muted. It is now
quieter than the Boxster, for example, although
Porsche does admit that this is partly due to the
911's different manifolds which fail to unleash the
wondrous bark of the Boxster's flat six just
before 6000rpm.

On the other hand, Porsche has executed
a quite exquisite job on the new car's cabin,
maintaining the basic 911 personality but at the
same time cleaning up many of the ergonomic hot
spots. The pedals are now proper non floor-hinged

items and are all the better for it. And, despite the more steeply raked windscreen, the view forwards is (almost) as clean and as panoramic as ever. The basic driving position is also now beyond serious criticism with a wheel and seats that adjust in multiple planes, as well as near-perfect placement of the controls and switches

Safety is the other area on which Porsche has concentrated hard. Not only will there will be driver and passenger airbags as standard, but side bags will also almost certainly be included in the basic price. Equally, this is the first 911 with traction control, although there remains some debate as to whether this will be standard on UK cars.

## MARKET & FINANCE ★★★★★
### A better investment than the stockmarket

Cash-strapped 911 fans should be rubbing their hands at the arrival of this new model. Nothing to do with the new car itself, more the effect it is likely to have on the prices of late-plate, outgoing 911s. If our price predictions are correct, the new car will cost little more than the old model and so be much better value. This should put the prices of old, late-plate models under pressure. Once used new-shape 911s come through – don't hold your breath, Porsche plans to sell just 750 between now and next August – old model 911s should get a little cheaper still. No such luck with the new car, however. Thanks to keen pricing, wider appeal, the scarcity factor and a sky-high image, we predict that the new 911's used values will be on the ceiling for many years to come.

Not so the new car's running costs. Porsche says that, thanks to new on-board electronics, service times for the new car have been reduced with intervals extended to 12,000 miles. A comparison of workshop rates for the old 911 and the new Boxster, on which the new 911 is based, gives a flavour of what's in store. Swindon Porsche dealer Dick Lovett quotes £438 (it takes 4.6 hours) for the old 911's 12,000-mile service, £694 for the 24,000-mile and £438 for the 36,000-mile service. Meanwhile, for the Boxster it quotes £188 for the 12,000-mile service (it takes just 1.5 hours), £380 for the 24,000 and £188 for the 36,000-mile service.

Savings here will help fund a punishing insurance bill. For a 40-year-old company director with one speeding conviction and full no claims living in Surrey, specialist brokers Bennetts Elite quotes a stiff £740 with a £500 excess.

## AUTOCAR VERDICT

So the Porsche 911 continues to live and breathe. And how. At the beginning of the decade Porsche was in such a state that the future of this most endearing of motor cars was seriously in doubt. There was talk of a proper four-seater that would replace the ageing and increasingly anachronistic 911, but fortunately such plans were shelved just in time to save Porsche from going under. Then the Boxster appeared, providing the world with what we now know to be a startlingly accurate clue as to what the next 911 would be like.

It's not just the 34-year history of this car that is fascinating, however. The dynamic evolution is just as intriguing, especially since this is the fastest, quietest, most effective 911 ever. You can almost gauge the shifts in world attitudes towards certain things by looking at the 911, never more so than right now, when the car is friendlier and more approachable than at any time in its existence.

In virtually all objective matters, the new 911 represents such a huge improvement over the car it directly replaces that it is difficult not to think that an entire model generation has gone missing somewhere in between. The jumps it makes in refinement, driveability, comfort and sheer straight-line speed are significant enough on their own to make you start to wonder where it will all eventually end.

But then, couple these aspects with the new car's better-mannered ride and handling and its subsequent searing cross-country pace, and you could be forgiven for thinking of the 911 as the finest sports car in the world right now.

The only reason you'd be wrong is this: so obviously has Porsche shifted the values of its footsoldier that, for the first time ever, it is no longer entirely accurate to call the 911 a sports car.

Although it lacks decent rear seat space, the 911 is more grand tourer than sports car now. And that can be regarded in two distinctly different ways: as a positive step forwards that will stand the model in fine stead come the next century; or as a crying shame that one of the most characterful and evocative cars of our time has all but disappeared. In reality, of course, it is both.

Porsche tried to replace the 911 with a GT car in the '70s. Now it has succeeded. Perhaps it should have changed the name, after all.

### The world's best sports GT car   ★★★★★

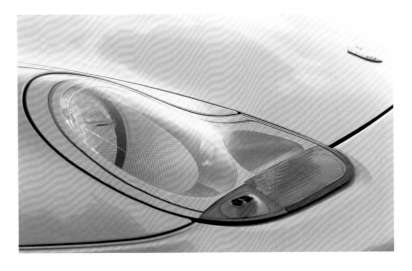

# GERMAN BITE

**911 CARRERA** More civilized and easier to drive, can the new 911 do justice to its name, asks Steve Cropley. Pictures by Stan Papior

There's a delicious moment of enlightenment which strikes every new driver in the latest Porsche 911. It's evidence that you're really starting to get to grips with the car, to understand its complex personality and feel the strength of its heartbeat.

It typically occurs within your first half-hour of serious driving. As your hand leaves the gearlever for the 100th or 200th time, you realise you've just swapped ratios precisely at the 7000rpm red line, judging the revs on engine note alone and not even looking at the tachometer.

In the beginning, you just don't have the confidence to take this brilliant new flat-six engine close to maximum without a weather-eye clamped on the tacho. It is uncommonly smooth, much quietened by its water jackets, and the tacho needle arcs so rapidly round the dial into the high numbers that without great care you're certain to hit the rev-limiter at 7300rpm; safe enough, but untidy and unsatisfying.

The Porsche 911 has always been a very special car to me. Drove my first in 1975 and have probably tried 50 more since then. Owned my first, a 1988 3.2-litre Carrera, in 1991, and have never really recovered from its departure in 1994. If I could wave the magic wand, it would be back there in the drive when I got home. The car is a true automotive phenomenon: brilliantly engined, idiosyncratic yet logical, terrifically well packaged, inspiring to drive and a peerless automotive investment. When the chance came for a long day out in the new, improved 911, I must say the old chest pump bounced about quite a bit. Pick it up at 7am from the Reading headquarters, said the man from Porsche. No need to give it back until mid-evening.

Amid the feelings of anticipation, there was time

to formulate some primary questions. Did this longer, taller, heavily Boxsterised new coupé have the purity of my old '88er? Did it still oversteer? Would the engine still shriek? Would the steering connect to the front wheels as if they were an extension of your arms? And would this new car be the same gold-plated investment my own 911 proved to be? I resolved to leave the road testing to my betters, and play the potential owner for the day.

With Mr Chief Smudger Papior, I duly pitched up to the Porsche emporium at seven. Fifteen minutes later we were parked at the exit, backsides in the Porsche buckets, noses in the road atlas, exhaust vapour boiling from two elliptical tailpipes, trying to decide where to go. Our inclination was Wales. Michael Fish said South Downs. Wales won. We turned west and headed down the M4 motorway.

What struck me straight away – and initially brought me scant pleasure – was the new 911's sheer conventionality. I expected lingering eccentricity, but this car felt like the Audi I'd just left behind. The seats, supportive, seemed softer than my 911. The steering, power assisted, no longer squirmed in my hands over odd cambers and ridges. Nor did it seem to offer the fine degree of control I remembered. The pedals no longer pivoted on the floor, so killing off the 911's last link with the VW Beetle, and were definitely softer under the feet. And the engine... I couldn't hear it.

This last feature was particularly hard to take: cruising at 90mph, my old 911 would emit a matey growl at 3400rpm which took your mind off its wind noise. This car – also pulling 3400 despite its six-speed 'box' and entirely different, tyres – had no engine note, and no wind noise either. You heard only the gravel roar from the road.

## 'DID THE NEW 911 STILL OVERSTEER? WOULD THE ENGINE STILL SHRIEK?'

# FEATURE

## 19 NOVEMBER 1997

Volume 214

No 7 | 5256

AUTOCAR
FIRST FOR NEW CARS

19 NOVEMBER 1997 £1.80

VOLVO C70
v MERC CLK v PEUGEOT 406
SUPER COUPE SPECIAL

EXCLUSIVE
10 best value
cars in Britain

DRIVE Dawn
to dusk in
new 911

PLUS RAC
Rally: your
full guide

INSIDE
OVER 3500
USED
CARS FOR
SALE

911 HUL

Porsche Cars Great Britain Limited

**ABOVE** More
conventional and more
civilized than ever, yet
still a true 911.

By the time we passed Bristol, 30 miles west, I
had wised up quite a bit. It's all very well to have
fond memories of a 10-year-old car, but it makes no
sense to suggest that a new car with the potential
of this one should be deliberately noisy, or should
do without conventional aids such as power-assisted
steering and brakes. It needs them all, along with
anti-lock and some form of traction control. I'll
never forget my disquiet when driving the McLaren
F1 (which I was too shy and retiring to trumpet at
the time) when I discovered what huge physical
strength and reserves of skill a driver needed to cope
competently with its quixotic lack of servo assistance
for steering or brakes.

This 911 seemed as loud as its predecessor
on the road noise front, but thumps caused by
bitumen joining strips seemed much more subdued.
The ride was still firm, but less prone to jitters
from the small surface ripples carefully built into all
British motorways. No doubt about it, though, on
motorways this was coming across as cruiser rather
than sports car. It was worrying.

About the time we crossed the bridge over the
Bristol Channel, I had caught sight for the first time
of a tiny silver dot just ahead, three or four inches

beyond the screen. Perhaps it was the way the sun
was striking the Porsche's body, or the fact that its
new-found straight-line integrity allowed the driver
more time for reflection. Whatever the reason, my
eye fell on the tiny, silvery sphere of paint covering
the point where the rear and side edges of the front
bootlid intersect and form an apex.

Panel ends and edges are always prime places for
a car's paint coverage to go wrong. It's where you
look for ridges, runs, bald spots and dried globules
– and usually find them. But the Porsche's painted
point was so even, so perfectly spherical that it
looked like a tiny dumbell. We'd already washed and
detailed the Porsche for photographs, and I found
myself thinking that the car's perfection at this tiny
point stood for the finish of the whole: the new 911
is built like a Swiss watch and coated with just about
the most lustrous paint you'll find.

With this discovery, one of my prime concerns
about the new 911 was dispelled. Ten years ago,
as I watched Porsches being built in the factory at
Zuffenhausen, I clearly remember our guide proudly
pointing out how much more mechanised the nearby
928 build process was, and how much less labour
intensive. One day the 911 would be like that, he said,

and it made me fear for that day. Now I can report, as one who for three years enjoyed observing Porsche quality through his kitchen window, that the new 911 has survived modernisation with no quality ill-effects at all.

Beyond Cardiff, we turned right, heading north through the Rhondda to roads we both know well from previous great days out. Once you're clear of civilisation, driving a 911 begins in earnest, with only a few raggy-coated sheep to witness your progress.

These are brake-gearchange-steer-throttle roads, where your speed and heading varies constantly and there's virtually no chance of steady-state motoring. The corners rush at you one after the other, most decently surfaced and so open that, as you apex in one, you can see the apex of the next. I'm always surprised, out there, not to encounter half a dozen others in quick cars, who have risen before dawn like us and headed as far as possible away from the smoke.

In the Porsche, on roads like these, it is easy to strike a rhythm. Once you spin the engine regularly beyond 4000rpm, it starts to sing, albeit more quietly than before. Its smoothness would dignify a turbine. The true joy of a car as powerful as this (173mph flat out, 0–100mph in 10.2sec) is that there is a far, far bigger difference than normal between full throttle and no throttle. To drive well, you have to be decisive with the power, both applying it and taking it off. The Porsche has a beautiful, dependable throttle – quite deliberate in its action and not too short in travel. It's especially good at metering engine braking, a vital tool in positioning the car in corners.

Point the new 911 at a bend, and you're instantly aware how much life has changed. This is a forgiving motor car. No need to watch for understeer on entry, or avoid throttling off mid-bend for fear of it swapping ends. This Porsche goes where you point it with such aplomb that you almost forget the engine weight is centred outside the wheelbase at the rear. At sane speeds there is just the gentlest whiff of stabilising understeer on turn-in, and no discernible pendulum effect on exit. The rear wheels can soak up your 296bhp out of a corner with barely a chirrup, especially when the traction control is doing its stuff. Switch it off and the car will slide sideways a foot or so, but only under the severest provocation.

Confession: I don't like the steering. Porsche talks of on-limit toe-out of the front wheels to help tame tail-happiness, but I believe this harms the ultimate

**BELOW** Power steering, supportive seats and no more floor-mounted pedals; 17-inch alloys carry mark of quality; six-speed manual 'box a delight to use.

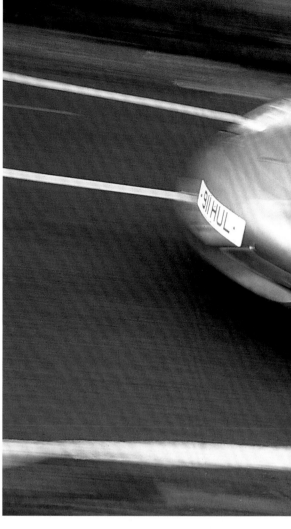

feeling of precision. It just does not have the sensitive, intimate steering of old-timer 911s. It's accurate, safe, nicely geared, even impressive. Against an older 911, well, it's dull.

Other complaints? The indicator stalk harks back to the Hillman Avenger: why would a Porsche driving control feel so unrefined? The engine is surprisingly easy to stall if you're reversing or manoeuvring at low speed, an annoying fault. The speedo mph gradations – 25, 50, 75, 100, 125 and 150 – are absurdly chosen: it's just as well drivers get a digital readout to use instead.

On the other hand, the brakes are simply superb. A bit over-servoed for my taste, but fully worthy of the old 911's reputation for top-class retardation and long life. The gearchange, reminiscent of a Honda NSX, has a shorter throw than it did, and is better located. You don't have to dip your left shoulder forward to pick up first or third. The action is fast but deliberate. Just right.

Few will fault the 911's ride. The springs are firm and the damper control is quite brilliant. While the car occasionally smacks into potholes rather hard, it copes with knobbly Wales back-roads – taken fast – as if developed especially for them. On smoother stuff it becomes true GT, poised yet composed. Is

**BELOW** Unlike old cars, the new 911 is quiet and easy to drive – perhaps too easy?

it too composed? The question crosses your mind when you recall that this new Porsche replaces both the previous 911 and the 928, notably more of a 'businessman's express'.

Papior and I did nearly 500 fundamentally enjoyable miles on a rainy, blustery day. We took in as many driving roads as possible, along with some windswept industrial and coastal locations for photography. Driving back at night along the M4, I struggled to summarise my feelings about this complex car. Of course, it was wonderful. Against a Ferrari F355 or anything else with this scale of performance it is fine value for money. But against my original list of primary questions things were different

Does the new 911 have the purity of the original? Yes, sort of. The Boxster connotations are no problem, but for my money there are a few too many 928 values mixed in there.

Does it oversteer? Not really. It can be made to, but that old feeling of having to control the car is gone. Good riddance, some will say. Not me. The latest model is indisputably faster point-to-point, but extra speed is hardly what we needed,

Does the engine note survive? It does not. Once it was wonderful. Now it's just pretty good.

Well, what about the steering, then? It's impressive, even great by other standards. And great against a 928. But definitely duller than its predecessor.

How will a 911 owner feel about the car from an investment angle? Very warm indeed, I'd say. This is a well-equipped, great value car with a sky-high reputation. It's highly desirable, brilliantly built, is in short supply and likely to stay that way. You could hardly buy better.

To sum up, I admired the 911 greatly. What impressed me most was the car's sheer honesty, the sensible price, the towering performance, the obvious quality and durability. Properly driven and serviced, this car will be in fine fettle in 10 years' time.

As far as buying a 911 goes, I'll have to cogitate a little longer. My view that the new 911 may have slightly too calm a nature for the purists is not the only one Stuttgart will have heard. I'm entirely confident that Porsche is taking it all rapidly on board – and will soon build me a Club Sport.

**ABOVE** New 911 proves its worth – but does it have the character of its forebears?

# 911 TOPS THE LOT

**911 CARRERA CABRIOLET** Forget the drama of an SLK's folding hard-top, the King's Road is in for a new slice of street theatre, courtesy of the latest 911 Carerra cabriolet

Picture the scene: a balmy summer's evening. The new 911 Carrera cabriolet waits by the kerb, roof up (only for security, naturally).

Key swinging nonchalantly in your hand as you approach, you press the remote. There's a click, a soft whirr, and the roof lifts back from the top of the windscreen. Simultaneously, the body panel behind the back window rises and then glides backwards, making room for the now folding roof to gently descend into the hollow between cockpit and engine. Then the flap panel returns to its original position, to hide the roof.

The entire process takes just 20 seconds and leaves all who see it in a state of bemused excitement. This remote control roof is worth the £6800 over the price of the 911 coupé alone.

It's a wonderful piece of engineering, the work of Car Top Systems (CTS), the joint Porsche-Mercedes company devoted to the design and production of convertible roofs, the same people who make the Boxster and Merc SLK tops.

The triple-layer roof matches the coupé's 0.30 Cd figure when it's erect, and delivers coupé-like refinement. No leaks, no wind whistles, no draughts, no ugly folding linkages. Ton-up cruising there's no need to raise your voice, which makes the standard, 32kg aluminium hardtop almost redundant. Of course, it has the advantage of a demistable glass

## QUICK FACTS

| Model | 911 Carrera Cabriolet |
|---|---|
| Price | £71,450 |
| On sale | May |
| Top speed | 175mph |
| 0–62mph | 5.4sec |
| MPG combined | 23.9mpg |
| Engine | 6 cyls horiz opposed, 3387cc |
| Power | 296bhp at 6800rpm |
| Torque | 251lb ft at 4600rpm |

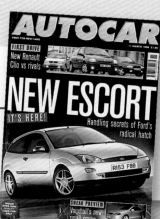

# NEW CARS

## 11 MARCH 1998

Volume 215

No 10 | 5271

rear window in place of the soft top's plastic screen. However, removing the hard-top is a two-person operation and inevitably means that al fresco driving isn't right on tap.

A shame, for the 911 works remarkably well as a convertible. There's no hint of cowl shimmy or body agitation, even on washboard surfaces. It feels as rigid as the coupé, though the figures prove otherwise:

where the new 911 coupé has torsional rigidity of a staggering 16,500Nm deg, the cabriolet manages 8200. That is still well above the old model's 6000. In bending rigidity, the difference is even more dramatic: 21,000N/mm for the coupé, 8900 for the cabrio. By comparison, the old 993 soft top reached 7200N/mm, and we always thought that was stiff. Whatever the figures suggest, the new 911 cabrio feels more rigid

than a Mercedes SL, the previous benchmark in the class.

Roof down, there's a little turbulence, more than in the Boxster. We didn't get a chance to try the wind-blocker, that Porsche promises reduces agitation to no more than a draught. Best of all, the lowered soft-top doesn't spoil the 911's sleek profile – say goodbye to the old Carrera's clumsy and exposed folding pram-style roof.

Porsche insists on providing two tiny rear seats, complete with three-point belts. A bar across the car, containing two spring-loaded roll loops that pop up whenever there's a risk of overturning, forces the seat backs into a vertical position, effectively rendering them useless for all but small children. Better to fold the seats down to supplement the trunk in the nose.

Porsche always claimed the same kerb weight for the old 911, whether as coupé or cabrio. Not so with the new models, the 75kg penalty of that trick electro-hydraulic roof and reinforced windscreen pillars. Instead of being 50kg lighter than the old 911, like the coupé, the new cabrio is 20kg heavier.

The extra mass is enough to add 0.2sec to Porsche's official 0–62mph time, but the 5.4sec claim will be conservative; we clocked the coupé to 60mph in 4.6sec. The 175mph top speed is unaffected by the weight increase and, despite the added bulk, Porsche also says fuel consumption is unchanged. Mechanically, coupé and cabrio are identical: the same superbly gutsy, 296bhp water-cooled flat-six is tied to either a six-speed manual or five-speed Tiptronic automatic.

What the cabrio brings is more sound, an intoxicating mix of induction and exhaust, two distinct layers of music that will appeal to those who find the new coupé a little too civilised.

Otherwise it's pure new 911, at once user-friendly, docile, seriously fast and sophisticated, yet responsive of handling. I suspect the arguments over the quality of steering will never be fully resolved. Yes, I admit it's lighter than the old car, and virtually all the unnecessary kickback, so beloved by some, has been eliminated. But you're left with the same proportionality between driver input and steering loads, what's really important.

Porsche plans to launch the new cabrio in the UK in May. By the end of the year, the rear-drive cars will be joined by all-wheel-drive Carrera 4 versions.

Either way, King's Road had better prepare for a new star.

# SPEC 911 CARRERA CABRIOLET

## DIMENSIONS

| | |
|---|---|
| Length | 4430mm |
| Width | 1765mm |
| Height | 1305mm |
| Wheelbase | 2350mm |
| Weight | 1395kg |
| Fuel tank | 64 litres (14 gal) |

## ENGINE

| | |
|---|---|
| Layout | 6-cyl horizontally opposed, 3387cc |
| Max power | 296bhp at 6800rpm |
| Max torque | 251lb ft at 4600rpm |
| Specific output | 87bhp per litre |
| Power to weight | 212bhp per tonne |
| Installation | Rear, longitudinal, rwd |
| Construction | Alloy head and block |
| Valve gear | 4-per cyl, dohc |
| Management | DME |
| Bore/stroke | 96/78mm |
| Compression ratio | 11.3:1 |

## GEARBOX

Type 6-speed manual
Ratios/mph per 1000rpm

| | | | |
|---|---|---|---|
| 1st 3.82/5.6 | | 2nd 2.20/9.8 | |
| 3rd 1.52/14.2 | | 4th 1.22/17.5 | |
| 5th 1.02/21.0 | | 6th 0.84/25.7 | |

Final drive 3.44:1

## ECONOMY

| | |
|---|---|
| Urban | 16.4mpg |
| Extra urban | 33.2mpg |
| Combined | 23.9mpg |

## STEERING

Type Rack and pinion, power assisted
Turns lock-to-lock 3.0

## SUSPENSION

Front MacPherson struts, lower control arms, coil springs/dampers, anti-roll bar
Rear Independent multi-link, coil springs/dampers, anti-roll bar

## BRAKES

Front 318mm ventilated discs
Rear 299mm ventilated discs
ABS Standard

## WHEELS AND TYRES

Size 7Jx17in (f), 9Jx17in(r)
Tyres 205/50ZR 17 (f), 255/40ZR 17 (r)

## AUTOCAR VERDICT

Highly sophisticated soft-top offers near 911 coupé levels of refinement. Exciting

# CUP WINNER

Porsche still knows how to make raw sports cars that score with hard-core 911 RS fans, as Colin Goodwin finds when he drives the 996-based Supercup racer

I don't really get the drift of what Roland Kussmaul is trying to tell me. He is explaining how I must take a particular corner at Porsche's Weissach test track in this spanking new 911 Supercup racing car.

The corner has everything you don't want, like an adverse camber, a crest in the middle of it and very little run-off area.

It is most important that I don't spanner this car, because Porsche is very busy building the Supercup cars for the one make series that chases the Formula 1 circus around Europe. There are lots of cars to be built and if I put them back by one I will not be popular.

Kussmaul knows Weissach as well as he knows his back yard. It is his back yard, in fact. And if he says that I must put on some opposite lock to make sure everything will be all right by the time I hit the apex of this blighter of a corner, I'm not going to argue. It sounds all wrong, but I put my faith in the talented test driver's experience.

So here we are, belting up to the corner in the silver racer and, woah, over we go. Just as Kussmaul has promised, the car lands sideways and then, because I have already put the correct lock on, goes shooting up the road in just the right direction for the next corner.

It's not much to do with me. It's down to the combination of an expert telling me what to do and a very competent racing car carrying out that command without any fuss.

Today is more than simply a drive in a rather wonderful racing Porsche 911. I'm looking for the answer to a question that has been in my mind since the first time that I drove Porsche's new water-cooled 996. The new 911 is a very fine car indeed. It's superbly built, very fast and even more friendly to drive than the old air-cooled 993. The trouble is, the new car is too sophisticated for the hard-core 911 fan. Perhaps it is a better car, but its raw spirit has been watered down.

There's no doubt that for many people – those who would previously have steered well clear of the 911 – the new car is a much more palatable proposition. But we hard-core 911 fans need something that's more raw and focused. This Supercup racing car might well hold the key to the car that we're after.

Porsche is not saying anything concrete, but the Supercup car, or 911 GT3 Cup to give it its proper name, is a pretty fair representation of the car that Porsche will build to replace the last 911 RS.

No one at Stuttgart will say whether the car will actually be called the RS, or whether it will wear some other badge, but we can be pretty sure that next year we will see a 996 that is directed straight at the committed driver.

## FACTFILE

| | |
|---|---|
| **Model** | 911 Supercup |
| **0–62mph** | n/a |
| **Top speed** | n/a |
| **Economy** | n/a |
| **Length** | 4430mm |
| **Width** | 1950mm |
| **Height** | 1305mm |
| **Wheelbase** | 2350mm |
| **Engine** | 6 cyls horizontally opposed, 3600cc |
| **Installation** | Rear, longitudinal, two-wheel drive |
| **Max power** | 360bhp at 7250rpm |
| **Max torque** | 265lb ft at 6000rpm |
| **Gearbox** | 6-spd manual |
| **Suspension** | Struts, lower control arms, coil springs/ dampers, anti-roll bar (f) multilink, coil springs/ dampers, anti-roll bar (r) |
| **Steering** | Rack and pinion, power assisted |

So what do we have to look forward to? Well, for one thing, there's no doubt that Porsche's designers and engineers are the absolute masters of building customer racing cars as well as full-house track stars. This Supercup car looks as though it has just rolled off the production line. The quality is right up there with the standard 996. There's no sign of bits that have had to be jiggled and tweaked to fit in the car.

Standard 996s are plucked off the production line and then wheeled over to the racing workshops at Weissach, where they are built up into 911 GT3 Cup cars.

At the heart of the racer is a 3.6-litre version of the 996's flat six, which has a slightly shorter stroke and larger bore than the road car's 3.4-litre motor. Power is up 64bhp from the standard 996, at 360bhp.

Porsche engines are usually disappointing to look at, but this one has a superb air intake trumpet that could ingest a small dog if it wasn't covered in fine mesh. The engine is fitted with a pair of free-breathing catalyst-equipped exhausts that, give the car back much of the bark that it had before water cooling arrived. This in itself livens up the experience a considerable amount.

The engine is fitted to the same six-speed

**BELOW** Dashboard from road car survives racer's radical diet.

transaxle that's used on the 911 GT2 racing car. It should prove bomb-proof, as the GT2 has almost double the Cup car engine's torque output.

Not surprisingly, the Supercup is substantially lighter than the road-going 996. Much of the sound deadening has been removed, and pretty much only the standard dashboard remains inside the car. The doors are glass fibre and the rear window perspex instead of glass. These and other weight savings have dropped the kerb weight from the road car's 1320kg to 1140kg for the racer.

If Porsche is to build an RS version of the 996 this is the tack we can expect Porsche's engineers to take. What makes the 911 Turbo go fast is raw horsepower. It is the sledgehammer approach. The Renn Sport cars have always used a mild increase in power, plus careful honing and refinement, to bring on their speed. Purists tend to prefer the latter method.

We'll talk about the other components that make this car special when we're on Weissach's test track, as that is the place to best appreciate them.

I've not been to Weissach before; it's not what I expected. It's completely different from Ferrari's Fiorano circuit, in that it is very narrow and only has a few yards of run-off before the thwack of panel and Armco. Goodness knows what a Porsche 956 Group C would be like around here. Hairy, I'd imagine. Very unlike the Supercup car.

Take most road-going supercars onto a race circuit and pound around for a few laps, and you'll feel the brakes begin to fade. Porsches are different. You can knock the daylights out of the brakes lap after lap and they still feel great. The Supercup car uses vast 330mm ventilated discs that are truly Herculean in stopping strength. Again and again. In this car, shod with slicks, you can brake ridiculously late for corners.

The Supercup is relaxing to drive by racing car standards. It has power steering that is perfectly weighted for feel, feedback and effort. This is one area where I reckon the road 996 is weak. The road car's steering is just not as sharp as a 993's. Of course, this car is wearing race tyres and has stiff Unibal joints in the front and rear suspension, as well as stiffer front shock absorber mounts, which add together to make a big difference to the steering.

I make plenty of mistakes around Weissach, which each time are forgiven by the very tolerant Supercup race car.

Johnny Mowlem, who won 17 out of 17 races driving a 993 in the British Porsche championship last year, and who now races a car exactly the same as this in the European Supercup championship, agrees that the 996 is a pretty friendly racing car.

He says that the old 993 was a car you chucked around a bit and one that made sure you knew whenever it was about to do something naughty. Mowlem says his Supercup car sends more subtle messages when letting him know what's about to happen, and requires a defter touch than his 993.

The GT3 Cup feels extremely safe, whatever speed I drive it at. It also has a lot more grunt than I had expected. Because it is relatively relaxing to drive it lulls me into thinking that it's a bit of a pussycat.

A thought that's soon swept aside when I crack open the throttle with too much vigour as we come onto Weissach's longest straight. The car slides worryingly, then straightens reassuringly as I manage to correct it.

Fortunately this is all out of sight of the Porsche people. Wisely they wave me in after about 10 laps,

as they quite rightly guess that I am having rather too much fun.

If Porsche actually does take what it has learnt from this car and transfers it to a road-going 911, then we're in for a treat.

I still mourn the passing of the last 911 RS. That was the best and most enjoyable sports car that I have ever driven, and until Porsche produces a 996 that embodies all the RS principles, then for me there will always be a large gap in the Porsche 911 catalogue.

I'm sure I'm not alone in this view, either. Go to a track day, like a Club 89 event, and you will see plenty of Porsche drivers giving their cars what for around the circuit.

Porsches can handle this sort of treatment better than most sports cars. It is these people who will break Porsche's doors down when the new version of the pure 911 arrives.

**ABOVE** Power steering makes Supercup deceptively relaxing for a racer.

## VERDICT

**A racing car, but shows what can be done with the 996 when driving is all that counts**

# 4 SURE

All-wheel drive doesn't just give Porsche's newest 911 extra stability and safety – it also boosts driver involvement. Peter Robinson reports

**Y**our fingers convey the information the instant you turn the wheel.

The steering is heavier, meatier, less sensitive. Not much, but enough for the difference to be immediately discernible to hands acquainted with the rear-drive Carrera.

The distinctions grew the longer we played with the Carrera 4 on the wonderfully demanding roads surrounding Porsche's Weissach proving ground. A bit more steering lock, a sense of mild understeer in a second-gear hairpin. Extra steering effort as increasing lateral forces amplify steering loads through a fourth-gear sweeper. A fraction less self-centring. Finally – and prepare for the on-going arguments – a perception that this steering is actually more involving than that of the Carrera 2.

Clearly, you don't need to notice that this 911 carries a titanium-coloured "4" on the engine hood and door sills, or that the brake calipers are also in a titanium hue, or that the newly designed 17in alloys' wheel centres are black, to appreciate that it's the new Carrera 4, the all-wheel-drive version of the latest 911. These are subtle differences, visual and dynamic, and they conceal the fact that the Carrera 4 brings a raft of new technology to the 911, including Porsche's first stability control system and the availability of an automatic transmission for the first time on an all-wheel-drive 911.

On the face of it, you might wonder why Porsche would want to build a four-wheel-drive 911 when the new Carrera is so brilliantly scare-free. But there was always going to be a four-wheel-drive 996. How could Porsche ignore the concept when 30 per cent of old 911 buyers chose all-wheel drive? Despite a £3050 price hike over the rear-drive Carrera, Porsche GB expects to have no trouble selling its 1999 allocation of 1200 C2s and 800 C4s.

The Carrera 4, given the green light by the Porsche board in February 1994, was developed in parallel with the C2, but project leader Thomas Herold admits it always ran a little behind the Boxster/C2. Putting drive to the front wheels as well as the rear meant finding room for the propeller shaft, front differential (which now includes the viscous clutch) and axles. From the windscreen forward, the Carrera 4 had to be totally re-engineered.

Only the chassis rails are carried over. The suspension struts have been inclined to the rear to make room for the driveshafts, although the rates for the now non-concentric spring/damper units are identical. To maintain the same 64-litre capacity, the fuel tank has been reshaped and the emergency folding spare wheel now sits on the floor of the boot, reducing its capacity by 30 litres to 100 litres.

Moving the viscous clutch from in front of the gearbox to the front differential means the same unit could be used for both the manual and Tiptronic automatic gearboxes, which share the same ratios and final drive as those of the C2. The extra mechanicals at the front also bring a small change to the weight distribution. It's now 40/60 with the shift of another two per cent to the nose, and one reason why the steering is heavier. The power transfer to the front wheels varies from five to 40 per cent, the ratio being a function of rear-wheel traction.

Drive no longer goes through a hollow transaxle tube, but a 3kg lighter shaft that's connected by

## QUICK FACTS

| | |
|---|---|
| **Model** | 911 Carrera 4 |
| **Price** | £67,850 |
| **Top speed** | 174mph |
| **0–62mph** | 5.2sec |
| **MPG combined** | 27.2mpg |
| **Engine** | 6 cyls horiz opposed, 3387cc |
| **Power** | 300bhp at 6800rpm |
| **Torque** | 258lb ft at 4600rpm |

# FEATURE

## 7 OCTOBER 1998

### Volume 218
No 1 | 5301

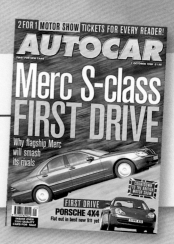

**ABOVE** Less understeer and more steering feel than rear-drive 911; the multi-function screen is an option.

rubber couplings at either end, to soften the drive take-up, and a central mounting joint to reduce vibration.

The Carrera 4 also introduces Porsche Stability Management (PSM). Made possible by the adoption of an electronic drive-by-wire throttle, the Bosch-built PSM combines the existing longitudinal controls – the anti-lock brakes and Automatic Brake Differential (ABD) – with a lateral control that, Porsche says, only cuts in briefly, if decisively, to support the driver in keeping the car stable in a corner. PSM brings wheel speed sensors able to detect the difference in speed from left to right (to "read" bends and their radius), a steering angle sensor, lateral acceleration sensor and a yaw sensor to detect drift angles. All very sophisticated and potentially intrusive. Not so, claims Porsche.

"Other cars are castrated by such systems," says Herold. "We didn't want the 911's entertainment factor to be influenced by the computer."

It hasn't. Not at all, and those drivers who indulge in 40deg slip angles – on a race track, of course – are able to turn it off. Touching the brakes "when the angle of the car becomes excessive" immediately reactivates the system. If the 911 begins to oversteer, PSM brakes the outer front wheel. If the car is understeering, it brakes the inner rear wheel, in both cases to stabilise the car's cornering attitude.

Is the C4 quicker with PSM on or off? Herold says that even with the system operational, the C4 reaches the same lateral acceleration on a skid pan as when it's deactivated. On the old Nürburgring, Porsche's quickest development test driver is always within the same second-long band, regardless.

It takes no more than a couple of corners to fall in love with the C4. It's the normal 911, only better. More stable, especially at the high speeds the Carrera so quickly attains, less nervous in

## 'WE DIDN'T WANT THE 911'S ENTERTAINMENT FACTOR TO BE INFLUENCED BY THE COMPUTER'

strong crosswinds, and even more consistent in its dynamics. At first it seems slightly less agile, because wheel movements are bigger, but experience reveals that its handling is actually more neutral, less oversteery.

Experimentation with the PSM reveals that the C4 responds to a smooth driving style and minimises the need for driver reactions, making it more relaxing to drive than the C2, not least at very high speeds on the autobahn. Aggressive driving inevitably activates the PSM unnecessarily, when the C4 is quite capable of coping with the situation without an excessive electronic invasion, thus slowing the car. There is no loss in the chassis' adjustability, and while the driver might momentarily sense a front wheel being braked, it's virtually impossible to know when a rear wheel is curtailed.

All the driver understands is that the nose is less prone to pushing wide. The engine management system is set up so that if you lift off suddenly in a bend, a degree of torque is maintained to smooth out the weight transfer and reduce the car's reactions. It all makes for a supercar that is as failsafe as any, yet remains fun to drive quickly, the electronics doing their job so unobtrusively that most drivers won't even notice, unless they attack corners with arms flailing. Even then, it's effectively impossible to throw the C4 off balance, at least on dry roads, though not even the C4 can defy the laws of physics.

Inevitably, the trick electronics and all-wheel drive hardware bear a weight penalty. The extra 55kg is 5kg more than the difference between the old C2 and C4. Porsche admits it's enough to increase the new 911's combined fuel consumption by 0.5mpg to 27.2mpg, but insists there is no change in the 0–60 time. Subjectively, I reckon you can detect a minor reduction in the rate of acceleration, though the C4 is still one of the fastest cars around.

The choice between C2 and C4 remains as complex as ever. The C4 is undoubtedly the more talented car, exuding an invincible air that many will find irresistible. Yet there will be those who prefer the lighter, more agile perception created by the cheaper C2. I prefer to hedge my bets until back-to-back testing is possible. I'll let my fingers make the decision.

And just in case you're wondering, Herold says there are absolutely no plans for an all-wheel-drive Boxster.

# SPECIFICATIONS 911 CARRERA 4

## DIMENSIONS

| | |
|---|---|
| Length | 4430mm |
| Width | 1765mm |
| Height | 1305mm |
| Wheelbase | 2350mm |
| Weight | 1375kg |
| Fuel tank | 64 litres |

## ENGINE

| | |
|---|---|
| Layout | 6-cyl horizontally opposed, 3387cc |
| Max power | 300bhp at 6800rpm |
| Max torque | 258lb ft at 4600rpm |
| Specific output | 88bhp per litre |
| Power to weight | 218bhp per tonne |
| Installation | Rear, longitudinal, rwd |
| Made of | Alloy heads and block |
| Bore/stroke | 96/78mm |
| Compression ratio | 11.3:1 |
| Valve gear | 4 per cyl, dohc per bank |
| Management | Bosch DME engine management sequential fuel injection |

## STEERING

**Type** Rack and pinion, power assisted
**Turns lock-to-lock** 3.0

## GEARBOX

**Type** 6-speed manual (or 5-speed auto)
**Ratios**/mph per 1000rpm
**Final drive** 3.44:1

| | | | |
|---|---|---|---|
| 1st 3.82/5.9 | | 2nd 2.20/10.3 | |
| 3rd 1.52/14.9 | | 4th 1.22/18.5 | |
| 5th 1.02/22.1 | | 6th 0.84/26.9 | |

## SUSPENSION

**Front** MacPherson struts, coil springs/dampers, anti-roll bar
**Rear** Multi-link, coil springs/dampers, anti-roll bar

## BRAKES

**Front** 318mm ventilated discs
**Rear** 299mm ventilated discs
**ABS** Standard

## WHEELS AND TYRES

**Size** 7Jx17in (f), 9Jx17in (r)
**Tyres** 205/50 ZR17 (f), 255/40 ZR17 (r)

## AUTOCAR VERDICT

All-wheel drive brings more stability and safety to the 911 – and more feel.

# PORSCHE 911

The theory was beautifully simple. Strip the interior, remove all sound deadening materials and provide a touch more power. But times have changed and Porsche has had to acknowledge the fact that even the most extreme road cars must offer at least some comfort for the driver.

So from its inception the GT3 was designed to be a different type of fast 911. Not a lightweight version – it is actually 30kg heavier than the standard car – but instead a meaner, more powerful 911, complete with sharper reactions from both engine and chassis.

Central to the GT3's metamorphosis is a completely new 3.6-litre engine, based on the unit that powered the GT1 Le Mans racer. The suspension and braking systems have also been uprated, while the body sprouts a multitude of wings and spoilers.

In short, the GT3 is Porsche's intended answer to criticism that the latest 911 has sold its soul in favour of an easier life. Just 40 will be made in right-hand-drive form and are expected to be priced at £76,500 when they go on sale next month.

### DESIGN & ENGINEERING ★★★★
**Race car technology, stunning engineering**

Not calling this car an RS is a wise decision, because Porsche's thinking behind the GT3 is different from

## QUICK FACTS

| | |
|---|---|
| **Model tested** | 911 GT3 |
| **Price** | £76,500 |
| **Top speed** | 188mph |
| **0–60mph** | 4.8sec |
| **60–0mph** | 2.7sec |
| **MPG** | 19.2 |
| **For** | Glorious engine, involved handling, brakes, still refined |
| **Against** | Lumpy town ride, poor ground clearance |

# ROAD TEST

## 4 AUGUST 1999

Volume 221

No 5 | 5343

**ABOVE** Unlike most hot 911s, refinement and ride quality barely suffer.

**OPPOSITE** It's no whale tail, but it's effective; new sill plates for an exclusive car.

that of previous hot 911s. Gone is the abundance of canny dietary fettling; as a result, the GT3 is 30kg heavier than the standard 911. To compensate, it has more power to achieve a power-to-weight ratio of 267bhp compared with the standard car's 224bhp per tonne.

If the engine's specification reads like that of a race car, that's because, fundamentally, it is one. Stroke is increased by 2mm over the GT1 lump on whose foundations the GT3 engine is built, giving a swept volume of 3600cc. Exotic materials abound, most notably in the lightweight titanium conrods that allow the GT3 to rev reliably to 7800rpm. As you'd expect, it also features lighter pistons than the norm.

Track use dictates the need for dry sump lubrication, but the oil tank is mounted on the engine rather than the chassis. The fuel tank has been increased in size to a massive 90 litres, but only on left-hand-drive examples. Right-hand-drive cars make do with the standard car's 64-litre tank.

A new six-speed gearbox is a development of the 1996 911 GT2's gearbox, albeit with a cable-operated change. Relatively easily changeable individual gear ratios are another concession to track use.

The chassis and suspension have come in for similar

treatment, although no actual geometry changes have taken place. For starters, the car has been lowered by 30mm over the standard Carrera and now has adjustable front and rear anti-roll bars. Axle geometry is quickly adjustable for road or race and all suspension mounting points are reinforced.

Move your foot from the throttle to the brakes and the GT3 continues to impress. There are larger ventilated discs all round. Disc diameter is up by 33mm and each disc is gripped by a stout monoblock four-pot caliper.

The car looks little different from many bespoilered 996s. There is a very low chin spoiler designed to limit air passing under the body at speed and maintain stability. Deep side skirts and a bold bi-plane rear wing improve the GT3's looks and aerodynamics.

### PERFORMANCE/BRAKES ★★★★
**A joy to use, but no quicker than standard 911**

As the laptop churned out the performance figures, faces dropped. What should have been one of the figuring highlights of the year was a disappointment: the GT3 wasn't as quick as we had hoped.

# ROAD TEST 911 GT3

## MAXIMUM SPEEDS

| | | | |
|---|---|---|---|
| **6th** 188mph/7200rpm | | **5th** 172/7800 | |
| **4th** 138/7800 | | **3rd** 106/7800 | |
| **2nd** 77/7800 | | **1st** 44/7800 | |

## ACCELERATION FROM REST

| True mph | seconds | speedo mph |
|---|---|---|
| 30 | 1.3 | 31 |
| 40 | 2.7 | 41 |
| 50 | 3.7 | 52 |
| 60 | 4.8 | 62 |
| 70 | 5.9 | 72 |
| 80 | 7.6 | 83 |
| 90 | 9.2 | 93 |
| 100 | 10.9 | 103 |

**Standing qtr mile** 13.2sec/109mph

**Standing km** 23.4sec/141mph

**30–70mph through gears** 4.1sec

## ACCELERATION IN GEAR

| MPH | 6th | 5th | 4th | 3rd | 2nd |
|---|---|---|---|---|---|
| 20–40 | 7.5 | 6.8 | 4.9 | 3.6 | 2.5 |
| 30–50 | 7.0 | 5.5 | 4.7 | 3.5 | 2.3 |
| 40–60 | 7.7 | 6.1 | 4.7 | 3.3 | 2.2 |
| 50–70 | 8.0 | 6.3 | 4.3 | 3.0 | 2.2 |
| 60–80 | 8.0 | 5.7 | 4.2 | 2.9 | - |
| 70–90 | 7.5 | 5.6 | 4.1 | 3.1 | - |
| 80–100 | 7.5 | 5.9 | 4.2 | 3.3 | - |

## BRAKES

| | |
|---|---|
| **30/50/70mph** | 9.6/25.5/48.5 metres |
| **60–0mph** | 2.7sec |

## FUEL CONSUMPTION

Average/touring/best/worst

19.2/24.7/24.7/14.6mpg

| | |
|---|---|
| Urban | 14.0mpg |
| Extra urban | 31.7mpg |
| Combined | 21.9mpg |
| Tank capacity | 90 litres |
| Touring range | 490 miles |

## NOISE

| | |
|---|---|
| **30/50/70mph** | 74/77/82/db |
| **Full acceleration** | 86db |
| Inside | 65db |

## TEST NOTES

Can't emphasise enough how much better this car looks in the flesh. Low ride height and body kit give it massive presence.

Sourcing rear tyres is a hassle. There are three different types of 285/30 ZR18 Pirelli P-Zero available for Porsches: N1, N2, and N3. The GT3 likes N3s only and they're the most difficult to find!

The dissenting voices that decried the GT3 as a poor substitute for a real RS Porsche soon settled once they had heard the engine at 6100rpm. It is one of motoring's best noises.

There are many reasons why. One, the grippy Millbrook mile straight was unavailable to us at the time. Two, the weather was Sahara hot. Three, the top three gear ratios are significantly taller than they are in the Carrera. Four, the GT3 weighs 30kg more than standard, a weight disadvantage that is roughly doubled when you brim the 90-litre fuel tank, which has long been a part of *Autocar* road test procedure.

Nevertheless, aided by its trademark 911 traction off the line, the GT3 hits 30mph in 1.8sec and 60mph in 4.8sec – a disappointing (but perhaps understandable given the circumstances) couple of tenths down on the regular Carrera. The magic ton comes up in 10.9sec, still in third gear. Through fourth gear the intensity never lets up and eventually the standing kilometre passes in a blur in 23.4sec, with the GT3 travelling at 141mph.

For an engine that offers 100bhp per litre, it has an unnatural dose of deportment, being less truculent at low speeds than many a hot hatch and remaining smooth throughout the rev range. In-gear times are impressive, but again slower than those the Carrera recorded. The benchmark 30–50mph in fourth and 50–70mph in top take 4.7sec and 8.0sec

# SPECIFICATIONS 911 GT3

## DIMENSIONS

Min/max front legroom 830/1090mm   Max front headroom 970mm
Interior width 1340mm   Max boot width 740mm   Boot length 420mm
Boot volume 130 litres/dm³   Front/rear tracks 1475/1495mm   Kerb weight 1350kg
Weight distribution front/rear n/a   Width with/without mirrors 1950/1475mm

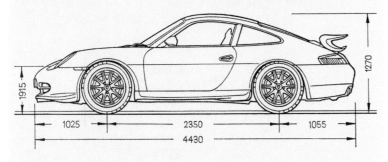

## ENGINE

| | |
|---|---|
| Layout | 6-cyl horizontally opposed, 3600cc |
| Max power | 360bhp at 7200rpm |
| Max torque | 273lb ft at 5000rpm |
| Specific output | 100bhp per litre |
| Power to weight | 267bhp per tonne |
| Torque to weight | 202lb ft per tonne |
| Installation | Rear, longitudinal, rwd |
| Construction | Alloy heads and block |
| Bore/stroke | 100.0/76.4mm |
| Valve gear | 4 per cyl, dohc |
| Compression ratio | 11.7:1 |
| Ignition and fuel | DME ignition, electronic sequential fuel injection |

## GEARBOX

Gearbox 6-speed manual
Ratios/mph per 1000rpm
Final drive 3.44:1

| | | | |
|---|---|---|---|
| 1st 3.83/5.6 | | 2nd 2.15/9.9 | |
| 3rd 1.56/13.7 | | 4th 1.21/17.7 | |
| 5th 0.97/22.1 | | 6th 0.82/26.1 | |

## SUSPENSION

**Front** MacPherson struts, coil springs anti-roll bar
**Rear** Multi-link, coil springs, anti-roll bar

## CHASSIS AND BODY

**Body** 2dr coupé
**Wheels** 8Jx18in (f), 10Jx18in (r)
**Made of** Cast alloy
**Tyres** 225/40 ZR18 (f), 285/30 ZR18 (r) Pirelli P-Zero
**Spare** Foam kit

## STEERING

**Type** Rack and pinion, power assisted
**Turns lock-to-lock** 3.0
**Turning circle** 10.6m

## BRAKES

**Front and rear** 330mm ventilated, cross drilled discs
**Anti-lock** Standard

---

respectively, the latter being particularly impressive for a ratio that will eventually allow 188mph.

Despite the slight stutter in the figures, extending the GT3 in second gear for the first time redresses any criticism that Porsche's latest generation of water-cooled engines sounds flat compared with the old air-cooled units. Few motors in our experience sound this good. From 3600cc it produces 360bhp at 7800rpm and 273lb ft at 5000rpm. There is a meaty resonance as the revs build from idle to 4000rpm, and at 6100rpm the engine's harmonics sustain the automotive equivalent of a top C until it hits the 7800rpm limiter.

Holding on to a lower gear just to experience it again and again is a frequent treat. Throttle response is noticeably quicker than that of the standard car, the revs rising and falling very quickly at the merest flex of a toe. In our experience it is one of the finest engines powering a road car.

Braking performance is chest crushing from any speed. Had the surface been cleaner the anti-lock system wouldn't have triggered as easily and whole tenths might have tumbled from the recorded 2.7sec 60-0mph time. The whole system feels more direct than the standard car's set-up. Pedal effort is greater and speed is wiped off so violently that a full harness would be welcome.

### HANDLING & RIDE ★★★★★
### More fun than a 996. Sensational steering

---

The big question was always going to be whether a 30mm reduction in ride height and stiffer suspension would render the GT3 incapable of coping with the UK's poorly surfaced roads.

Much of the time the GT3's ride quality teeters on acceptable. Pottering around town isn't a comfortable experience, the Porsche's nose sniffing out every rut and ridge possible, but as speeds increase the ride relaxes. Cruising well within the legal limit is far from soothing, but even after three hours the ride wasn't being cursed by driver or passenger. The payback is stunning body control on any given road, with no body roll to speak of, just grip and composure in such large doses that reaching beyond the limits regularly would require either an unusually brave or a very foolish driver.

The cornering experience itself is very different from that of the Carrera. The steering is sharper – much sharper. The slightest nudge of the three-spoke wheel sends the front end slicing into an imaginary

**ABOVE** Wheel adjusts for reach only; it's good to hold and perfectly placed.

**LEFT** Six-speed 'box derived from GT2; tasteful GT3 logo on handbrake.

apex. As you hold the rim, the GT3 feels like an uncensored version on the regular car, so much more vivid is the dialogue between driver's palms and tarmac.

Next there is the chassis' reaction to throttle inputs. Whereas a standard 996 leans towards initial understeer, the GT3 is more on its toes with front-end bite, allowing judicious use of the throttle – the GT3 isn't offered with traction control – to balance the car with a dose of opposite lock through corners. Acclimatised to the balance of power and traction of 285/30 ZR18 Pirelli P-Zeros at the back and 225/40 ZR18 P-Zeros at the front, it doesn't take a bucketload of skill to deputise much of the steering work from the hands to the right foot.

## WHAT IT COSTS

### PORSCHE 911 GT3

| | |
|---|---|
| **On-the-road price** | £76,500 |
| **Price as tested** | £80,375 |
| **Cost per mile** | n/a |
| **Insurance group** | 20 |
| **Typical quote** | n/a |
| **Contract hire rate** | n/a |

### EQUIPMENT CHECKLIST

| | |
|---|---|
| Anti-lock brakes | ■ |
| Metallic paint | £745 |
| Airbag driver/passenger | ■/■ |

| | |
|---|---|
| RDS stereo/CD player | ■/£95 |
| Alarm/immobiliser | ■/■ |
| Central locking/remote | ■/■ |
| Air conditioning | ■ |
| Leather upholstery | ■ |
| **Full leather/** | |
| **carbon fibre package** | **£3875** |
| Traction control | n/a |
| Automatic gearbox | n/a |

Options in **bold** fitted to test car

■ = Standard  na = not available

## COMFORT, EQUIPMENT & SAFETY ★★★
### Flawless seats and driving position

Every car with sporting pretensions should have the seats and driving position of the GT3. It makes accessing the performance all the more comfortable and enjoyable.

Driver and passenger share identical Recaro buckets with fixed backs and slots for a full harness. Lateral support from these glass fibre, leather-covered seats is superb and it has been achieved without any damage to the comfort level they offer over long distances.

Such vice-like support hinders the driver's ability to turn around during parking, and the huge wraparound wings at the top of the seat backs impair rearward visibility, but we wouldn't be without them.

From these seats the driving position has changed for the better. The driver sits low, the reach-adjustable wheel sitting at a comfortable level and the gear lever in comfortable proximity too. Best of all, the driver's legs now hit the pedals at a lower trajectory than in the Carrera and that makes heel-and-toe gearchanging even more of a pleasure.

Apart from this, the GT3 is virtually identical to the standard car. The central cubby between the dash and centre tunnel is deleted, but the rest of the interior,

**ABOVE** Front boot is big enough to call the GT3 a practical supercar.

**BELOW** Deeply sculptured, high-backed Recaro buckets are mounted low for a spot-on driving position.

This adjustability alone is compensation enough for the harsher ride.

Through general sharpening and tweaking in the right places, Porsche has made the GT3 more pointable than the base 996, but it can't disguise the GT3's weight penalty.

Whereas the 2.7 RS, Club Sport and most recently the 993 RS feel more wieldy than their standard production contemporaries, the GT3 merely feels sharper than a Carrera. For us it's a small but important difference.

door handles and all, remains unaltered. There are some tasteful GT3 inscriptions on the instrument faces to remind those who can't hear the engine that this is a special 911. Air conditioning, a Becker stereo, four airbags and no reduction of sound deadening material contribute to a cabin that is far more civilised than any previous 911 with road and track pretensions.

Instead of rear seats there is a useful area capable of swallowing a fair amount of luggage. Combined with the front boot, the GT3 has enough luggage space to double as a sensible grand tourer.

We can't think of many vehicles that impart the same sense of solidity as the standard 911. That the GT3 comes without traction control is a statement of the GT3's driver bias. However, the anti-lock brakes are simply awesome. Plus points, too, for the twin front airbags, side airbags and inherent strength of the bucket seats.

## ECONOMY ★★★★
### Tiny thirst for a car with this performance

For a car that's capable of 188mph, the GT3 has a meagre thirst for fuel. During testing and hard road use the consumption fell to 14.6mpg. This increased significantly at a steady (Continental) 100mph cruise to around 22mpg. Over the standard touring route we recorded our best figure of 24.7mpg. The overall figure of 19.2mpg is a superb result considering the performance. Add to this a 90-litre fuel tank and a huge 490-mile touring range is available. What a shame that right-hand-drive models must make do with the smaller 64-litre tank.

## MARKET & FINANCE ★★★★★
### Unbeatable combination of rarity and image

After the initial sales success of the 996, used values have softened in recent months. But limited-edition 911s are a rather different ball game.

Demand for the GT3 is predictably strong. Only 40 are destined for the UK from a limited production run of between 1300 and 1400 cars – and they've all been snapped up.

Sheer speed has always been expensive, but the GT3 attains an impressive level of performance without an exorbitant increase in price – £11,700 above the standard 996. Considering that the GT3 achieves such heights without losing a stitch of equipment over the standard car, the £76,500 price starts to look like some sort of bargain.

# THE **AUTOCAR** VERDICT

Having a bloodline as strong as any Ferrari can have negative as well as positive effects. For every new product, expectations are inevitably higher, and the possibility of failure becomes increasingly likely. But that certainly isn't the fate of the 911 GT3.

We'll admit to being apprehensive on discovering that the GT3 would not be a lightweight RS version of the 996 and would instead weigh more than the standard car. But we needn't have worried.

Where Porsche has surpassed itself is in creating a car that offers greater dynamic capabilities and deeper tactile qualities than a regular 996, without sacrificing more than 10 per cent of that car's impressive refinement. Driving the GT3 on a favourite road is a much more rewarding experience, but not necessarily a more painful one.

Central to this extraordinary breadth of appeal is the all-new engine, which blends an addictive top-end explosiveness with a suprising level of decorum at low revs. It's a fine example of how to use, but not abuse, race track technology in a road car.

Despite its extra weight, the GT3 also feels significantly sharper than the standard car through the twisties, yet its ride always remains just the right side of acceptable. The steering deserves particular praise. Porsche has reinstated a level of feel into the 911's helm that we feared had been banished forever. As an object to arouse the committed driver's senses, the GT3 is everything that the regular 996 isn't.

But there's a crucial extra element to the GT3's appeal that was missing from its more single-minded ancestors: civility. It may not be the last word in refinement, but the GT3 can munch motorways nearly as effectively as it can race tracks. That it has sound deadening, gas struts for the bonnet, air conditioning and a host of other features that would have been scrapped had the car worn an RS badge is actually a bonus. The GT3 is a fast 911 for the next century, and the fact that it's not as raw as some of its forebears merely means you're in a more comfortable position to enjoy the experience.

Six months ago we didn't think it possible that the Ferrari 360 Modena could be rivalled. How rapidly things change.

## Best 911 since the 2.7 RS     ★★★★★

# CANARY WARP

**911 TURBO** The new 911 Turbo is as technically brilliant under its skin as it is beautiful. Gert Hack discovers what lies beneath the striking exterior

This is the car that Porsche fans have been waiting for. If you can ignore the finely honed Carrera 4 and race-raw GT3, the Turbo has been the evocative centrepiece of the 911 line-up ever since the first blown model broke cover almost 25 years ago.

The all-new 996 version promises to be a fitting continuation of the tradition when it goes on sale in Britain next summer priced at less than £100,000.

It is dramatically different from its predecessors beneath the skin. And the new car's striking exterior; leaves you in no doubt that this is a very special 911 indeed.

It follows Turbo tradition by being noticeably wider front and rear than the naturally aspirated coupé and cabrio 911s. The huge tyres, 295/30 R18s on 11in-wide rims, have been moved further outwards and are covered by wings 30mm wider than the Carrera's. That makes the Turbo as wide as a 928.

Project leader Friedrich Bezner says this is about as wide as a 911 can ever be, as the production line simply won't allow any further increases. As it is, the Turbo looks noticeably different to the standard car and, apart from the bonnet and doors, all of its external panels have been redesigned. This was unavoidable, as the Turbo has different headlights and larger rear lights, and also needs more cooling than its naturally aspirated brother.

Three enormous vents dominate the front end, hiding a trio of water coolers for the engine, along with two condensers for the air conditioning system. At 62mph, around 1000 litres of air per second will pass through this system; almost three times this amount at the top speed of 189mph.

There are two further vents in the rear wings to feed the pair of intercoolers beneath – a design solution that has allowed the 911 to sport surprisingly

sleek lines at the rear. The wing is now divided into two planes, with the upper section rising by 60mm above 74mph.

This has a crucial effect on the Turbo's stability. The theory is that the wing creates a very slight negative lift at the rear of the car which, when combined with a slight lift at its front end, should give it ideal balance at high speed.

Its drag coefficient (Cd 0.31) has been improved so that, despite only a slight increase in power – 420bhp compared to its predecessor's 408 – its top speed is considerably improved. Porsche's quoted maximum of 189mph compares with 180mph for the old.

As a result, the new Turbo is among the fastest production cars in the world. It is also one of the fastest accelerating, with a quoted 0–62mph time of 4.2sec. It should arrive at 125mph in less than 15sec and should be capable of a standing kilometre in 22.4sec.

These figures apply to the car when equipped with its revised six-speed gearbox. For the five-speed Tiptronic 'box – available for the first time in the Turbo – times are significantly slower, but the system compensates by being more versatile than ever.

For instance, in the Drive position, gearchanges can now be made on the steering wheel, without the gearstick having to be moved to manual mode as before. Furthermore, there are no longer five predetermined transmission programmes in the auto mode, but a continuously variable number of speeds dictated by driving style.

To harness its power on the road, the Turbo couples four-wheel drive with the Porsche Stability Programme (PSM) electronic stability system first seen on the Carrera 4.

PSM is designed to complement on-the-edge

## 'THE NEW TURBO IS AMONG THE FASTEST PRODUCTION CARS IN THE WORLD'

# ANALYSIS

**1 DECEMBER 1999**

Volume 222

No 9 | 5360

**ABOVE** Increased track makes Turbo 30mm wider than Carrera.

## FACTFILE

| Model | Porsche 911 Turbo |
|---|---|
| **Price** | £78,000 (in Germany) |
| **Top speed** | 189mph |
| **0–60mph** | 4.2sec |
| **Length** | 4435mm |
| **Width** | 1890mm |
| **Height** | 1295mm |
| **Wheelbase** | 2350mm |
| **Weight** | 1885kg |
| **Engine layout** | 6 cyls horizontally opposed, twin turbochargers, 3600cc |
| **Max Power** | 420bhp at 6000rpm |
| **Max Torque** | 413lb ft at 2700rpm |
| **Transmission** | Four-wheel drive, six-speed manual/ five-speed Tiptronic |
| **Suspension front** | Transverse arms, MacPherson struts |
| **Suspension rear** | Transverse & longitudinal control arms, spring shock absorber units |
| **Tyres** | 225/40 ZR18 (f), 295/30 ZR18 (r) |

driving styles. It only comes into force when the car is right on the limit of adhesion and only then to help keep the car in control by selective braking of individual wheels.

And make no mistake, these limits are very high with the Turbo. This is because the brake discs have become even larger and stronger, and the dynamic abilities of the Turbo's running gear – which has been based on the Carrera Sport's – far exceed those offered by the basic 911s.

Another contributory factor is the four-wheel-drive system, again based on the Carrera 4's. It is designed to operate without electronic interference, to have power distribution controlled independently by a viscous coupling in the front differential, and to work in harmony with the anti-lock brake system.

At normal driving speeds with minimal rear-wheel slip, only around five per cent of torque is transmitted to the front axle. This will increase to 40 per cent at high speeds or on more slippery surfaces. This makes the Turbo design "rear dominant", similar to that of the Carrera 4, according to Porsche. That helps keep the driving experience largely similar to that of a rear-drive 911. Maximum traction was emphatically not a priority.

The Turbo's engine, by contrast, is completely new. Water-cooled with four valves per cylinder, it shares

# TECHNICAL HIGHLIGHTS OF THE NEW 911 TURBO

**1** New six-speed gearbox with propshaft to rear differential

**2** First water-cooled 3.6-litre twin-turbo 911 engine churns out 420bhp

**3** Familiar telescopic rear wing extends above 74mph to curb lift and improve airflow

**4** Intercoolers for both turbos nestle under wide rear wings

**5** New 18-inch alloy wheels are hollow-cast for light weight

**6** Door sills and air scoops on rear wings are among biggest visual changes

**7** Viscous coupling on front differential can handle up to 40 per cent of torque at high speeds

**8** Enormous air-cooling vents and all-new bi-xenon headlights make for distinctive front end

**9** Engine cooling needs no less than three heat exchangers

almost nothing with the Carrera's horizontally opposed unit other than shape.

Its construction owes much to the race-ready GT3's powerplant. Its vertically divided crankcase is a solid and proven component that has coped with 600bhp or more in competition trim. On either side is a group of three cast cylinders covered by four-valve cylinder heads. This allows Porsche more flexibility in piston displacement, upwards as well as downwards. The latter might become relevant for racing, but as it leaves the factory the new water-cooled engine corresponds exactly to its air-cooled predecessor, with the same bore-stroke ratio for its 3.6 litres. As before, it has race-type dry sump lubrication.

Two turbochargers, four-valve technology and performance-controlled valve lift all promise great things in the power department, although this has clearly not been exploited to maximum effect: 420bhp and 413lb ft aren't that much more than the old Turbo had under the bonnet.

But Porsche promises that both will be available at lower revs, with much flatter power and torque curves than before.

And if this is not enough for you, it will be possible to buy in more performance direct from the factory. How much all this will cost is not yet certain, but it definitely won't come cheap.

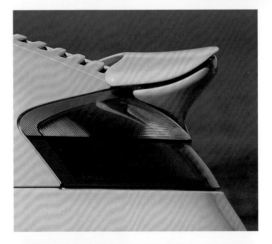

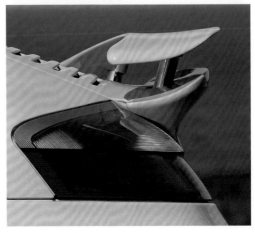

**LEFT** Rear spoiler unobtrusive on Turbo... ...until 74mph, when top section lifts.

# HORN BLOWER

**911 TURBO** The latest Porsche supercar has the awesome performance you expect from a twin-turbo 911, but also a level of refinement that's all new. Peter Robinson reports

Excuse me, but I'm about to be altogether politically incorrect. Three miles a minute is so easily achieved in the new Porsche 911 Turbo that you're constantly looking for a suitable stretch of blacktop.

You see, the Turbo's performance is totally, intoxicatingly, wonderfully addictive. Invariably, you want to stretch this fantastic engine, to push it closer to the limits, to feel again the pulverising sensations it brings, all the while knowing that this 911 can out-accelerate any opposition.

The intrinsic difficulty, therefore, in driving the Turbo is this: I simply don't know how anyone will keep their licence intact. Not only is the new, fifth-generation Turbo the fastest ever street-legal 911, but it's also the most refined. One hundred and twenty five miles per hour – on the autobahn, of course – is utterly effortless, and the urge to go even faster, to tap deeper into its extraordinary acceleration, is almost impossible to resist.

Creating this thump-in-the-back feeling doesn't demand constant working of the six-speed gearbox. So broad and strong is the torque spread that even in the very tall sixth gear you still experience real thrust. Above 70mph you can leave the Turbo in top, forget the lower ratios, and still crush any rivals. Of course, dropping down a cog or two serves up even more blistering performance. Subjectively, this 911 feels closer in character to a big-capacity motorbike than a civilised supercar that weighs 1540kg.

And because Porsche has worked hard on the aerodynamics, the Turbo tracks dead straight above

## QUICK FACTS

| | |
|---|---|
| **Model tested** | 911 Turbo |
| **Price** | £94,749 |
| **0–62mph** | 4.2sec |
| **Top speed** | 189mph |
| **Economy** | 21.9mpg |

# FIRST DRIVE

## 9 FEBRUARY 2000

Volume 223

No 6 I 5369

AUTOCAR
FIRST FOR NEW CARS
9 FEBRUARY 2000 £2

911 TURBO
FIRST DRIVE

FREE
PORSCHE
PULL-OUT
POSTER

100
TEST CARS
ON THE WAY
INSIDE

S·PR 905

414BHP 190MPH 0-60 4SEC
THE ONE NOTHING WILL CATCH

ALL-NEW
MONDEO
THE CAR FORD SAYS WILL OUTHANDLE THE GERMANS

THIS WEEK
MERC SLK V6
NEW TOYOTA
MR2 vs ELISE
SKODA FABIA
E72 RENAULT

PR 905

150mph. Forget the constant corrections and intense
alertness needed in the previous all-wheel-drive
model, let alone the wayward early cars.

But what's missing is the charismatic symphony
of a 911 and, especially, the GT3. Muted by two
intercooled turbochargers, the blown 911's sound
is hushed and so civilised that it doesn't sing like a
Porsche any more. No howl, no adrenalin-pumping
scream, more an almost BMW-like mechanical hum
that builds gently and is eventually, if you keep the
loud pedal down, almost overwhelmed by wind
noise above 140mph. Besides, the source of the
noise can't easily be defined. Close your eyes and this
could even be a front-engined car.

In every other way the new twin-turbo engine
is truly impressive. Now water-cooled and finally
with four valves per cylinder, the 3.6-litre boxer is, in
fact, a turbo version of the dry-sump 911 GT3/GT1
engine, rather than a blown and enlarged variant of
the normally aspirated 911's 3.4-litre unit.

It is, therefore, more closely related to the old
air-cooled 911s. At the beginning of the 996 Turbo
programme in 1996, Porsche looked at blowing the
3.4-litre engine. Turbo engine project engineer Peter
Zickwolf says: "We could have achieved the desired

power." But Porsche realised the 3.4 block would
need extra strengthening, while the GT3's could be
carried over.

The Turbo shares the block, pistons and chain
drive for the camshafts with the GT3, while using
the same head castings, smaller valves and different
combustion chamber shape and induction pipes.
Since it revs to 6750rpm, there's no need for the
GT3's titanium conrods (necessary with a 7800rpm
cut-out). Instead the Turbo gets forged conrods.
For the Turbo, Porsche's VarioCam Plus system
offers two intake timing positions, rather than GT3's
infinitely variable set-up.

Each KKK K64 turbo and intercooler serves
its own cylinder bank and works in parallel to
a maximum boost of 0.8bar, on a much higher
compression ratio of 9.4:1 (the old car was 8.0:1) to
produce 414bhp at 6000rpm and, more significantly,
413lb ft of torque across a wide plateau from
2700rpm to 4600rpm. Porsche boasts that the
Turbo offers an extra 14bhp and 15lb ft over the old
model, preferring to forget that the limited edition
Turbo S had 424bhp and weighed 40kg less. Still, the
turbo boost is now so progressive that it's almost
linear. It begins to build softly at 1800rpm, kicks a

little at 2600rpm, and then delivers a smooth torrent of power to the 6600rpm redline, and on to the 6750rpm fuel cut-out. Lag, while not quite eliminated, is not an issue.

Porsche's own, often pessimistic, figures reveal that the Turbo blasts to 62mph in 4.2sec, 0.6sec faster than the GT3 and 0.3sec ahead of the old Turbo. At just 9.2sec to 100mph, it's a full second quicker than the GT3, and 50-75mph in fifth vanishes in just 5.0sec, 1.7sec less than the GT3, and 0.9sec quicker than a BMW M5. But the figures, impressive as they are, can't hope to convey the immense, yet seemingly effortless, energy of the Turbo. The 189mph top speed is 9mph faster than the old Turbo and 15mph up on the semi-racing GT3. And since it takes just 22.4sec (GT3 23.2sec) to cover a standing kilometre, it makes 150mph possible just about anywhere on the open road. See what I mean about politically incorrect?

According to the official figures, the new Turbo also uses 18 per cent less fuel, with a combined cycle of 21.9mpg. This enables Porsche to justify retaining the regular 911's 64-litre fuel tank, even when it is down 7.5 litres on the old Turbo and 25 litres below left-hand-drive versions of the GT3. The problem is packaging. Fitting three radiators, a driveshaft and axles into the nose doesn't allow any room for a bigger tank, left or right-hand drive. Make full use of the Turbo's performance and you'll struggle to top a miserable 200 miles between fills, if our average of 17.4mpg is typical. A shame, for it rather defeats the purpose of what is otherwise a brilliant GT car

Visually, the Turbo is easily the most radical of the new 911s, and instantly recognisable. Inevitably, given the styling heritage of the Turbo, the rear wheel arches are swollen by 65mm over the Carrera. This time a twin rear wing is created by an active spoiler that rises 60mm on hydraulic dampers built into the engine cover when the car hits 75mph. The extendable wing contributes 9kg of downforce at the 189mph top speed. The clumsy looking side scoops at the trailing edge of the doors feed air to the intercoolers. Son-of-959 vents behind the rear wheels add to its meaner, more squared-off and wider appearance. Yet, the nose is rounder and longer to accommodate a third radiator, and the 911 gets Ferrari 360 Modena-like vents at the front to increase cooling capacity by 50 per cent. A small black chin spoiler, with openings for brake cooling, is styled to minimise lift.

Finally, the headlights, so far unique to the Turbo, arch down into the bumper. Bi-xenon lights are used for the first time, even on low beam. Headlight quality,

**ABOVE** Direct, precise steering suffers no significant kickback and is almost as communitive as the more focused GT3. Turbo's ride is firm but comfortable.

once a serious 911 weakness, is now a real strength. Porsche says the Turbo's drag coefficient has improved from 0.34 to 0.31, a notable achievement since it's only 0.1 higher than the standard Carrera.

Compared with the Carrera 4, the Turbo sits 10mm lower and rides on the 911's firmer optional Sports suspension. The Turbo's brakes are from the GT3 and are as impressive as its acceleration. Massive 330mm cross-drilled, ventilated, four-caliper discs do the job. Later this year, for the first time on a production car, the options list includes ceramic composite brakes which weigh 50 per cent less than the standard discs and have a lifespan of 186,000 miles

For the first time on a 911 Turbo, Porsche offers an automatic option – a Mercedes-Benz five-speed unit set up to function as a Tiptronic via steering wheel buttons – or a wholly revised slick six-speed manual. Drive is fed via a viscous coupling to the front and rear axles. In normal conditions, just five per cent of power is delivered to the front wheels, but that can increase to 40 per cent to discourage oversteer. In reality, the Turbo simply charges around corners, oblivious to g-forces, following exactly the chosen path and seemingly never, running short of traction. It is remarkably easy to drive gently, with a progressive, fluent clutch, and precise and direct steering.

The limits are so high that seemingly insane speeds are required before Porsche's PSM electronic stability control system cuts in. Even if you switch off PSM, you need only to brake to reintroduce the system, which then brakes each wheel individually to correct any loss of traction. It can't defeat physics, of course, but gives the Turbo near drama-free handling. Find a damp airfield, and I'm sure power slides will come naturally, provided you stay off the brakes.

The tyres, noisy on coarse surfaces, hint at tramlining on less than smooth tarmac, but just when you expect the nose to wander it straightens up. Kickback is never a problem, yet the steering almost matches the GT3 (they share the same servo pump) in its ability to serve up a constant stream of information. With 225/40 ZR18 tyres at the front and 295/30 ZR18s at the rear, you'd expect the ride to be firm, and it is. But it's firm rather than harsh, although it can jolt over sharp bumps at low speeds. Mostly, the Turbo delivers a comfortable ride that's ideally suited to long-distance motoring. Since there is enough power to lift the nose under full noise, subjectively the Turbo seems to lack the superb body control of the GT3. Conversely, it has superior traction, especially in slippery conditions.

To help justify the £94,749 price, Porsche throws

## SPECIFICATIONS 911 TURBO

### ECONOMY
| | |
|---|---|
| Urban | 14.4mpg |
| Extra urban | 30.7mpg |
| Combined | 21.9mpg |

### DIMENSIONS
| | |
|---|---|
| Length | 4435mm |
| Width (exc. mirrors) | 1830mm |
| Height | 1295mm |
| Wheelbase | 2350mm |
| Weight | 1540kg |
| Fuel tank | 64 litres |

### ENGINE
| | |
|---|---|
| Layout | 6 cyls opposed, 3600cc |
| Max power | 414bhp at 6000rpm |
| Max torque | 413lb ft at 2700–4600rpm |
| Specific output | 115bhp per litre |
| Power to weight | 265bhp per tonne |
| Installation | Rear, longitudinal, 4WD |
| Bore/stroke | 100/76.4mm |
| Made of | Alloy heads and block |
| Compression ratio | 9.4:1 |
| Valve gear | 4 per cyl, dohc per bank |
| Ignition and fuel | Bosch ME 7.8 engine management, two turbos, two intercoolers |

### STEERING
| | |
|---|---|
| Type | Rack and pinion, power assisted |
| Turns lock-to-lock | 3.0 |

### GEARBOX
**Type** 6-speed manual
(or 5-speed automatic)
**Ratios/mph per 1000rpm**
**Final drive ratio** 3.44:1

| | | | |
|---|---|---|---|
| 1st 3.82/5.6 | | 2nd 2.05/10.5 | |
| 3rd 1.41/15.3 | | 4th 1.12/19.3 | |
| 5th 0.92/23.5 | | 6th 0.75/28.8 | |

### SUSPENSION
**Front** MacPherson struts, coil springs
**Rear** Independent multi-link, coil springs, anti-roll bar

### BRAKES
**Front** 330mm ventilated discs
**Rear** 330mm ventilated discs

### WHEELS AND TYRES
**Made of** Aluminium
**Size** 8Jx18in (f), 11Jx18in (r)
**Tyres** 225/40 ZR18N3 (f), 295/30 ZR18 N3 (r), Pirelli P-Zero

### THE **AUTOCAR** VERDICT
This level of performance demands respect. Easily the best 911 Turbo ever, though its character is now determinedly refined rather than adventurously exciting.

in a day's advanced driving course with every Turbo sold in the UK, and loads the new top-of-the-range 911 with a full leather interior, Alcantara headlining, electric seats with key-operated memory, trip computer, automatic air conditioning, an alarm and immobiliser. The digital speedo has been moved out of the central revcounter into the conventional speedometer to allow the trip computer to display more information. Small LEDs are used to light the ignition lock, light switch and door handles. Electric switches on the driver's door sill replace the handles for the bonnet and engine cover.

Mostly the changes work in lifting the perception of cabin quality by ridding the dashboard of virtually every shiny plastic surface. But the seats lack lateral support (deep GT3 buckets are an option), and the cushion seems shallow, while the seat back doesn't provide enough support for the shoulders.

The Turbo adds another desirable branch to the 911 tree. It's obviously not as sporting in its focus as the GT3, yet offers noticeably more performance and comfort, which makes the skimpy touring range even more frustrating.

But speed rarely comes as refined as in the new 911 Turbo. I'm totally hooked. When do we get another go?

# PORSCHE 911 TURBO

The Turbo has been the evocative centrepiece of the 911 line-up for 25 years. We find out if the all-new four-wheel drive version is a fitting successor to its forebears

This car needs little introduction. It is the latest version of the most famous sports car of all time, continuing a tradition of turbocharged 911s that began in 1975. For 25 years the 911 Turbo has been the fastest and most expensive car in the range. Strange, then, that it hasn't always offered the same driving thrills as a regular normally aspirated Carrera.

But there is a twist this time. With the launch of the new 911 in 1997, the traditional Porsche recipe was altered – and not necessarily to everyone's taste. It was bigger, faster and water-cooled. Could forced induction and a four-wheel-drive chassis make the new Turbo the most complete 911 ever made, and one of the best to drive?

## DESIGN & ENGINEERING ★★★★★
**Tech eliminates lag and gives peerless safety**

This being the new all-singing, all-dancing Turbo, it seems odd not to be crowing about huge power and torque gains over the outgoing Turbo. Yes there is a massive 414bhp at 6000rpm and 413lb ft of torque from 2700-4600rpm (up 14bhp and 15lb ft) but they aren't stunning gains.

But scrutinise the engine specification and the method behind this uncharacteristically cautious

| QUICK FACTS | |
|---|---|
| **Model tested** | 911 Turbo |
| **Price** | £86,000 |
| **Top speed** | 189mph |
| **30–70mph** | 3.4sec |
| **0–60mph** | 3.9sec |
| **60–0mph** | 2.4sec |
| **MPG** | 19.6mpg |
| **For** | Performance, brakes, steering, build quality, ride |
| **Against** | Thirst, poor range, lack of flair in styling detail |

# ROAD TEST

## 12 JULY 2000

Volume 225

No 2 | 5391

Four-wheel drive weighs 55kg. Viscous coupling gives 95 per cent of drive to the rear in normal driving.

At 189mph the extendable rear wing generates 9kg of downforce. In normal driving it appears at 75mph.

Ventilated steel brake discs standard. But later Turbos will be available with ceramic composite discs.

Twin KKK turbos and air-to-air intercoolers help 3600cc water-cooled flat six produce 414bhp and 413lb ft.

**ABOVE** 3.6 engine from GT3 given virtually lag-free turbo boost, translating into effortless power in every gear.

**OPPOSITE TOP** Plastic intake inserts look cheap; Turbo recorded 60–0mph in 2.4sec.

approach to turbocharging emerges. Porsche was after unrivalled driveability, a blown engine that simply didn't feel turbocharged.

The regular 911's block would have needed strengthening, so Porsche started with the dry-sump 3.6-litre engine from the GT3 and added a single KKK K64 turbocharger for each of the horizontally opposed banks of cylinders. Given how fantastic the GT3 unit is, that's an appealing combination.

Some of the GT3's trick internals were deemed

surplus to this lower-revving unit – it has a 6750rpm limiter, against the GT3's 7800rpm. So the titanium conrods went back to the motorsport shelf and are replaced by forged items, and the variable inlet valve timing system has two positions rather than the fully variable set-up on the GT3.

But if you want evidence of how much Porsche wanted to eliminate lag, just look at the 9.4:1 compression ratio. It's comparable with a regular normally aspirated saloon car.

It's about the only thing that is, though. Since 1993, Porsche has thought it prudent to supply its fastest car with permanent four-wheel drive. It still does. Driven in a straight line the Turbo is effectively rear-wheel drive, with just five per cent of drive going to the front wheels. But that can rise to as much as 40 per cent if the system senses a loss of traction.

On top of this is Porsche's PSM traction and stability control system, first seen on the 1998 Carrera 4. It can operate on each wheel individually and, in conjunction with the awesome active safety of the four-wheel-drive system, must make the Turbo one of the safest-handling supercars ever. New front lights, twin air intakes in the front bumper and just in front of the rear wheels identify the car on the road.

## HISTORY

Motorsport success in the early '70s with turbochargers saw the first 911 Turbo arrive in 1975. It had 260bhp, and thanks to fearsome turbo lag and an unforgiving rear-engined chassis many ended up in hedges. Through the '80s its power climbed to 300bhp and in 1988 it got a five-speed gearbox. An all-new Turbo arrived in 1992 with 360bhp. The outgoing 400bhp 993 Turbo dates from 1995. Awesome special editions have included the 1992 380bhp Turbo S and the stunning 1995 420bhp GT2.

Add the duck tail wing and 959-style ducting on the underside of the rear wings, and the car makes a very different statement to the standard Carrera on the road. If Porsche wanted the Turbo to look as hard as nails it's succeeded.

## PERFORMANCE AND BRAKES ★★★★
**Slower, but power delivery is sweet?**

Here's a lesson in not getting too tied up in the raw data churned out by the computer.

The figures will tell you the following: that the Turbo rockets from rest to 30mph in 1.4sec and 60mph in 3.9sec. That the all important 0-100mph run is dispatched in just 9.4sec, and that by the time the standing kilometre has flashed past in 21.9sec the 1549kg Porsche is travelling at 149mph. Impressive stuff.

But then you remember that the old 993 Turbo managed 1.5sec, 3.7sec and 9.2sec over the same increments back in 1995. And the Ferrari 360 Modena (without the benefit of four-wheel drive) may be slower to 30 and 60mph but is 0.6sec faster to the magic ton. We have no doubts about the Porsche's claimed 189mph maximum.

# ROAD TEST 911 TURBO

## MAXIMUM SPEEDS

| | | | |
|---|---|---|---|
| **6th** 189mph/6560rpm | | **5th** 153/6500 | |
| **4th** 125/6500 | | **3rd** 100/6500 | |
| **2nd** 69/6500 | | **1st** 36/6500 | |

## ACCELERATION FROM REST

| True mph | seconds | speedo mph |
|---|---|---|
| 30 | 1.4 | 31 |
| 40 | 2.3 | 41 |
| 50 | 3.0 | 51 |
| 60 | 3.9 | 61 |
| 70 | 4.9 | 72 |
| 80 | 6.1 | 82 |
| 90 | 7.4 | 92 |
| 100 | 9.4 | 102 |
| 110 | 11.3 | 113 |
| 120 | 13.1 | 123 |
| 130 | 15.8 | 133 |
| 140 | 18.8 | 143 |
| 150 | 22.1 | 154 |

Standing qtr mile 12.3sec/115mph
Standing km 21.9sec/149mph
30–70mph through gears 3.4sec

## ACCELERATION IN GEAR

| MPH | 6th | 5th | 4th | 3rd | 2nd |
|---|---|---|---|---|---|
| 30–50 | 9.0 | 5.7 | 3.9 | 2.8 | 1.7 |
| 40–60 | 7.0 | 4.7 | 3.2 | 2.4 | 1.7 |
| 50–70 | 5.7 | 3.9 | 3.0 | 2.3 | - |
| 60–80 | 4.9 | 3.5 | 3.0 | 2.4 | - |
| 70–90 | 4.7 | 3.7 | 3.0 | 2.5 | - |
| 80–100 | 4.9 | 4.0 | 3.1 | 2.6 | - |
| 90–110 | 5.1 | 4.0 | 3.3 | - | - |
| 100–120 | 5.4 | 4.5 | 3.6 | - | - |
| 110–130 | 6.3 | 5.1 | - | - | - |
| 120–140 | 6.9 | 5.6 | - | - | - |
| 130–150 | 7.3 | 6.8 | - | - | - |

## FUEL CONSUMPTION

Average/best/worst/touring
19.6/22.1/22.1/12.8mpg

| | |
|---|---|
| Urban | 14.4mpg |
| Extra urban | 30.7mpg |
| Combined | 21.9mpg |
| Tank capacity | 64 litres |
| Touring range | 310 miles |

## BRAKES

| | |
|---|---|
| 30/50/70mph | 8.5/23.1/45.0 metres |
| 60–0mph | 2.4sec |

## NOISE

| | |
|---|---|
| Idle/max revs | 54/80dbA |
| 30/50/70mph | 71/73/75dbA |

## TEST NOTES

It's another reincarnation for the good old 911 HUL plate. Oddly enough, the first 911 Turbo *Autocar* tested arrived in 1975 with the plate 2 GOO, and it wasn't until '83 that the now famous Turbo press car plate became tradition. It reappeared in '89, '91 and most recently in 1995.

Spent a day in the Turbo with our long term Evo 6 in Wales. The Porsche had too much pace and grip for even the mighty Mitsubishi.

The low chin spoiler can be a pain. Of the three examples we've driven, every one was badly damaged.

Nice to see a car designed for sustained high speeds. The windscreen wipers worked perfectly, even on the wrong side of 170mph.

# SPECIFICATIONS 911 TURBO

## DIMENSIONS

Min/max front legroom 830/1090mm  Max front headroom 970mm
Interior width front/rear 1340/1250mm  Max boot width 740mm  Boot length 420mm
Boot volume 130dm³  Front/rear tracks 1465/1522mm  Kerb weight 1549kg
Weight distribution front/rear 41/59  Width with/without mirrors 1930/1465mm

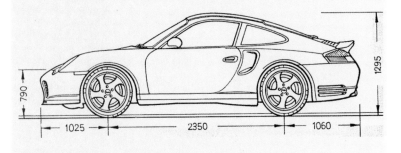

790    1025    2350    1060    1295

## ENGINE

| | |
|---|---|
| Layout | 6-cyl horizontally opposed, 3600cc |
| Max power | 414bhp at 6000rpm |
| Max torque | 413lb ft at 2700–4600rpm |
| Power to weight | 276bhp per tonne |
| Torque to weight | 266lb ft per tonne |
| Installation | Rear, longitudinal, 4WD |
| Construction | Alloy heads and block |
| Bore/stroke | 100.0/76.4mm |
| Valve gear | 4 per cyl, dohc |
| Compression ratio | 9.4:1 |
| Ignition and fuel | Bosch ME 7.8 engine management, multi-point fuel injection |

## GEARBOX

Gearbox 6-speed manual
Ratios/mph per 1000rpm
Final drive 3.44:1

| | | | |
|---|---|---|---|
| 1st | 3.82/5.6 | 2nd | 2.05/10.5 |
| 3rd | 1.41/15.3 | 4th | 1.12/19.3 |
| 5th | 0.92/23.5 | 6th | 0.75/28.8 |

## SUSPENSION

Front Struts, coil springs, anti-roll bar
Rear Multi-link, coil springs, anti-roll bar

## CHASSIS AND BODY

Body 2dr coupé
Wheels 8Jx18in (f), 11Jx18in (r)
Made of Cast alloy
Tyres 225/40 ZR18 (f), 295/30 ZR18 (r)
Spare Space saver

## STEERING

Type Rack and pinion, power assisted
Turns lock-to-lock 3.0
Turning circle 10.6m

## BRAKES

Front 330mm ventilated discs
Rear 330mm ventilated discs
Anti-lock Standard

So why do we have nothing but high praise for a motor that seems to have taken a backwards stumble? Because it is probably the best turbo installation ever, and provides effortless power in every gear from as little as 1800rpm. Because throttle response is so crisp that it's possible to blip the engine on a downchange – be it heel-and-toeing or simply de-clutching – as if it was a normally aspirated Carrera.

The in-gear times support this to an extent but still don't paint a clear enough picture of the massive torque that seems to lob you down the road until your sense of responsibility makes you back off. In fourth gear, 30-50mph takes 3.9sec – exactly the same as the Ferrari – and 50-70mph in top takes just 5.7sec – a full 1.2sec less than the Modena can manage.

It makes great noises too. Just the right amount of turbo whoosh mixes with a deeper, meaner engine note than the standard Carrera to leave occupants and passers-by in no doubt that this is a bona fide supercar.

But it can switch off and play the comfortable cruiser surprisingly well too. The gearbox and clutch have a deliberate mechanical feel, but are light enough to be used in traffic all day. As in all 911s, engine noise simply isn't a factor at speed, and what wind noise there is doesn't intrude much.

It seems every new Porsche is a showcase for braking technology these days. The Turbo is no different. Ventilated, cross-drilled discs measuring 330mm sit at each corner and remain imperious no matter how you treat them. A 2.4sec 60-0mph time is only a tiny part of their fantastic repertoire.

### HANDLING AND RIDE ★★★★★
**Balance of driver involvement and comfort**

The 911 Turbo does things other cars can't do, with huge amounts of grip, poise and steering ability. The days are gone when 911 Turbos were blindingly fast cross-country tools let down by inferior steering and power delivery that made it difficult to get the best from the chassis.

It only takes a few miles to realise the 3.0-turn lock-to-lock rack on the Turbo is at least as sweet as that of a Carrera 2. There's real consistency in the way it loads up and just the right amount of patter though the leather-bound rim to inform the driver of surface changes and altering levels of grip.

**Air con and traction control are standard, but CD is extra.**

**Steering wheel is reach and rake-adjustable, feels great in the hands.**

**Red line appears at 6500rpm and engine is still strong at 6800rpm.**

Not that they really matter in a car with such other worldly amounts of grip anyway. On a dry road it is near impossible to reach the Turbo's limits, let alone breach them. The car just turns in on instruction, remains neutral under a constant throttle or tucks in under a trailing throttle, and then fires up the road in search of the next tricky apex. And this time it's not a dull experience. Because throttle response is so good the chassis feels infinitely more adjustable, even though gratuitous powerslides are off the agenda.

But the most impressive thing about the car is the balance it strikes between ultimate driver involvement and comfort. There's a suppleness in the car's whole demeanour that just isn't present in any other 911. At first the car feels too soft and then you quickly realise that the Turbo rides the most obnoxious of surfaces with no complaint. The movements are so well controlled you can travel at remarkable speed on even the most treacherous B-roads.

And when the weather gets nasty, you've only got to slow down a little bit.

High-speed stability is superb, and the improved ride comfort means that motorway journeys are far less tiresome than they once were, even if the

**ABOVE** Driver's seat is superb but adjustment is only partly electric.

**LEFT** Seats not class best, but driving position is excellent. Buyers shorn of £86k could bemoan lack of gadgets, though.

## WHAT IT COSTS

### PORSCHE 911 TURBO

| | | | |
|---|---|---|---|
| **On-the-road price** | £86,000 | Leather trim | ■ |
| **Price as tested** | £86,095 | Height/tilt-adjust steering column | ■/■ |
| **Cost per mile** | £165 | Anti-lock brakes | ■ |
| **Insurance group** | 20 | Airbag driver/passenger/side | ■/■/■ |
| **Typical quote** | £1,200 | Cruise control | £450 |
| | | Alarm/immobiliser | ■/■ |
| | | RDS stereo/**CD player** | ■/**£95** |

### EQUIPMENT CHECKLIST

| | | | |
|---|---|---|---|
| Air conditioning | ■ | Options in **bold** fitted to test car | |
| Traction control | ■ | ■ = Standard  na = not available | |

295/30 ZR18 rear Pirelli P-Zeros do want to be heard too much of the time.

Only the extra size of the 996 bodyshell lets the side down. The 911 Turbo is just too big, and feels unwieldy on our narrower blacktop. In light of the car's all-round ability, though, it's a small compromise.

### SAFETY AND EQUIPMENT ★★★★
**Front seats adequate, cabin lacks design flair**

Don't be fooled by the sumptuously trimmed rear seats – the Turbo is a two-seater with space for a couple of vertically challenged four-year-olds in the back. Far better to fold the back seats down and add to the rather small boot.

It's a good workplace, though. The standard sports seats aren't the last word in comfort or support but everyone found them good enough, despite the odd mixture of electric and manual adjustment. The driving position is excellent but the steering wheel only adjusts for reach, so some will inevitably find it set too low.

The now familiar overlapping instrument cluster has been slightly altered for the Turbo,

with questionable success. Porsche's central rev counter with digital speed read-out at the bottom has long been one of the clearest systems around. So it's a shame to see that a more extensive trip computer display has usurped the digital speed read-out. It now takes two glances to check road and engine speed. Not a welcome change in such a rapid car.

The rest of the cabin is standard 911. The centre console is ergonomically sound but the plastics aren't of the highest quality and the switchgear isn't the most tactile. It all works well enough, but we'd like a little more titillation for our £86,000.

Standard equipment includes leather seats, climate control and a gaggle of airbags. One notable omission for a car with GT pretensions is cruise control, a substantial £450 option.

It doesn't matter if you prize active or passive safety, or a combination of the two. The Turbo is about as safe as it gets. Twin front airbags and side airbags protect the occupants, and a supremely safe four-wheel-drive chassis with stability and traction control give the driver a good chance of avoiding the incident in the first place.

**BELOW** Four-wheel drive and unshakeable control make for safe thrills on B-roads; digital speed read-out is now left of its perfect position under revcounter; materials not always top quality.

## MARKET AND FINANCE ★★★★
### Good value but not the best 911 to resale

There's no doubt the 911 Turbo offers value for money against its established rivals. Mainly because it's £11,000 cheaper than was first expected, thanks to Porsche UK's recent across-the-range price cuts.

No doubt the car will be supplied in numbers so small, used values won't be badly affected. And the usual comprehensive Porsche two-year, unlimited mileage warranty adds peace of mind into the equation.

Our only concern is that used values of the current 911 haven't been too stable of late, and the Turbo variant of every 911 is always hit the hardest come resale time. A good but not rock solid investment.

## ECONOMY ★★★
### Acceptable thirst thwarted by miniscule tank

As you might expect, fuel economy is not the Turbo's strong point. Even on the touring route it could only manage 22.1mpg and that figure fell to a dismal 12.8mpg at the test track.

Our overall test average of 19.6mpg wouldn't

seem too bad if it was supported by a decent sized tank. Unfortunately, there's only room for 64 litres of super unleaded, leaving a range of 183 miles with a heavy right foot and 311 miles in fuel miser mode.

**ABOVE** Turbo is brilliant all-rounder that both cossets and exhilarates the driver.

---

## THE **AUTOCAR** VERDICT

It takes a while to understand exactly what Porsche has achieved with the new 911 Turbo.

The new car is a massive improvement over the old one. Granted, those who thrived on the sheer pace of the old Turbo won't find the straight-line speed reason enough to buy one, but that's one of the only two glitches.

Finally, 30 years after it started forcing compressed air into engines, Porsche has produced an almost lag-free motor. What the bald figures can't tell you is just how usable every one of those 414 horses is. And that's before you've considered the astonishingly capable chassis that copes with rotten B-roads without blinking.

And the whole package is more impressive than its parts. It is equally rewarding on that favourite section of the journey home or a trans-continental thrash. Nothing with a 911 badge has ever been able to boast that. Which makes the tiny fuel tank even more unforgiveable. Despite this, the Turbo is the best 996 yet and another truly great Porsche.

### First Turbo with genuine all-round ability  ★★★★★

# GT2 MUCH

**911 GT2** The awesomely powerful GT2 is Porsche's fastest production car. But it's also the most expensive. *By Steve Sutcliffe*

Four hundred and fifty-seven brake horsepower. In a rear-engined, rear-wheel-drive car. Without traction control. Blimey. Even Porsche's resident wheelman Walter Rohrl squints slightly when I ask him how fast the new 911 GT2 is on the road. Just for a moment I think he's going to be coy but then, like a light bulb coming on, his expression changes when I ask him how quick it is around the Nürburgring. The smile isn't wholly revealing, but you can still tell: even Walter thinks the GT2 is quick with a capital F.

And the stopwatch proves it. Unofficially, Rohrl has done a swift 7min 47sec lap. "But I wasn't really trying and the car wasn't quite set up properly" he says. There will, however, be an official time set in the spring. And yes, we'll be there to report on it.

That even a man like Rohrl thinks the GT2 is rapid is hardly surprising, considering Porsche reckons this to be the fastest production car it has ever built. Yes, the various GT1 incarnations were quicker, as no doubt was Count Rossi's one and only road legal 917, a photo of which I used to carry in my wallet for reference purposes whenever the question "what is the silliest car ever?" arose in my youth.

But none of these were fully fledged production machines, which means in the real world the GT2 truly is the fastest ever Porsche.

## QUICK FACTS

| | |
|---|---|
| **Model tested** | 911 GT2 |
| **Price** | £118,000 (est) |
| **On sale** | May |
| **0–62mph** | 4.1sec |
| **0–100mph** | 8.5sec |
| **0–124mph** | 12.9sec |
| **Top speed** | 196mph |
| **Urban** | 14.9mpg |
| **Extra urban** | 30.4mpg |
| **Combined** | 21.9mpg |

Whether it's also the best product ever to emerge from Porsche's development centre in Weissach, Germany, is another matter. Having spent the day driving a GT2 just outside Venice I'd say it's not, though the roads were rather limiting, so to be sure I'll wait until we drive the car on familiar UK roads before venturing a definitive verdict.

What I can tell you here and now is this: the GT2 is not as good a road car as the latest 911 Turbo on which it is based. Neither is it as good value.

I'll come to the reasons for the former statement in a while, but explaining the latter requires nothing more than maths and plain common sense. In Germany the GT2 has just gone on sale for a whopping DM339,000 as opposed to DM243,000 for the regular Turbo. In English money that's a premium of £32,000 over the Turbo's £86,000 price – for a car that isn't four-wheel-drive, doesn't feature as much equipment inside and which has only 10 per cent more power.

Ah, but the GT2 is designed to appeal to a completely different type of customer, says Porsche. That's why its suspension owes more to the raw and raucous GT3 than it does to the Turbo. Hence also the bucket seats, huge rear wing, acres of carbonfibre inside and the quasi Le Mans racer aero kit, which is said to improve airflow through the car for its cooling qualities as well as produce active downforce over the front and rear axles.

But, big wing and extra spoilers aside, truth is you can tell the GT2 is little more than a pumped-up 911 Turbo. It looks like the same car fundamentally, albeit lower and with a little more attitude around the nose and tail. Underneath too, despite having slightly more power and therefore even greater go, the mechanical differences aren't that great beyond the fitment of Porsche's ceramic composite brake discs, which are optional on the Turbo anyway.

So it's hardly surprising that, visually at least, the GT2 carries nothing like the clout of the original

# FEATURE

28 FEBRUARY 2001

Volume 227

No 9 | 5423

AUTOCAR
FIRST FOR NEW CARS

20-page special

Formula 1 preview
20 extra pages

Exclusive We ride in Schuey's Seicento!

Inside story
Aston builds a Ferrari

Vanquish New British hero targets Maranello

car of the same name. That car was magnificently outrageous in every way – and although it cost the price of a well specified BMW 5-series more than any other 911 at the time it somehow justified its price by being so utterly extreme.

Sadly, that's no longer the case. According to Rohrl the latest GT2 is a surprisingly comfortable car on the road, much like the Turbo in fact. The springs, and dampers are around 12 per cent stiffer and the ride height is a meaningful 20mm lower front and rear.

"But it's still an easy car to drive every day. Not as sporting or responsive as the GT3," says Rohrl. "But faster, quieter and more comfortable."

Hmm.

So, it's got an engine that produces 43bhp more than the 189mph Turbo and it weighs 100kg less because the all-wheel-drive system has been binned along with much of the sound deadening material (including the rear seats). And it'll go sideways at the flex of a big toe thanks to a new limited-slip differential – the only form of traction aid beyond your imagination.

Why, then, am I not having a ball in this car? Because by Porsche's own admission this is not a fully focused driver's delight like the old 911 GT2, or even the recently discontinued GT3. Instead, it's merely a faster, two-wheel-drive incarnation of the current Turbo with extra understeer dialled in to keep you on the straight and narrow. Although frankly, it understeers so much in slower corners that this in itself becomes a rather worrying trait, especially when the roads are slippery like those we used around Venice.

I wish I could say I was joking about all this. Sadly, I'm not. I had barely been able to sleep the night before driving this car. I thought it would be one of the year's most exciting four-wheeled experiences. But in reality, although the roads I drove it on didn't help one bit, I came away chronically disappointed.

## 'PERFORMANCE IS MONUMENTAL – WITH THE EMPHASIS ON THE SECOND HALF OF THAT WORD'

Straight-line performance from GT2 is awesome, with a top speed of 196mph and 0–62mph covered in just 4.1 seconds. Brakes are just as impressive.

Not because the GT2 is in any way a bad car to drive, but because it isn't an incredible one.

Like the Cayenne Range Rover rival due to go on sale next year, this model is, I suspect, indicative of the shift in core values currently occurring at Porsche. Without wishing to sound too naive or old fashioned, I'm saddened by the fact that hardcore enthusiasts are no longer top of the list of people that Weissach wants to satisfy, not even when it comes to models as extreme as this.

Having said all that, the GT2 does have its moments, though usually only on long, straight, flat pieces of road. Put simply, the performance is monumental – with the emphasis on the second half of that word.

According to Porsche it'll do 60mph in four and a bit seconds, 100mph in 8.5sec and 124mph (0-200km/h) in 12.9sec. The quoted top speed is, somewhat enigmatically, 4mph shy of the magic 200mph. Apparently the greens would have gone very red indeed had a 200mph top speed been quoted, so the car was geared to hit its limiter in sixth at 196mph (as if 196mph is some kind of sane speed compared with 200mph).

Unsurprisingly for a Porsche, it also stops rather

**ABOVE** Cabin features bucket seats and aims for a real racer feel, with specification levels in fact lower than donor 911 Turbo despite the GT2's higher price.

**LEFT** Subtle logo on handbrake lever denotes a special 911; Boxer six produces a scorching 457bhp peak output.

**ABOVE** GT2 shares most of its componentry with the Turbo although suspension set-up is stiffer, as on the GT3.

**OPPOSITE TOP** Huge wing dominates the rear end; nose looks more aggresive than on 911 Turbo.

well. Very well in fact. The ceramic discs don't improve actual braking power by that much, but considering the regular Turbo with steel brakes stops violently enough to stretch your retinas, that's not a complaint. The main benefit of the composite discs is their superior longevity. Porsche reckons they're good for about 150,000 miles, as opposed to anything between 35,000-50,000 for the steel equivalents. At £250 per disc that's a significant chunk of cash saved in the long run.

Like the 911 Turbo, only more so, the GT2 has no weak areas to its performance subjectively, apart from its lack of any real aural thrill. Sadly turbocharging has hushed the operations of the water-cooled horizontally opposed six.

It starts to pull meaningfully from as little as 2000rpm in any of the first four gears, and by 3500rpm the surge borders on the ridiculous in any gear. Mid-range overtaking performance is genuinely titanic and would be hilarious were it not necessary to have every last one of your wits about you to avoid an engagement with the passing scenery.

There's so much acceleration available below 100mph that even on a dry road you need to think hard about whether full throttle is strictly necessary when overtaking. Most of the time it isn't. Wheelspin, even with the engine hung out over the rear tyres and a limited-slip diff to aid traction, is not exactly uncommon. I can't imagine what it would be like in the middle of the night, in the rain, on a dark and unfamiliar road. Fantastically-scary, no doubt.

Which would be perfectly fine and dandy in a warped kind of way, so long as the chassis was of a similarly crisp calibre. But it isn't. Not, at any rate, when it comes to communicating what's happening beneath you and controlling the inertia that the engine is capable of creating.

In my opinion, you can forget ride comfort, tyre roar, suspension rumble and all the other traditional concessions to refinement in a car like this, because none of them really matters. This is the ultimate 911 so it should be just that dynamically, and who cares if the ride's hard and tyre roar is a bit raucous?

Yet Porsche has deliberately tried to make it

'YOU NEED TO THINK HARD ABOUT WHETHER FULL THROTTLE IS STRICTLY NECESSARY WHEN OVERTAKING'

# SPECIFICATIONS 911 GT2

## DIMENSIONS

| | |
|---|---|
| Length | 4446mm |
| Width | 1830mm |
| Height | 1275mm |
| Wheelbase | 2355mm |
| Weight | 1440kg |
| Fuel tank | 89 litres (lhd), |
| | 64 litres (rhd) |

## ENGINE

| | |
|---|---|
| Layout | 6 cyls opposed, 3600cc |
| Max power | 457bhp at 5700rpm |
| Max torque | 457lb ft at 3500- |
| | 4500rpm |
| Specific output | 127bhp per litre |
| Power to weight | 317bhp per tonne |
| Installation | Rear, longitudinal, rwd |
| Bore/stroke | 100/76mm |
| Made of | Alloy heads and block |
| Compression ratio | 9.4:1 |
| Valve gear | 4 per cyl, dohc per |
| | bank |
| Ignition and fuel | Motronic ME 7.8 |
| | engine management, |
| | twin KKK turbos |

## STEERING

**Type** Rack and pinion, power assisted
**Turns lock-to-lock** 3.0

## GEARBOX

**Type** 6-speed manual
**Ratios/mph per 1000rpm**
**Final drive ratio** 3.44:1

| | | | |
|---|---|---|---|
| 1st 3.82/5.7 | | 2nd 2.05/10.7 | |
| 3rd 1.41/15.6 | | 4th 1.12/19.6 | |
| 5th 0.92/23.9 | | 6th 0.75/29.3 | |

## SUSPENSION

**Front** MacPherson struts, coil springs, anti-roll bar
**Rear** Multi-link, coil springs, adjustable anti-roll bar

## BRAKES

**Front and rear** 350mm ceramic composite discs
**Anti-lock** Standard

## WHEELS AND TYRES

**Made of** Alloy
**Size** 8.5J x18in (f), 12.0J x18in (r)
**Tyres** 235/40 ZR18 (f), 315/30 ZR18 (r)
Pirelli P-Zero Rosso

## THE VERDICT

Should be the ultimate 911. But massive acceleration and braking ability aside, it's not as good as the Turbo. Shame.

a car for all seasons in terms of its chassis, hence the surprisingly supple ride and the peculiarly soft rear end. And the strange lack of control to the suspension through fast sweeping corners.

What the GT2 ends up being as a result is neither one thing nor the other. It's neither an effective grand tourer nor an ultimate sports car.

Because much of the sound deadening has been removed, it's not a good long-distance cruiser, especially not in right-hand-drive form, where the fuel tank shrinks from 89 litres to an inadequate 64 litres (for packaging and crash safety reasons, apparently). Nor is it the thinly disguised road racer you expect and so desperately want it to be. It's too soft, too comfortable and too civilised for that.

Which ironically is why it will appeal to, and be bought by, many more people than the old GT2. The accountants at Porsche will no doubt consider this a result, as will the company's shareholders. And in a way they'll be right.

But the engineers on whose reputation the company was founded will surely be less proud of their latest creation. The GT2 should be the most exciting Porsche ever built, as well as the fastest and most expensive. It may well be the latter, but the former it is not. Shame, but at least I now know why Walter Rohrl prefers the GT3.

# FASTER, BETTER

**911 3.6 CARRERA** The 911 Carrera has undergone a continuous programme of improvement. Could the latest incarnation be the best 911 yet?

Funny this, and just a bit sad: Porsche is especially proud of the 911's new cupholder. It slots neatly, almost hidden, into the surround below the centre air-vents of the otherwise barely revised dashboard. Push the right end and, first, a spring-loaded arm swings out to reveal a single cupholder. Pull that and it extends to release a second one. Clever, and more effective than the previous afterthought device that attached to the side vents.

We can thank the Americans for that. Don't you love 'em? Here we have possibly the world's greatest sports car and the improvement they identified as the most crucial for the first facelift of the nearly four-year-old 996 Carrera was cupholders that work.

Fair enough, I guess, if you drink coffee on your drive to work. We enthusiasts (is this European arrogance?) can take solace, though, that Porsche hasn't gone soft in its panderings to its biggest market. Bottom line: this is a better 911, faster, more powerful and economical, visually more attractive and less likely to be confused with the Boxster. And, of course, it's better equipped. There will be no price increase, either, when the range of coupé and cabriolet models in Carrera 2 and 4 form reach UK dealers in September, while the new Targa and Turbo-look 4S follow a couple of months later.

Perhaps more than any other, the 911 has benefited from unceasing development and refinement throughout its life – almost 38 years. This version, the first revision of the water-cooled model, conforms to the same house philosophy.

The immediate clue to the enlarged engine capacity is a deeper engine note at low to medium revs, what Porsche calls a "more voluminous sound body". This harder noise develops as the rev counter needle sweeps past 4000rpm, reaches a peak that almost hurts at 4600rpm, and is then replaced by an exciting resonance at 5300rpm, one effectively carried over from the less-muffled air-cooled model. The sound then grows ever more electrifying en route to the 7200rpm red line.

Even the idle has a new aural potency that's entirely justified by the flatter, beefier torque curve. This in turn triggers an improved engine response you'll notice the instant you move off. The old 911 was quick and flexible, but the new car beats it easily, slotting its performance between the old 911's and the mighty Turbo's. Each gear, as snapper Tim Wren exclaimed, offers a different driving experience.

Stretching the stroke from 78mm to 82.8mm increases the horizontally opposed six-cylinder engine's capacity from 3.4 to 3.6 litres. VarioCam technology, introduced on the 911 Turbo last year, has now been applied to the normally aspirated engine, providing seamless two-stage variable inlet-valve timing that switches over at 2800rpm.

Tuning the exhausts to improve the 911's unique sound stage has been helped by lowering the back pressure. This work also hoists maximum power by a healthy 19bhp to 315bhp at 6800rpm, while the torque climbs to 373lb ft at 4250rpm, up 22lb ft and peaking a useful 350rpm lower in the rev range. In fact, there's more torque throughout the range, and increased power from 2400rpm.

The result? Officially, zero to 62mph is cut by 0.2sec to 5.0sec for the C2 and C4 coupé (the cabrio is slower by the same amount) and top speed rises

## QUICK FACTS

| | |
|---|---|
| **Model tested** | 911 3.6 Carrera |
| **Price** | £55,950 |
| **On sale** | September |
| **0–62mph** | 5.0sec |
| **Top speed** | 177mph |
| **Urban** | 17.5mpg |
| **Extra urban** | 34.8mpg |
| **Combined** | 25.5mpg |
| **CO₂ emissions** | 158g/km |

# NEW CARS

## 11 JULY 2001

Volume 229

No 2 | 5442

AUTOCAR
Every Wednesday
11 July 2001 £2.10

FIRST DRIVE
New Porsche 911
Better than ever

British GP special
15 EXTRA PAGES

# Hot new MGs
12-PAGE MEGATEST Can reborn Rovers cut it on the road?

Y928 BJW

Plus At the limit in MG's
500bhp firebreather

**ABOVE** Three-spoke wheel, previously optional, is now standard. No improvements to steering thought necessary.

**OPPOSITE** Exhaust retuned to deliver something of the old air-cooled bellow.

by 3mph to 177. At the same time the combined fuel cycle improves from 23.9mpg to 25.5mpg. August Achleitner, the Carrera project leader, says, "We could have offered even more speed, but that wasn't our goal. It's important to reduce emissions and fuel consumption, as well as improve power and torque. We have the same gear ratios and consumption is now lower at the same engine revs."

Subjectively, the new 911 feels more refined and tractable, marvellously easy to drive gently in traffic – who needs the Tiptronic automatic when the driveline and gearshift are so effortlessly fluent? – and a superb long-distance cruiser, all without compromising the car's crucial sports car purity.

Porsche has justifiably left the brakes well alone. But a new alloy wheel design, especially the optional 18in variety fitted to our test cars, have such slim spokes that the view of the cross-drilled, vented discs is virtually unimpeded. New casting methods allow very thin spokes which reduce the unsprung weight of the 10-spoke 17in rims by 3.6kg and the 5-spoke 18in rims by 10.6kg. The 18s, chosen by the majority of customers, also introduce wider front wheels and bigger rubber, which now sits flush with the body sides. Doesn't sound important, but it makes

a surprisingly obvious visual difference that, together with the Turbo's headlights, gives the new car a more attractive and assertive appearance.

On the standard 17s the front track has been increased by 10mm, the wider tyres necessitating the fitting of the Turbo's subtly bulging front fenders. At the back, the optional 285/30 ZR18 rears (up from the old 265/35s), especially, fill the wheel arches handsomely, giving the prodigiously able chassis even greater grip. The suspension is otherwise virtually unchanged, though Porsche says subtle mods to the damper valving improve small bump absorption and reduce yaw and roll. Nor did the engineers see any reason to revise the steering.

Why would you, when the dynamics are as progressive and talented as the 911's? You forget, until you come back to the car, just how tactile and sensitive the Carrera driving experience is. The 3.6 is superior because it has more grip, and if anything is a touch more communicative; and it has lost none of its progressive, on-the-limit manners. Lift off suddenly at the apex and the rear still goes momentarily light, but get back on the throttle and it quickly settles. While the C4 pushes the nose wide more readily than the C2, there is power enough to compensate, because this car's attitude can truly be adjusted on the throttle. The way the 911 changes direction, a wrist flick this way then that, flowing through corners, urged on by an engine touched with genius, all the driver's sensors totally connected to the car, is one of motoring's great experiences.

Achleitner claims that on a grippy surface, Porsche's PSM stability control system doesn't cut in until the car is generating 1.4g lateral acceleration. This is not an intrusive system and few owners will bother to turn it off.

Subtle modifications to the styling, especially around the nose, improve cooling by 15 per cent, while revisions to the front wheel arches, including small lips on the spoilers' trailing edges, reduce lift on the front axle by 25 per cent and by 40 per cent at the rear. At the same time the 0.30 drag coefficient is unchanged. Sure enough, for what it's worth, stability at 150mph is noticeably improved

Think brakes and you think Porsche. At once powerful, progressive and responsive yet with a pedal movement that's astonishingly short. Nobody, absolutely nobody, does brakes better than Porsche.

Inside, too, the 911 is unmistakably created by enthusiasts for enthusiasts, cupholders notwithstanding. Some will be disappointed that the basic layout remains so similar to the Boxster's; but it works well and although it's now better finished, still doesn't offer the visual delights of the Audi TT. A three-spoke wheel, optional on the previous model, is now standard. The 3.6 gets Turbo instruments and Porsche's comprehensive and easyto read trip computer is, at last, fitted to all cars. There's even a small glovebox and, as on the Turbo, both bonnet and boot lids are now opened electrically. Other changes include a demisted glass rear window for the cabrio. It's 18 per cent smaller in area, though Porsche claims the driver's view is reduced by just 5 per cent.

Despite the lightweight wheels, the increases in equipment and body reinforcement to ensure the 911 passes the 40mph offset crash test mean the C2 weighs 1345kg, up 25kg.

Faults? The seat belt always slips off the shoulder in the cabriolet; I reckon the 911 deserves a new, less-Boxstery interior; and Porsche's options are still excessively priced. By then you're down to the real nit-picking. Four years on, the water-cooled 911 remains the defining Porsche, perhaps the defining sports car.

# SPECIFICATIONS 911 3.6 CARRERA

## DIMENSIONS

| | |
|---|---|
| Length | 4430mm |
| Width | 1770mm |
| Height | 1305mm |
| Wheelbase | 2350mm |
| Weight | 1345kg |
| Fuel tank | 64 litres |

## ENGINE

| | |
|---|---|
| Layout | 6 cyls horizontally opposed, water cooled 3596cc |
| Max power | 315bhp at 6800rpm |
| Max torque | 273lb ft at 4250rpm |
| Specific output | 88bhp per litre |
| Power to weight | 234bhp per tonne |
| Installation | Longitudinal, rwd |
| Bore/stroke | 96.0/82.8mm |
| Made of | Alloy heads and block |
| Compression ratio | 11.3:1 |
| Valve gear | 4 per cyl, dohc |
| Ignition and fuel | Bosch ME 7.8 |

## SUSPENSION

**Front** MacPherson struts, lower control arms, coil springs, anti-roll bar
**Rear** Multi-link, coil springs, anti-roll bar

## GEARBOX

**Type** 6-speed manual
**Ratios/mph per 1000rpm**
**Final drive ratio** 3.44:1

| | | | |
|---|---|---|---|
| 1st | 3.82/5.6 | 2nd | 2.20/9.7 |
| 3rd | 1.52/14.1 | 4th | 1.22/17.5 |
| 5th | 1.02/20.9 | 6th | 0.84/25.5 |

## STEERING

**Type** Rack and pinion, power assisted
**Turns lock-to-lock** 3.0

## BRAKES

**Front** 318mm ventilated cross-drilled discs
**Rear** 299mm ventilated cross-drilled discs
**Anti-lock** Standard

## WHEELS AND TYRES

**Made of** Alloy
**Size** 8Jx18in (f), 10Jx18in (r)
**Tyres** 225/40 ZR18 (f), 285/30 ZR18 (r)

## THE VERDICT

Judicious evolution has produced an even better 911. Charismatic, quicker, cleaner and more exciting than ever.

# HATS OFF TO NEW 911

**911 TARGA** The previous 911 Targa combined the Carrera's speed with the Cabrio's open-air appeal, so it's no surprise to see Porsche carrying the process one stage further

The new 911 Targa, due in UK showrooms by December, won't disappoint you. Everything you'd expect from a Porsche – exceptional dynamics, head-turning looks, faultless build – along with new features you won't have anticipated, make this Targa a more desirable and practical proposition than ever.

The previous version turned tradition on its head, replacing the classic roof architecture dating back to 1965 with a much more user-friendly glass arrangement. Combining the Carrera 2's speed and safety with the Cabrio's open-air appeal made it the automatic choice for many 911 buyers – almost one in 10, in fact. So it's no surprise to see Porsche now carrying the process one step further.

Much of the new Targa's excellence is a tribute to the fact that it was part of the clean-sheet plan when the current 911 line-up was conceived – something that couldn't be claimed for its predecessor. In fact, not one component from the old model's roof has been retained, and it is far better integrated into the 911's voluptuous steel body than it was first time round. And just as impressively, it can now claim an excellent 0.30 drag coefficient, exactly the same as its fixed-roof siblings'. To some eyes the sharp-cornered rear-side windows and thick cant rails (the strip roof outboard of the glass panel running from windscreen to C-pillar) are even more handsome than those adorning the Carrera 2; though the seams cutting the base of the C-pillars are regrettable.

The overall operation of the Targa's roof is virtually

## QUICK FACTS

| | |
|---|---|
| **Model tested** | 911 Targa |
| **Price** | £61,000 |
| **On sale** | December |
| **0–62mph** | 5.2sec |
| **Top speed** | 177mph |
| **Combined** | 25.5mpg |
| **CO$_2$ emissions** | 158g/km |

# NEW CARS

## 10 OCTOBER 2001

Volume 230

No 2 | 5455

**ABOVE** Glass panel slides back in front of rear window; blind ensures privacy.

**OPPOSITE** 911 first: rear window opens to improve loading access to rear seats.

unchanged. You press the switch on the centre console, either at a standstill or on the move, and two electric motors lower the front section of glass a couple of millimetres before sliding it rearwards. At the same time, an integral wind deflector flips up from atop the windscreen to reduce wind buffeting. Keep the switch depressed and the large pane of laminated safety glass continues its rearward path before resting neatly inside the back window. The process is incredibly slick, taking a mere eight seconds in all – less than half the time required to fold and stow the 911 Cabriolet's more complex fabric hood.

For added kerb-side drama, you can now open the Targa's roof from outside the car using a remote key-fob. Press it for more than three seconds and it unlocks the doors and opens the glass and side windows. To shield occupants from glaring sun and provide a greater degree of privacy, Porsche has also retained the previous model's full-length roller blind.

The most significant development, however,

is the addition of a hinged rear window – the first to be offered on any 911. Operated either by a button on the driver's side door sill or the key fob, it lifts skywards, hatchback style, to provide more convenient external access to a small parcel shelf and the rear seats.

It may sound gimmicky, but the Targa's rear window is a great asset for those who regularly use the 911's tiny rear seats as luggage space, adding greatly to the car's practicality. When the rear window is opened, two additional interior lights mounted in the seat-belt units illuminate to help you find your belongings at night.

The new Targa shares its mechanical package with the recently face-lifted Carrera 2. Perched in the back is Porsche's brilliant 24-valve 3.6-litre flat six-cylinder engine. The new water-cooled unit, complete with the Variocam variable valve timing technology introduced on the Turbo last year, delivers 315bhp at 6800rpm and 273lb ft of torque at 4250rpm.

## 'NOTHING SO CRUDE AS OLDE WORLDE SCUTTLE SHAKE OR CHASSIS FLEXING THREATENS THE BRILLIANT HANDLING'

The new unit sounds as menacing as ever at idle – though diehard air-cooled 993 fans will probably disagree – but under hard acceleration it now emits a noticeably deeper and more seductively throaty bellow than the earlier 3.4-litre engine. With the roof open, the urge to drop down a gear and wind the engine out to its 7200rpm red line for a dose of that sound track is almost irresistible.

In normal going the Targa's extra 70kg is barely apparent. Our test car came with a standard six-speed manual gearbox, which delivers the 0–62mph sprint in 5.2sec – just 0.2sec slower than the coupé and the same as the Cabriolet – and a top speed of 177mph.

The weight penalty can be blamed on the Targa's use of the Cabrio's reinforced platform. To ensure sufficient chassis stiffness a sturdy 30mm thick steel tube has been threaded through the A-pillars and back through the Targa's cant rails to the base of the C-pillars. Porsche claims the torsional rigidity of the Targa falls roughly halfway between the Carrera 2's and Cabriolet's. But you'll look in vain for signs of dynamic weakness brought on by the compromised roof structure. Nothing so crude as olde worlde scuttle shake or chassis flexing threatens the brilliant handling. In short, it feels like a Carrera 2.

The power-assisted steering is as tactile as ever. Stiffer anti-roll bars and firmer springs make the ride a little harsher, but only the most experienced 911 hands will notice any difference.

Open the roller blind and the interior instantly feels friendlier. It's largely psychological, of course, but the added brightness really does improve the ambience of the cabin. Those wanting genuine wind-in-the-hair experience could be excused for feeling a little disappointed when the glass roof is finally retracted back. Whether it's the fixed cant rails or the fact that wind turbulence is never an issue, the Targa feels almost too civilised

Flaws? There are one or two. Retracting the roof all the way back greatly reduces rearward visibility, because the twin layers of tinted and laminated safety glass allow just 35 per cent light transmission. And the already marginal rear seat headroom is further reduced. At higher speeds, wind noise is also more of a problem than it is in the Carrera 2.

The Targa is the 911 that lets you have it both ways. While the Carrera 2 offers supreme dynamic ability and the Cabrio uncompromised wind-in-the-hair pleasure, the Targa is the truly accomplished all-rounder, offering a compelling mix of both these cars, along with much improved practicality and refinement

# SPECIFICATIONS 911 TARGA

## DIMENSIONS

| | |
|---|---|
| Length | 4430mm |
| Width | 1770mm |
| Height | 1305mm |
| Wheelbase | 2365mm |
| Weight | 1415kg |
| Fuel tank | 64 litres |

## ENGINE

| | |
|---|---|
| Layout | 6 cyls horizontally opposed, water cooled 3596cc |
| Max power | 315bhp at 6800rpm |
| Max torque | 273lb ft at 4250rpm |
| Specific output | 88bhp per litre |
| Power to weight | 223bhp per tonne |
| Installation | Rear, longitudinal, rwd |
| Bore/stroke | 96.0/82.8mm |
| Made of | Alloy heads and block |
| Compression ratio | 11.3:1 |
| Valve gear | 4 per cyl, dohc |
| Ignition and fuel | Motronic ME 7.8 |

## SUSPENSION

**Front** MacPherson struts, lower control arms, coil springs, anti-roll bar
**Rear** Multi-link, coil springs, anti-roll bar

## GEARBOX

**Type** 6-speed manual
**Ratios/mph per 1000rpm**
**Final drive ratio** 3.44:1

| | | | |
|---|---|---|---|
| 1st | 3.82/5.6 | 2nd | 2.20/9.7 |
| 3rd | 1.52/14.1 | 4th | 1.22/17.5 |
| 5th | 1.02/20.9 | 6th | 0.84/25.5 |

## STEERING

**Type** Rack and pinion, power assisted
**Turns lock-to-lock** 3.0

## BRAKES

**Front** 318mm ventilated cross-drilled discs
**Rear** 299mm ventilated cross-drilled discs
**Anti-lock** Standard

## WHEELS AND TYRES

**Made of** Alloy
**Size** 8Jx18in (f), 10Jx18in (r)
**Tyres** 225/40 ZR18 (f), 285/30 ZR18 (r)

## THE **AUTOCAR** VERDICT

Accomplished all-rounder offering an enticing mix of performance and thrills with the practicality of a hinged rear window.

# OLD-SCHOOL HIGH

**911 3.6 CARRERA** The 996 comes of age with next year's Carrera. It's as 911 as they come but with even more sound and fury. So who needs air-cooled?

Ever since emissions regulations forced Porsche to stop blowing cold air over the crankcase of its most famous sports car, the 911 has been liquid cooled. Water replaced the fan, power went up, the car got a fraction bigger, it was treated to a new codename, 996, and Porschephiles did what they always do when the company interferes with their deity: they got stroppy.

They moaned about a different noise, bigger dimensions (still far more manageable than anything else pretending to be a sports car) and croaked on about a chassis that had lost the ability to communicate.

Until mid-October 1998 I was in no position to comment. Then came my first 996 experience over Dartmoor in a cooking Carrera 4. It was enlightening. I simply couldn't conceive how the car could be bettered. And yet every Zuffenhausen sage on the planet, and plenty of younger enthusiasts, too, was convinced that the last-generation air-cooled car (codename 993) was a more entertaining package.

That car must have been sensational. And it was, back in 1994. But not better than the 996, which was a more able sprinter and heaps more relaxing over long distances. Call me a heretic, but I've always preferred the water-cooled car. Not just because it was a more complete car, either: I found that first 996 more entertaining to drive.

Porsche is showing signs of getting ever more impatient with the old-school moans, too. Because it has just revised the 996 and provided the antidote to the air-cooled mob's whinging. The new car's a belter: a palpable improvement on the current 3.4-litre car and – this is the really juicy bit – possibly the best normally aspirated machine the company has ever made.

The Carrera 2002 gets a bigger 3.6-litre engine producing 315bhp – up 19bhp – and 273lb ft of torque courtesy of the latest version of Porsche's Variocam valve timing system. Other than marginally revised damper settings to make traversing smaller

# FEATURE

## 19/26 DECEMBER 2001

Volume 230

No 12 I 5465

bumps less noticeable, the chassis and steering remain as before.

The majority of the alterations are cosmetic. New turbo-style front lights with a teardrop bottom edge help distinguish the car from the Boxster, and the previous generation Carrera for that matter. This, combined with some clever restyling of the front and rear bumpers, has sharpened the Carrera's appearance immeasurably.

The nose is now far less blunt and tapers back to meet the A-pillars more gracefully. As is often the case, you'll struggle to spot the tweakery on the page, but you'll be surprised how different the car looks on the road.

The 996's interior, however, is the one area that is worthy of a whinge. Sensible ergonomics may have replaced the mad-house layout that hadn't changed since the dinosaurs, but it was all ruined by less than perfect build quality and some thin, unbecoming, plastic-work. The first 996's cabin felt fragile.

Much of that has now been redressed. Substantial materials and more lovingly finished switchgear lift the cabin noticeably, but it's still not worthy enough

to share house-room with the driving experience. Or the noise. The test car had a good portion of the options' list thrown at it: sports suspension (£1727), leather sports seats(£459) and a less than discreet aero kit (£2333). But it's the optional sports exhaust (£1149) that's had us giggling for a month now.

Instructions for making your friends laugh with you are as follows: keep your right foot off the throttle, twist the key slowly and allow the Porsche engine management team its moment of humour. One second later the flat-six fires with a colossal, instantaneous bark: the kind of noise you'd swear was illegal and certainly hasn't been heard coming out of a Porsche road car tailpipe since the late-'60s. It's fantastic: it makes children smile and blokes jealous. And it sounds even better at the top end. But there should be no hurry to get there: low-speed Carrera driving is a pleasure.

The weighting of the controls has been optimised for high-speed responses and reassurance, and does a fine job of making stop-start driving comfortable. Considering the 30mm reduction in ride height over the standard car, the urban ride quality is astonishing.

Tyre width causes more problems over drainage covers than any inability on the suspension's part. But it's still one of the world's best supercoupés in which to get stuck in a traffic jam. Important stuff in the vocabulary of the everyday sportster.

Then you shuffle out of concrete- and camera-land and dawdle on the motorway, waiting for the traffic to disperse. Take time to concentrate on the ride quality: it's vintage Porsche. The kind that makes you realise there's an important difference between smoothness and actual comfort. You'd never call the way the Carrera fidgets on UK three-laners smooth, but then you register a distinct lack of fatigue even if you spend hours at the wheel. Odd that.

Look to the vertical damping control for the reason why. Each small movement up and down is perfectly controlled, and the ultra-firm seat cushion means your body doesn't move independently of this damping masterclass. Cruise 1000 miles in this car and you'll arrive as supple as the moment you left. Just don't make use of the new cup holder at speed – it'll plaster your pretty new dash plastic with whatever's in the can.

You choose your first accelerative hit in the new 911 with sports exhaust carefully, not because the car is uncontrollably fast in a straight line but because you need to experience a sustained hit of its noise and staggeringly linear acceleration. The tune builds in second gear from about 4000rpm – which, incidentally, is the last point at which any irritating little Evo from the East can live with you – swells at four-six, fades slightly and then comes back for a sustained yelp until the 7200rpm limiter forces you to grab third. Then you do it all again for a second helping of genetically modified induction and exhaust noise that's better than any air-cooled 911 I've driven.

It's so captivating you probably won't have noticed the speedo needle's new found athleticism: the new 911 is a very fast car. Brilliant traction is a factor in the 1.6sec 0-30mph time, but nothing more than raw power can take credit for a 4.6sec 0-60mph sprint and the ability to fire from rest to 100mph in 10.1sec. Think I'll repeat that last little pearl: next year's boggo 911 Carrera, not the Turbo or GT2 mind, will run 10.0sec flat to the ton. Lummy.

And this car is so friendly, so willing to manipulate its performance credentials into your way of operating. It's perfectly happy even if you just want to lug, save fuel or avoid using the lever by your left thigh too much, in which case you'll miss out on a gearchange that every other maker aspires to. The engine is

# ROAD TEST 911 3.6 CARRERA

## ACCELERATION FROM REST

| True mph | seconds | speedo mph |
|---|---|---|
| 30 | 1.6 | 30 |
| 40 | 2.5 | 41 |
| 50 | 3.5 | 51 |
| 60 | 4.6 | 61 |
| 70 | 5.5 | 72 |
| 80 | 7.0 | 82 |
| 90 | 8.2 | 92 |
| 100 | 10.1 | 102 |

Standing qtr mile 12.9sec/112mph
Standing km 22.7sec/147mph
30–70mph through gears 3.7sec

## ACCELERATION IN GEAR

| MPH | 6th | 5th | 4th | 3rd | 2nd |
|---|---|---|---|---|---|
| 20–40 | - | 5.6 | 4.1 | 3.3 | 2.2 |
| 30–50 | 6.9 | 5.3 | 3.9 | 3.2 | 1.9 |
| 40–60 | 6.8 | 5.3 | 3.8 | 2.9 | 1.9 |
| 50–70 | 6.8 | 5.1 | 3.7 | 2.7 | 2.0 |
| 60–80 | 7.0 | 5.1 | 3.6 | 2.6 | - |
| 70–90 | 7.1 | 5.2 | 3.6 | 2.7 | - |
| 80–100 | 7.2 | 5.0 | 3.6 | 3.0 | - |

## MAXIMUM SPEEDS

| | | | |
|---|---|---|---|
| 6th | 177mph/6950rpm | 5th | 151/7200 |
| 4th | 126/7200 | 3rd | 102/7200 |
| 2nd | 70/7200 | 1st | 40/7200 |

## FUEL CONSUMPTION

Average/best/worst/touring
19/26.1/12.1/26.1mpg

| | |
|---|---|
| Urban | 17.5mpg |
| Extra urban | 34.8mpg |
| Combined | 25.5mpg |
| Tank capacity | 64 litres |
| Touring range | 368 miles |
| $CO_2$ | 158g/km |

## BRAKES

| | |
|---|---|
| 30/50/70mph | 9.5/25.1/48.4 metres |
| 60–0mph | 2.5sec |

## NOISE

| | |
|---|---|
| Idle revs | 49dbA |
| Max revs | 89dbA |
| 30/50/70mph | 74/77/82dbA |

# SPECIFICATIONS 911 3.6 CARRERA

## DIMENSIONS

Min/max front legroom 830/1090mm  Max front headroom 970mm
Interior width 1340mm  Boot width 740mm  Boot length 420mm
Boot volume 130dm³  Front/rear tracks 1455/1500mm  Kerb weight 1345kg
Weight distribution front/rear na  Width with/without mirrors 1950/1475mm

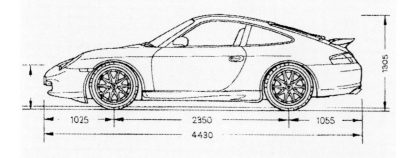

1025   2350   1055
4430
1305

## ENGINE

| | |
|---|---|
| Layout | 6 cyls horizontally opposed, 3596cc |
| Max power | 315bhp at 6800rpm |
| Max torque | 273lb ft at 4250rpm |
| Specific output | 88bhp per litre |
| Power to weight | 234bhp per tonne |
| Torque to weight | 203lb ft per tonne |
| Installation | Rear, transverse, rear-wheel drive |
| Construction | Alloy heads and block |
| Bore/stroke | 96.0/82.8mm |
| Valve gear | 4 per cyl, dohc |
| Compression ratio | 11.3:1 |
| Ignition and fuel | Bosch ME 7.8 engine and injection management |

## CHASSIS AND BODY

| | |
|---|---|
| Body | 3dr coupé |
| Wheels | 8Jx18in (f), 10Jx18in (r) |
| Made of | Alloy |
| Tyres | 225/40 ZR18 (f), 285/30 ZR18 (r) Pirelli P-Zero Rosso |

## TRANSMISSION

Gearbox 6-speed manual
Ratios/mph per 1000rpm
Final drive 3.44

| | | | |
|---|---|---|---|
| 1st 3.82/5.6 | | 2nd 2.20/9.7 | |
| 3rd 1.52/14.1 | | 4th 1.22/17.5 | |
| 5th 1.02/20.9 | | 6th 0.84/25.5 | |

## STEERING

Type Rack and pinion, power assisted
Turns lock-to-lock  3.0
Turning circle  10.6m

## SUSPENSION

Front MacPherson struts, coil springs, anti-roll bar
Rear Independent, multi-link, coil springs, anti-roll bar

## BRAKES

Front 318mm ventilated, drilled discs
Rear 299mm ventilated, drilled discs
Anti-lock Standard

---

constantly poised to let you take its rev needle up to the red zone whenever you feel inclined.

This truly is a great engine: one that basks in its heritage and by every objective measure improves on its predecessor. It also demolishes every air-cooled normally aspirated lump the company has ever made.

More worryingly for rival car makers, Porsche has infused the chassis with an equal dose of brilliance. To experience it working over a road, filtering out the unnecessary, passing on the necessary, is to experience one of motoring's finer offerings. As before, control is the key. From small to massive speeds the Porsche's body movements are resolutely kept in check, leaving the driver to savour a steering rack of rare brilliance.

So transparent is its appeal, you know you're going to love changing direction in the Carrera even just palming it around in a car park. It doesn't disappoint. All traces of the power assistance that make it possible to move the front 205/40 ZR18 tyres at low speed seem to evaporate above 40mph. Real, reassuring weight that requires two hands all the time means pin-point accuracy and that unique 911 signature-tune: a streaming dialogue of information about grip and surface changes that no computer-controlled active system will ever match.

And it's fun. Fun in a way that lets the driver exploit that list of abilities, and revel in the fact that Porsche continues to manage the impossible; namely, disguise the fact that this car's engine is in entirely the wrong place. So you get all the traction benefits and none of the horror stories of the old car. Sure, a silly entry speed and a trailing throttle will still create an interesting angle of approach, but leave the stability and traction control on and even that's taken care of. Grip wet or dry is ample and the optional seats are more than capable of coping with the forces.

Size isn't a problem in this particular application either. Some additional strengthening to the bodyshell has increased the kerb weight by 25kg over the outgoing model, but it's still lighter than a 993. So despite being a bigger car than it was, it's a perfect size for our roads: manageable on B-roads, great on A-roads and eminently parkable.

There are a few gripes to air, though. Why has Porsche meddled with the best instrument layout in the business? For 2002 the 911 gets the same dash layout as the Turbo, switching the digital speed readout from the rev-counter to the analogue speedo. Where's the logic in that? It's now impossible to get that momentary glance at your road speed, important in something that has a claimed maximum of 177mph.

Understeer is an unexpected irritant, too. We drove the car on Pirelli P-Zero Rosso and Continental Sport Contact 2 tyres and both allowed the front end to break traction significantly before the rears would let go. It takes a concerted thump of throttle in second gear to get some oversteer, but once there the Porsche is perfectly balanced. Good thing, too: 'sideways action' has always been listed alongside 'taking candy from a baby' in the 996 performance handbook.

But other than that, there's little to carp about. This car is quite possibly the supreme expression of performance motoring. It offers as much sheer kick as most supercars and promises the kind of reliability that the Porsche brand was built on. But where the Carrera hits hardest is on a less tangible level. At a time when manufacturers are desperate to engineer personality into their cars, the 911 has real, sustainable character right from the moment it moves. The kind that makes you want to own one, and live with one.

Which leads to the most devastating blow of the lot: it costs £55,950 (or £61,618 if you include all the toys on the test car). It's a dangerous sport calling such expensive machinery a bargain, but no other word does the new 911 justice. It's a stunner.

**ABOVE** Reprofiled bumpers sharpen looks; test car with optional body kit and lower sports suspension.

**LEFT** Out goes the cheap plasticky feel of old 996; turbo-style teardrop lights mark 2002 model.

# SILVER BULLET

**911 TURBO CABRIOLET** Can the world's greatest A-to-B supercar hack it as a soft-top? David Vivian drives the new 190mph 911 Turbo convertible across Italy to find out.

The best car Porsche makes? 911 Turbo. Why? Purity of purpose fused with breadth of ability. There isn't another car currently in production that takes a demanding road apart with quite the surgical precision and devastating efficiency of Porsche's incandescently rapid all-drive supercar. It doesn't matter what kind of road it is: fast and open, twisty and technical, humped, dipped and wickedly cambered; the Turbo is capable of blitzing any and all varieties of black top. Throw in a wet and slippery surface and the pace it manages to preserve verges on the supernatural.

If you need to put the squeeze on the distance between where you are and where you want to be with black hole-like force – and this has been proved come home-time on numerous supercar group tests – it's the Porsche's fob you reach for. Scooby and Evo keys spin off the table in the scrum. There may be faster, lighter and lither 911s, but none that gets the job done quite as effectively for any given input of driver skill. It's the jewel in the Zuffenhausen car maker's crown and, with the optional 30bhp factory performance upgrade (450bhp total), virtually uncatchable A to B unless you happen to be at the controls of a turbine-engined helicopter. I dig it absolutely. Just the way it is.

So I reckon slicing the roof off a 911 – any 911

and however skilfully done – must be a Bad Idea. Bad because Butzi Porsche designed the 911 as a coupé to epitomise the notion of 'pure and simple'. Bad because these days sunshine is almost as dangerous as inhaling other vehicles' exhaust fumes. Bad because convertibles are sometimes driven by sun-tanned poseurs and 911 credibility rests firmly on the shoulders of people who take their driving stone-cold seriously. Bad because, as delivered by Porsche's current design team, it spectacularly trashes the 911's beautiful, iconic and timeless profile. Bad because all measures to shore up the loss of rigidity always add weight. And bad because, well, you wouldn't order a pint of Guinness and then scoop off the head with a spoon, would you?

I'd like to think Porsche agrees, but it knows it doesn't have to. It's merely meeting a demand in the market. For the years 2001-02, a third of all 911s sold were cabrios. Add Boxster production and 60 per cent of new Porsches that year were soft-tops. You can't knock it. Porsche is a small, independent car maker. It must do what it needs to remain independent and survive. Despite having to cut production of 911 and Boxster in the face of the global economic downturn, it seems to be doing fine with healthy profit margins. The C4S Cabrio launched last month proved that it is possible to stop short of throwing the talent out with the tin-top and joins the plain Carrera and glass-roofed Targa models in the fresh-air 911 line-up. But the new 911 Turbo Cabrio (£96,130 when it hits UK showrooms in October) is the statement car – not just the fastest-ever soft-top 911 but, with its claimed 189mph top speed and 4.3sec 0–62mph time, the fastest production convertible on the planet. Even Merc's mighty twins, the SL55 and SL600, would feel the tug of its slipstream on the autobahn, though Ferrari's 360 Spider would be much harder to shake off.

But I'm standing in the courtyard of the new Residenza La Canonica hotel complex at Tenuta La Bagnaia just outside Siena in the heart of Tuscany

## FACTFILE

| Model | 911 Turbo Cabriolet |
| --- | --- |
| Price | £96,130 |
| 0–62mph | 4.3sec |
| 0–100mph | 9.5sec |
| Top speed | 189mph |
| Urban | 14.9mpg |
| Extra urban | 30.7mpg |
| Combined | 21.9mpg |
| CO$_2$ emissions | 309g/km |

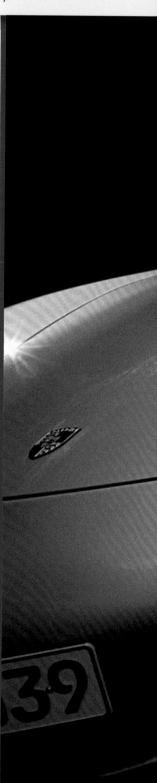

# FEATURE

## 6 AUGUST 2003

Volume 237

No 6 | 5548

and Porsche's driving agenda for today is almost exclusively twisty. Waiting for photographer Matt Vosper to snap some final details as the pale gas-burner blue of the early morning sky starts to haze over with the building heat, there's time to ponder the shape, detailing and cabin and it's an oddly unsettling process. Porsche has brought along an original 1989 (930) 911 Turbo Cabrio to illustrate just how far things have progressed in the ensuing 14 years. The old-timer, with its 3.3-litre air-cooled engine, has just 300bhp, 317lb ft of torque and a four-speed gearbox. It would trail the 996 by over a second in a race to 60, and disappear backwards at a rate of 28mph in its rear-view mirror flat out.

The distance between the two cars' technologies can only be calculated by astronomers, but there's no doubt which is the hornier looking. It isn't merely that the original is so obviously fat and in-yer-face. Just as effective (maybe fortuitous) is the way that hopelessly undainty hump of hood, concealed by only a black tonneau, balances the extravagance of the lower bodywork. Proper sod-off whale-tail spoiler, too. With the 996 Turbo Cab, the smoothly integrated metal cowling into which the powered hood so swiftly folds adds an unfortunate impression

of mass to the tail. It's almost as if the car has been clamped by its nose and spun in a centrifuge until all the fat has been forced into its arse. The sense of bulk is accentuated by the tail spoiler with its elevating upper surface, which isn't subtle enough to be cool or substantial enough to be dramatic. Despite its undoubted aerodynamic effectiveness, it looks disappointingly 'technical' and deeply un-sexy.

Silver's a good look for the exterior, to some extent de-emphasising the bulkiness, but the milky terracotta colour of the cabin (an oddly popular choice for German press cars) is distractingly awful. It's hard fully to appreciate the generally sussed ergonomics, large clear dials, terrific driving position and seats, brilliant build and immaculate finish when you're surrounded by a colour that's giving your retinas so much grief. The flashy carbon gearknob and handbrake grip feel better than they look, too. I never thought I'd say this, but for me Porsche styling has become a consuming issue. These days the company is incapable of building anything other than brilliant cars. Ugly? Not a problem. With the Cayenne Porsche owns ugly – has taken it places BMW's Chris Bangle only dreams about. Stunning achievement though an

SUV with supercar grunt is, I can't get a lock on its form – not so much looking through a glass darkly as through a malfunctioning autofocus lens. Same with the new 911 Turbo Cab. Apart from the perceived bulk problem, it simply isn't quite right. From any angle, it only ever *nearly* gels.

No matter. The sound of a many 3.6-litre, twin-turbo flat six firing up and accelerating down the hotel's dead-straight, half-mile-long drive to the main road goes some way to compensating for the lack of aesthetic intoxication. There are two components to the engine noise: a granite hardcore cocooned by the low-pass whoosh of an F16 jet. It isn't a musical sound in the way that Motorhead isn't a musical sound. But it is gloriously gruff, gravelly and macho. The obvious advantage of the Cabrio, perhaps the only one that adds to the potency of the driving experience, is that you can hear more of it.

Time to find out, anyway. This, after all, is the acid test, the reason we're here. Can the world's great

A-to-B supercar hack it as a soft-top? If anyone can pull it off, Porsche can. Along with the C4S Cabrio, the Turbo has the stiffest and strongest of all open-top 911 bodyshells. Spot-welded steel panel reinforcements behind the B-pillars grant it 4.5 per cent more torsional and 3 per cent more flexural stiffness than other Carrera Cabrio models. At the kerb the Turbo Cabrio is 110kg heavier than the coupé, or about the same as an excessively rotund passenger. The 253bhp per tonne power to weight ratio (knocked back from 272bhp per tonne) remains formidable.

And as we strike out for the Tuscan hills, it isn't any harder to understand why the 911 encapsulates arguably the best idea anyone has ever had about travelling quickly on four wheels. What matters isn't speed per se but speed-to-size ratio. The Turbo Cab might be 2.4 inches wider than a regular Carrera at the hips but it's still ultra compact by supercar standards, and the supercar that takes up least amount of road is the one that can use it most

## 'EVEN THE MOST DETERMINED HANGERS-ON FALL AWAY LIKE PARATROOPERS LEAVING A PLANE'

The latest Cabrio may not be the most aesthetically perfect 911 convertible to emerge from Porsche's design studio, but there's no arguing that it sets new standards for topless performance.

effectively. It has more space, more options, more chances to exploit traffic dynamics.

Satisfaction flows almost immediately from a depth of character and a sense of identity evolved over decades: the timbre and feel of the engine, the easy precision of the gearchange, the tactile rewards associated with build and finish and, with the Turbo, of course, unfettered access to numbing speed. As the road starts to climb towards Monticiano, the almost disdainful effortlessness of the Turbo's delivery is a genuine jaw-slackener. The first thing that hits you is the massive flexibility that seems to build from nowhere, registered as an increase of linear strain on your neck muscles, and then a sharper exponential surge of pace as the VarioCam Plus valvegear starts to adjust the camshaft angle and the turbos really bite. No need for short cogs and high revs here: fourth and fifth have more than enough urge to dial up three figures in the time it would take to grab a lower gear in a lesser car.

At the top of the hill, the road opens out and the curves are better sighted. So far the Turbo Cab has given an almost perfect does-what-it-says-on-the-box, adding only headroom, ventilation and decibels to the coupé's familiar repertoire. The overriding impressions are of exquisite helm feel, enormous grip, brilliantly judged damping and colossal afterburner grunt. No shudder, wobble or diminution of intent. And this is where the Porsche starts to corner at a quite ridiculous lick – all the time feeding back finely resolved information about the road surface to the rim of the wheel. A series of sweeping semi-hairpins blends into a section of manic S-bends through which the Turbo Cab scythes with frankly amazing speed and precision. It's as extreme and addictive as you could want. Even my antipathy towards the apparent oxymoron of a soft-top Turbo is beginning to melt as I steep myself in the feel of the thing. Braking demands a confident push on the pedal but, even without the optional ceramic discs and six-pot front calipers, the

'THE ALMOST DISDAINFUL EFFORTLESSNESS OF THE TURBO'S DELIVERY IS A GENUINE JAW-SLACKENER' standard cross-drilled and inner-vented steel discs are phenomenally powerful and seemingly tireless.

The all-drive chassis' grunt/grip balance, kept in check so effectively by the PSM stability control, is a thing of beauty up here in the hills. Despite the considerable acreage of sticky, ZR-rated, rubber on the road, there's an almost sensual subtly about the way the car changes direction and the steering which resolves kickback not so much as a tugging at the rim, but a hermetically sealed bond between hands and road. And, as if to bury the qualms of doubters like me, it rides with more than reasonable comfort, too.

Briefly the roads are flatter and faster as we head east for a blast on the A1 autostrada. Out of roundabouts, the Turbo Cab's immense torque punches it away from just about anything that has decided to latch on. And when the bark of the squashed oval exhausts turns belligerent at about 4000rpm, even the most determined hangers-on fall away like paratroopers leaving a plane.

There's more high-speed traffic as we feed onto the A1 (having already closed the roof on the hoof), most interestingly, a bright yellow 360 Modena humming along at what looks like a steady ton. We pull into the fast lane about 200 metres ahead. Suddenly, and rather aggressively, the Fezza is filling the mirror. This is Italy, after all, and Porsches have to be taught some respect. But this 360 driver has clearly miscalculated. Perhaps it's something to do with the feeble-looking spoiler or black fabric bubble just above it. I slot fourth and acquaint the pedal with the metal. I imagine the Ferrari driver behind is doing exactly the same. Is the 360 left for dust? No. It's much better than that. The Ferrari gets dropped with the kind of glacial speed and inevitability that milks the agony for all its worth. Flashing a glance back, I swear its driver is rocking back and forth in his seat, trying to generate the extra impetus he needs to stick with me. But traffic calls a halt to the trial of strength before things get too hairy and we peel off at the next junction, leaving the 360 to wail and blur its way south.

That's how the Turbo usually feels. Invincible. Later in the day, the Cabrio's front wheels encounter a succession of truly nasty expansion joints that send shudders through the steering column and a thrap of vibration down the body structure. It's a reminder that, stiff as it is, there's still a bleedin' great hole where the roof should be. I'll stick with the word 'should', too. Proper 911s are coupés, cabrios are abberations. That said, they really don't come any faster or better than this.

# SPECIFICATIONS 911 TURBO CABRIO

## DIMENSIONS

| | |
|---|---|
| Length | 4435mm |
| Width | 1830mm |
| Height | 1295mm |
| Wheelbase | 2350mm |
| Weight | 1660kg |
| Fuel tank | 64 litres |
| Boot space | 100 litres |

## ENGINE

| | |
|---|---|
| Layout | 6 cyls, 3600cc |
| Max power | 420bhp at 6800rpm |
| Max torque | 413lb ft at 4250rpm |
| Specific output | 117bhp per litre |
| Power to weight | 253bhp per tonne (manual) |
| Installation | Rear, longitudinal, 4-wd |
| Bore/stroke | 100.0/76.4mm |
| Made of | Alloy heads and block |
| Compression ratio | 9.4:1 |
| Valve gear | 4 per cyl, dohc per bank |
| Ignition and fuel | Motronic ME 7.8 electronic ignition, sequential multi-point fuel injection |

## STEERING

| | |
|---|---|
| Type | Rack and pinion, power assisted |
| Turns lock-to-lock | 3.0 |

## GEARBOX

**Type** 6-speed manual
**Ratios/mph per 1000rpm**
**Final drive ratio** 3.44:1

| | | | |
|---|---|---|---|
| **1st** 3.82/5.6 | | **2nd** 2.05/10.5 | |
| **3rd** 1.41/15.3 | | **4th** 1.12/19.3 | |
| **5th** 0.92/23.5 | | **6th** 0.75/28.8 | |

## SUSPENSION

**Front** MacPherson struts, coil springs, anti-roll bar
**Rear** Multi-link, coils, anti-roll bar

## BRAKES

**Front/rear** 330mm ventilated discs
**Anti-lock** Standard

## WHEELS AND TYRES

**Made of** Alloy
**Size** 8.0Jx18in (f) 11.0Jx18in (r)
**Tyres** 225/40 ZR18 (front)
295/30 ZR18 (rear)

## THE AUTOCAR VERDICT

The worse of the two Turbos is still an astonishing sports car; Porsche just seems incapable of making a bad one.

# WHITE RIOT

**911 GT3 RS** On previous outings, Rennsport 911s have turned in spectacular results. Can the new GT3 RS do the same, asks Chris Harris

Sometimes in life it's better just to sit back and watch for a while. On any other occasion, and with any other car, a 10-lap blast would be the highlight of the day, but with the new £84,230 Porsche 911 GT3 RS – the Porsche I've been itching to drive since 1996 – the experience is different. To truly appreciate what this car is capable of, you need to observe it at work first. And only then should you climb aboard. It's just that kind of car.

In historical terms the GT3 RS was either a poorly kept secret or a macro-run special, knocked out at the last minute to counter a few loose-lips at the latest GT3 launch earlier this year. One day I'll find out which. Either way, while being presented with the most aggressive 996 variant to date, a few hacks rightly pointed out that for all its 375bhp and 1380kg, the GT3 still wasn't quite the real-deal. Followed by the statement that brings out an inspector Dreyfus-style twitch in Stuttgart's chassis engineers: "It still isn't a replacement for the 993 RS." Andrew Flintoff is less weary of being the perennial next-Botham than Porsche is of hearing that whatever it does isn't the new 993 RS. Bet it wished the bloody thing hadn't been so good after all. But this time it came armed with an off-but-on-the-record response to the GT3 jibes: just wait for the RS version. The almost pornographic representation of the current Carrera you're looking at is Porsche's final word on the subject.

More than anything else, Porsche is proud (almost obsessed) with its heritage. And that's why in 1999, when it launched a Carrera shorn of some equipment and with an extra 60bhp, it resisted the temptation to resurrect the RS label. You see Rennsport is much more than a signifier of increased performance potential; it's a performance philosophy unto itself. More power brings more pace, but only if overall mass is reduced through race-car technology can a Porsche earn the most respected tag. This is one of those cars.

Waving two fingers at Newton's hard graft, the RS places the same 3600cc flat-six as the GT3 over the rear axle. Peak power of 381bhp yowls into focus at 7300rpm (6bhp up and 100rpm lower than a GT3) and the torque curve is a carbon-copy of the standard car's: 284lb ft at 5000rpm. Miniscule gains in percentage terms, but then RS has never been about large specific power gains (the geek in me can confirm that for 911/964/993 RS variants the average is 15bhp over the respective standard car). For some reason Porsche decided that this car needed a lightweight, single-mass flywheel, even though a GT3 doesn't exactly suffer from a recalcitrant rev counter needle, and it also needed to homologate a new rear spoiler lip. So it gulps a little more $O_2$, and it revs even quicker.

Perhaps the basic 996's greatest single achievement is its humble approachability: see it, open door, start, blitz everything else on four wheels. All ruined by the RS I'm afraid. There is so much detail to imbibe, so many aspects that deserve a grinning nod of approval that get-in-and-go isn't an option. Like me, you're trying to look beyond the redness of it all, but that's not easy. You may think the writing crass, the wheel centres OTT and wonder about those fading sticker sections at either end, but I just adore such touches. Mixed in with a huge carbon rear wing, a nostrilled front bumper straight off a Supercup race car and an overall 10mm reduction in ride height, it has unrivalled road and pit-lane presence. Other shapes are more attractive,

## FACTFILE

| Model | 911 GT3 RS |
|---|---|
| Price | £84,230 |
| Insurance group | 20 |
| 0–60mph | 4.4sec |
| Top speed | 190mph |
| Economy | 12.0/24.9mpg |
| CO$_2$ emissions | 328g/km |

# FIRST DRIVE

## 2 DECEMBER 2003

Volume 238

No 10 | 5565

**ABOVE** As with standard GT3, handling is fairly senior. But in the right hands, RS is about as good as it gets; engine is stock GT3 but with a lighter flywheel so it revs even more freely: outputs are 381bhp/ 284lb ft; full cage, fire extinguisher, six-point harness: not exactly your average tally of NCAP safety equipment.

better suited to making school children whoop and point, but the GT3 RS is the most enticing-looking device out there. It's a battle of wills: do you resist salivating over other RS details like the Porsche logo on the bonnet (that's actually a sticker to supplement the weight saving of the carbonfibre panel itself) or do you shuffle between the roll-cage and Recaro bucket to sample what this car's really all about? Oh, the agony.

Full cage, fire extinguisher, six-point harness. Not your average tally of NCAP-friendly safety-equipment, but then no number of airbaggy pretensioner things can match the womb-like security of what is essentially a race-car cabin. There's also some carpet, a hi-fi and this example has air-con. A few more outward signs of specialness – Alcantara trim for the wheel and gearlever – finish what is certainly a workmanlike cabin, but somehow you wish it was a little further removed from the cooking car. Still feels generic GT3 as you adjust the seat for length (fixed backrest only in the RS), pull the wheel as far towards your chest as possible (still no height adjustment, but then there's no need for it). However, you then adjust the electric wing mirrors and notice that they're carbonfibre. Nice. But the driver's seat

Rennsport connection is only fully justified when the rear-view mirror is tweaked to reveal a world as seen through vapourising petrol. A Perspex rear screen may not help visibility, but it shaves pounds, looks trick and that's why this car, with a full tank of gas, weighs 50kg less than a GT3 Clubsport.

Familiar key, familiar fleshy action in the lock-barrel. New noises as the engine fires, though; louder from the inside because there's precious little sound deadening and the flywheel chunters away when the car's idling in neutral. The circuit is drying fast, but we're on Pirelli P-Zero Corsas: best take it easy then. The RS doesn't understand easy though. As soon as the oil temperature gauge has risen to a level that makes me feel less guilty about caning Brendan Corr's thousand-mile-old baby, it's impossible not to push. The RS is a multi-layered sports car in the way only the most talented are, but like everything else that comes with soft-compound, lightly treaded tyres, it's the rubber that defines the driving experience. When cold it's not the 295/30 ZR18 Corsas that need watching because the 911's inherent traction advantage means that even out of the first hairpin on the first dampish lap, the RS can handle just about all of 8300rpm in second. It's the 235/40 ZR18 fronts that require attention; until there's some heat in 'em it's understeer city. That doesn't affect a full-bore hit down the straight. Everything in second, third, fourth and a couple of seconds in fifth. Bedford's longest straight is a little under a kilometre long, I entered it at 45mph and backed off rather earlier than necessary with the speedo reading 149mph. A 911 Turbo Powerkit would only manage 151mph earlier this year. For flexibility, noise, choice of gear ratios, shift action and punch this is the best 911 drivetrain ever. And at 149mph you think it must be the RS's finest aspect, until you drill the middle pedal to the floor and feel the optional £5355-worth of PCCB (Porsche Carbon Composite Brakes) do their thing. The retardation is mighty and the pedal feel bang-on. But I haven't been sanctioned to run all day and therefore can't test what every GT3 owner would like to know – their resistance to fade. Shame.

Three laps in and we have temperature. The understeer doesn't disappear, you just build corner speed up to it, the nose pushes on a little, the rubber bites and the rear tyres just hook up. Once settled it feels like mild oversteer, but is in fact the RS finding its own very special steady state cornering posture.

Do you notice any lack of mass? A little: the RS is keener to change direction than the standard car, but it's the revised spring and damper rates that matter more. My biggest gripe with the standard car is an unacceptable amount of rear-end movement – dare I say it's too soft – and the RS is much better tied down, doesn't meander like the GT3. If I already had a GT3, I'd be finding out what exactly does constitute 'rear geometry changes' and finding if they could be fitted ASAP. Because while you'd expect the extra rigidity to manifest itself on the road as a torrid lack of compliance, it simply doesn't appear.

Yes, the RS is firmer than a GT3 on ordinary terra firma, ie away from the confines of a billiard-table smooth test track. On B-roads it snaffles out the slightest camber changes and feels like it wants to tramline badly under brakes (in fact, it doesn't). But the fact is, the standard GT3 isn't a great road car in the first place, and the RS is only very marginally worse. It has maybe two per cent less ride comfort. In the great scheme of things, it hardly matters.

What does is that despite its stiff ride and edgy front end, the RS is still perfectly usable on the road if you're that way inclined. Okay, show it a really rough surface and the suspension shows you its track roots, and it hardly absorbs anything. And of course there are still creature comforts: air

# SPECIFICATIONS 911 GT3 RS

## DIMENSIONS

| | |
|---|---|
| Length | 4435mm |
| Width | 1950mm |
| Height | 1265mm |
| Wheelbase | 2355mm |
| Weight | 1350kg |
| Fuel tank | 64 litres |

## ENGINE

| | |
|---|---|
| Layout | Flat, 6 cyls, 3600cc |
| Max power | 381bhp at 7300rpm |
| Max torque | 284bhp at 5000rpm |
| Power to weight | 282bhp per tonne |
| Installation | Rear, longitudinal, 4WD |
| Management | Bosch Motronic ME 2.8 |
| Bore/stroke | 100.0/76.4mm |
| Compression ratio | 11.7:1 |
| Gearbox | 6-speed manual |

## GEARBOX

**Type** 6-speed manual

## STEERING

**Type** Rack and pinion, power assisted
**Turns lock-to-lock** 3.0

## SUSPENSION

**Front/rear** Struts, coil springs, anti-roll bar/multi-link, coil springs, anti-roll bar

## BRAKES

**Front** 350mm ventilated discs
**Rear** 330mm ventilated discs

## WHEELS AND TYRES

**Size** 8.5Jx18in (f), 11Jx18in (r)
**Tyres** 235/40 ZR18 (f) 295/30 ZR18 (r)
Pirelli P-Zero Corsa

## THE **AUTOCAR** VERDICT

Wears the RS badge with pride and is a surprisingly big step up over the regular GT3. As a raw driving experience this is about as pure as it gets nowadays.

conditioning, hi-fi, electric windows and mirrors mean that if you've got the cash and a strong spine, you *could* use it every day – although I suspect dealing with the attention it attracts might be a more important issue to deal with in coming to such a decision.

Two questions, then. What if you own a GT3 and are wondering whether the RS is nothing more then a sticker and wing-fest: is the RS worth the extra £12k? Used M3 CSL values are in free-fall, and the market seems unhappy with these limited editions of already small-volume models. But remember, Porsche invented this game, and therefore knows precisely how far it has to go to keep the customer sweet. What matters is that for various cumulative reasons, the RS feels a *lot* more special than the GT3. Only the £133k Ferrari 360 Challenge Stradale gets close.

It is the supreme lightweight, track-attack 996 and in so being rights nearly all of the GT3's problematic areas. Which leads us on to the really big question: is it better than 993 RS? No, not quite. But being a close second best to the finest 911 ever – at a time when legislation makes this kind of exercise infinitely more difficult than it was in 1995 – is still a mighty achievement.

# BETTER THAN EVER

**911 CARRERA S** The first drive of a new Porsche 911 is always a momentous occasion and the 997 doesn't disappoint. *By Peter Robinson*

This is 911 heaven. The 997, responding perfectly to every input, doing exactly what you want, when you want, is in its element. The scenic road, following the winding eastern shores of False Bay, about an hour from Cape Town, might have been created for Porsche's new 350bhp Carrera S.

Early Monday morning, free of tourists, this is a dream road, set between rugged mountains and azure sea, twisting, climbing, dipping, with straights long enough to snatch fourth. Here, the new 911 shrugs off any initial concerns that the steering has lost its Porsche-ness precision on turn-in. The engine – glorious of response, ferocious of pace, exhaust echoes ripping off the hillside, induction yowl saturating the cabin – leaves me breathless. The grip never lets up, and I'm pushing ever faster, hoping to unsettle the back end as the car belts to-and-fro, through the same intimately linked series of corners, for the photographer.

No more perfect test could be conceived. With each run, I'm gaining in confidence and speed, discovering the outer limits of adhesion are appreciably higher than ever. Confidence turns to trust. Yes, yet again, Porsche has built a significantly faster 911. But that's not really the 997's achievement. This is also a better handling, more predictable – yes, more rewarding – 911, with a chassis poise that essentially refutes its tail-heavy weight bias. In these circumstances, tottering on the limit, the 996 gently bobbed the nose vertically. The 997 stays flatter, biting first at the nose, then sticking resolutely at both ends, the brakes smashing into the speed and seemingly unconcerned at their continual near-abuse.

For those familiar with the 996, and all its ancestors, nothing less than a 911 recalibration is required. It's as if everything (well, *almost* everything) the S does is 10 to 15 per cent better, faster.

I came to South Africa to lay hands on the still-secret, mildly disguised (although masking tape can't conceal the engineering mule's more voluptuous curves) latest-gen 911 Carrera for the first time, coincidentally on the same roads Mercedes chose to launch the McMerc SLR. Three months later, to confirm our first impressions and capture the uncloaked styling on film, we picked-up a production S from Zuffenhausen. Two 997 workouts before the official press launch. Spoiled.

Apart from thoroughly revised styling (only the roof panel is carried over from the 996) that obviously draws its inspiration from the 993, highlights include a now 3.8-litre flat-six for the S version we're testing, a new interior and Porsche's first attempt at adaptive damping in a 911.

Styling first. In profile, the glass-house hovers over the bulging hipster wheel arches (adding 38mm to the width, but needed to accommodate the S's 19inch alloys and bigger brakes), so it appears slimmer, even longer, though it's actually a tad (3mm) shorter, and more rounded, front and rear. An enormous amount of work has gone into the aerodynamics, not just in lowering the drag coefficient (from 0.30 to 0.28 for the Carrera, 0.29 on the S) and reducing lift, but also in improving the airflow under the car, from the front radiators and around the wheel arches.

Visually, this might be the successor to the 993, rather than the conservative, knee-jerk reaction to criticism of the 996's avant-garde 'broken egg-yolk' headlights that it is. It remains a 911 and, importantly, won't be confused with either predecessor, but it

## FACTFILE

| Model | 911 Carrera S |
|---|---|
| Price | £65,000 |
| On sale | October |
| Top speed | 182mph |
| 0–62mph | 4.8sec |
| Economy | 24.6mpg |
| CO$_2$ emissions | 277g/km |
| Insurance group | 20 |

# FIRST DRIVE

## 15 JUNE 2004

Volume 240

No 11 | 5592

**ABOVE** Acceleration and top speed are better than ever: S hits 62mph in 4.8sec on its way to 182mph..

**OPPOSITE** Expanded flat six (up to 3.8 litres from 3.6) sounds better, goes better; discreet boot spoiler raises at speed; Xenon lights standard on S, Turbo.

also suggests the need for a bolder design direction for Porsche's iconic coupé. The 997 is set down for at least a six-year life-cycle, more than enough time for new design boss Michael Mauer (ex-Saab, Smart and Mercedes) to work his persuasive inspiration.

For the new Porsche Active Suspension Management (PASM) Zuffenhausen makes the usual, seemingly contradictory claims for adaptive dampers: improved ride comfort with sharper handling. Standard on the £65,000 S (optional on the 3.6-litre Carrera that puts out 321bhp – up 6bhp – and costs £58,380 – up £1750), and developed with Bilstein, the continuously variable dampers offer a choice of normal or sport settings based on vertical suspension movements and longitudinal and lateral acceleration.

The new dampers are part of a package of chassis changes that includes variable-ratio steering, revisions to the rear suspension geometry and bigger Michelins – Pilot Sport N1 235/35 ZR19 front

and 295/30ZR19 rear on the S (the Carrera gets 18s), developed specially for this car. Bridgestone, Pirelli and Continental rubber comes later.

It's been just three days since I drove the previous 911, and I'm immediately aware that the S is operating on a higher level across virtually the entire dynamic spectrum. The truth, unpalatable though it may be to those obsessed by the air-cooled variety, is that each successive water-cooled 911 has moved the game forward.

Already I'm conscious the new S is quieter and more comfortable of ride, most notably in normal mode, the suspension absorbing bumps that would have jarred the rear end of the old model. The notably stiffer sport setting feels as firm as any regular 996's, yet still with less initial impact harshness. The gear change is faster and lighter, sweeter, full of character and a joy to operate. Yet a flatter and beefier torque curve reduces the need, if not the inclination, for cog-swapping. Pushing the flat six to

'WE DON'T SEE ANY NEED TO CHANGE THE CONCEPT...
IT WOULDN'T BE A 911 WITHOUT THE REAR ENGINE'

295lb ft at 4600rpm, up 350rpm on the 273lb ft 3.6, meant exceeding the torque capacity of the old gearbox and thus required development of an all-new 'box, one that reduces shift travel by 15 per cent, in combination with a self-adjusting clutch.

The big-bore engine is more gutsy and responsive around 3000rpm, where it begins to tap into the flat six's intoxicating induction snort, and it's equally happily to rev, despite those 350 horses being developed at 6600rpm, 200rpm below the 3.6-litre's power peak. There is real power from 2500rpm, thanks to the variable intake-valve timing and a total redesign of the induction system that brings shorter intake manifolds and a two-piece resonance chamber, with a patented resonator that's activated between 5000-6000rpm to reduce oscillations of induction noise to within 260 hertz. The effect is a constantly volatile induction howl that takes on a harder character at 5600rpm, in synch with a power kick, and builds in volume to a deep scream by 7300rpm that seems to spring from the very heart of the engine.

August Achleitner, director of 911 development, insists the S is set up to reach its 182mph top speed exactly at the 7300rpm fuel cut-out, something the 177mph Carrera (they share gearing) can't achieve. Porsche claims the S's 4.8sec run from 0–62mph is a mere 0.2sec quicker than the Carrera's, the difference widening to over a second by 124mph, which the 3.8 hits in 16.5sec. That's almost a Ferrari 360 time and we've yet to see the circa-475bhp 997 Turbo, due in 2006. The 997 feels stronger than the numbers suggest. So much more gutsy, I was frequently aware of running one gear higher than if I'd been in a 996.

Weissach has taken advantage of many of the potential systems off-shoots of modern electronics. A sports mode alters the accelerator pedal movement and introduces an even higher threshold of intrusion by the stability management system (now standard, even on the Carrera) and switches the PASM to a firmer damper set-up. Maybe the faster throttle – and faster-closing butterfly on a trailing right foot – works in improving responses on a race track. On the road, especially in traffic, the action is too abrupt and hinders smooth progress.

A day's outing in Germany left me asking, again, how Porsche can move the next 911 forward from the 997. I find it hard to imagine any sane driver running out of adhesion in the new Carrera, at least on the road. It sticks at both ends, PSM rarely intruding and then so subtly it never spoils the

Handling is better than ever; sport mode heightens responses, minimises body roll; grip is phenomenal.

# SPECIFICATIONS 911 CARRERA S

## DIMENSIONS

| | |
|---|---|
| Length | 4427mm |
| Width | 1808mm |
| Height | 1300mm |
| Wheelbase | 2350mm |
| Weight | 1420kg |
| Fuel tank | 64 litres |

## ENGINE

| | |
|---|---|
| Layout | 6 cyls, 3824cc |
| Max power | 350bhp at 6600rpm |
| Max torque | 295lb ft at 4600rpm |
| Power to weight | 246bhp per tonne |
| Installation | Rear, longitudinal, 4WD |
| Bore/stroke | 96.0/82.8mm |
| Compression ratio | 11.8:1 |
| Gearbox | 6-speed manual |

## STEERING

**Type** Rack and pinion, power assisted
**Turns lock-to-lock** 2.6

## SUSPENSION

**Front/rear** MacPherson struts, coil springs, anti-roll bar/multi-link, coil springs, anti-roll bar

## BRAKES

**Front/rear** 330/330mm ventilated cross-drilled discs

## TYRES

**Tyres** 235/35 ZR19 (f), 295/30 ZR19 (r)
Michelin Pilot Sport N1

action. Magazine editors love oversteer, but, despite my best efforts on a variety of corners, I couldn't get the tail to move sideways for more than a few fleeting seconds. Attack second-gear hairpins and the Porsche's traction advantage means hurtling out of the bend, right foot buried through the firewall. Lift off and it merely tightens the line by tucking the nose neatly, without worrying the driver. The engineers' claim that on the brilliant new Michelins, the 997 has 10 per cent more cornering speed than the 996. Utterly believable.

My only puzzlement concerns the steering. Because the variable-ratio steering is lighter and slightly less direct around the straight-ahead, the immediacy and linearity of responses in that crucial first movement off-centre, taken for granted by longtime 911 drivers, are reduced. This is the biggest change to the steering since the adoption of power assistance on the 964 in 1988 and, at first experience, just as controversial. I spent day one in South Africa confused by the rack's messages, even admitting to missing the constant joggling of the wheel, a 911 peculiarity for more than 40 years that has finally been eliminated. Initial turn-in seemed slower, less urgent, and I was sawing at the wheel through third-gear sweepers, convincing myself I could feel the rack's ratio changing. By the end of the second day, after belting the S over the challenging Franschhoek Pass and tapping into the car's greater agility at the limit, taking advantage of its superior grip and more adjustable handling, I'd come to terms with the new set-up. Everywhere beyond the first 30 degrees of wheel movement the steering is quicker and more precise. Body control is brilliant. The 911 stays flat, linking corners in a series of incisive, flowing movements, the suspension soaking up bumps and surface changes that would upset the previous 911's poise. Be warned, 996 owners need to accept that the 997 feels different. It took me until the third morning to accept that the changes to the steering truly worked.

Porsche's 350mm ceramic brake discs are now optional across the 911 range. To justify the high expense you need to be a determined track-day attendee, for the S gets the current Turbo's terrific 330mm cross-drilled discs. Still, the ceramic brakes deliver even more immediate responses, a progressive-feeling pedal, reduce unsprung weight by 14kg, and function without the squealing that was once unavoidable from such systems.

Add wider, more supportive bucket seats, greater adjustability of the driving position, courtesy of the now height- and reach-adjustable wheel, and pedals

that are 10mm forward, and a new interior design that's notably superior in material quality and fit, and the cockpit news is virtually all positive. If the dashboard styling is conservative – again, borrowing its theme from earlier 911s – the ergonomics, largely shared with the Cayenne, are easier to fathom. A couple of small, welcome touches: the digital speedo's returned to the lower section of the central rev counter, where it's easier to read, and you can now (finally) hear the turn indicator click.

In 997 S form, the 911 Carrera is faster, more stable, more precise, and forgiving, an altogether superior – make that more efficient – sports car than the 996. Still, I suspect this anaesthetising of traditional Porsche traits – flaws if you must – will be missed by some obsessive 911 drivers. It is almost too good, a genuine supercar at an un-supercar price, that retains all the practicality that has made the 911 unique for over 40 years, and is capable of true greatness.

**ABOVE** Familiar 911 shape looks little changed from the 996's, but the roof panel is the only body part carried over.

**OPPOSITE** 19in five-spoke alloys; 911's front boot isn't massive, but it's supplemented by rear-seat storage; conservatively styled dash is well put together and laid out; digital speedo returns to lower section of rev counter.

## AUTOCAR'S CHECKLIST

### STYLING ★★★★
No minor facelift this, more a sleekly professional mix of 996 and 993 that perpetuates the classic 911 profile.

### ENGINE ★★★★★
Better than ever. Mid-range response sharper; more tractable, eager to rev. At some cost to economy.

### HANDLING/RIDE ★★★★★
Adaptive dampers make for huge improvement in ride; massive grip. New steering an acquired taste.

### BRAKES ★★★★★
As good as they get. Optional ceramic discs brilliant without noise penalty.

### CABIN QUALITY ★★★★
Better put together, feels solid. But conservative in back-to-the-993 styling. Leather standard in UK.

### PRACTICALITY ★★★
Supercars don't come more practical. Rear seats for children or luggage, boot bigger without spare wheel.

### VALUE FOR MONEY ★★★★
Long options list impossible to resist. S certain to be in short supply in first year. Excellent residuals.

### SO WHAT DO WE THINK?
Faster, more stable, more precise.
Everything you expect from a new 911

# THE BUSINESS. AS USUAL

**911 CARRERA** The 911 is *the* motoring icon and the new 997 is the best one yet.
Steve Sutcliffe takes the opportunity to sample the first 997 on UK roads

itting, waiting in a lay-by somewhere just
outside Oxford. Wondering what the new
Porsche 911 will be like to drive. Wondering
whether it will be a step forwards or backwards.
Or maybe, even, a step sideways.

My mind fizzes with anticipation. Will it look
good in the metal? Will it steer like a 911? Will it
sound like a 911? Of course it'll stop like a 911. But
will it feel like a 911? Will it intimidate *like a 911*?

And then it appears, nose bobbing a little as
photographer Stan Papior gives it a decent portion
of vegetables around the far side of the roundabout
at which we are to meet.

I can't make up my mind quite how to react to
the 'new' 911 when it finally draws up alongside
me, its exhaust system pinging as it cools. I'm
so shocked I forget to say hello to its driver and
just gawp at the car. Has he collected the wrong
Porsche, I begin to wonder. I thought I'd been
commissioned to write a story about driving the
first 'new' 911 in the UK, yet Stan would appear
to have turned up in an old 911 — a deliciously
bright red example, I'll grant you, but an old 911
all the same.

Oh hang on, the nose is different, sort of. And
so are the rear wheel arches. And the lights. And
the door mirrors. But overall, well, it just looks so

## QUICK FACTS

| | |
|---|---|
| **Model tested** | 911 Carrera |
| **Price** | £58,380 |
| **Top speed** | 177mph |
| **0–62mph** | 5.0sec |
| **MPG combined** | 25.7mpg |
| **CO₂ emissions** | 266g/km |
| **Insurance group** | 20 |
| **Engine** | Flat-six, 3596cc |
| **Power** | 321bhp at 6800rpm |
| **Torque** | 273lb ft at 4250rpm |

familiar. Question one, it seems, has already been answered. And if you don't believe me, make your own mind up the first time you see one on the road – if indeed you clock that it's a new one you're looking at.

"What's it like then?" I ask Stanley. "Fast," he replies through a very big grin. Most of you will not have had the pleasure of our Stanley but, trust me, grins of this calibre are not often contained within his everyday repertoire. Which means it's time for me to find out and for Stan to drive the Honda NSX I've just arrived in for the rest of today.

A pull on the new door handle confirms immediately that, although the styling evolution may have stalled somewhat at Porsche, the engineering evolution has not. From the moment you touch the new 911 it feels, yes, like an old 911; but at the same time tougher and more durable than the 996. I always had the sneaking suspicion that the 996 was nowhere near as well built as it's predecessors: the

doors would never shut with quite the same thunk; the switchgear never felt as if it'd last forever; and the gearchange always felt light and (whisper it) even a tad notchy beside the 993's. But all that has changed on the 997. Statically, this car feels every inch like the real deal. Like a genuine 911.

Take the cabin. You climb in, realise how snugly you fit the seats and how Cayenne-like the centre console is, and also how much clearer the basic ergonomics are. Yet the overwhelming impression is that you've somehow been here before.

This is no coincidence. This is Porsche admitting to a rare mistake. This is Porsche saying: "We got the 996 cabin wrong – slightly – because it didn't really feel like a 911 inside. But don't worry folks, because we've adjusted the settings, moved things around a bit (specifically the rev counter and the digital speedo) and now everything is – how you say – hunky-dory once more." So we'll just ignore the exceedingly naff stopwatch on top of the dash

for the time being – even Porsche can continuously make mistakes, after all.

Key in the ignition (mounted on the right of the steering column, note), twist and, what was that? Blimey, it's so smooth. So calm. Prod the throttle just to make sure it's actually alive and, sure enough, there's that sound. That same old chainsaw-in-cotton-wool rush as six horizontally opposed pistons (water-cooled, just as they were in the 996) begin to pump at one another. Same electric response to the throttle, too. No, make that an even better response to the throttle this time round. Yes, this is a 911. But it's also a new kind of 911. A more refined 911.

I dip the clutch and get ready to engage first gear and another minor realisation occurs: the pedal is way lighter than before, the gearlever far easier to manipulate around its gate. Changing gear in this car, you imagine, will not be much more taxing than it is in a Honda Civic.

And so it proves. I pull away, listening carefully to the engine's more muted yet still inimitable machinations, and move the lever easily into second and then third. And twig that never before has a 911 been so damn easy to drive. Soon, maybe, BSM will be buying these things.

Half a mile up the road, having not yet gone above 30mph, it's already obvious how much more comfortable this car is compared with any other to have worn the magic number. It rides so well it's hard to believe it'll actually handle when I start to throw it around. So perfectly matched are the springs of the seats to those of the suspension, and so soothing is the damping, you just don't notice you're riding across a road that is, by and large, dreadfully lumpy. The only giveaway is the tail spoiler of the NSX you're following: it bobs violently up and down in front while you glide serenely over the same Tarmac.

Then you notice the steering. Or more specifically, you notice that you haven't noticed the steering. Haven't yet thought to yourself: what lovely steering this car has. This is because, to begin with, you just aim the new 911 and it steers. It goes in the exact direction you want it to, without any particular sensation of doing so other than visual confirmation through the windscreen. Feel, you think to yourself, is missing from this car's steering – even though it's accurate to within one quarter of half a millimetre.

The rear of the NSX squats a fraction in front and a clear thought begins to form: that this is the

## 'NO PREVIOUS 911 HAS BEEN SO DAMN EASY TO DRIVE. SOON, BSM WILL BE BUYING THESE THINGS'

**ABOVE** 997 is more comfortable and refined than old model, but don't worry: the handling's even better, too.

**RIGHT** Latest 911 a dynamic masterstroke, but is it now time for something new?

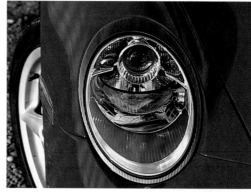

**ABOVE** Cabin better made than before, ergonomics also far superior to 996's; famous oval headlamps make a welcome return; ceramic brakes a £5349 option.

**OPPOSITE** Carrera's 3.6-litre flat-six makes 321bhp and 273lb ft.

time to find the answers to the more important questions concerning the new 911. Namely, does it do the business when you need it to do the business? Or does it – because it is so much smoother and more refined than before at low speeds – fall apart when you need it to crystallise at high speed?

It takes about eight seconds or just one decent fourth-gear corner to find out, and it goes something like this. From three figures you lean on the middle pedal hard and immediately lose 30mph, taking you down to a nice speed to turn in at. You turn in gently and the inside front tyre takes a great big bite at the apex while the outside front tyre takes all the load without a deflection. The body then rolls a fraction and settles on its suspension, and the dampers take a breath and allow the body to breathe beautifully with the road below. And then finally you realise that through the palms of your hands you can feel it: feel the steering; feel the tyres clawing at the Tarmac; feel the 911-ness going on beneath you.

Soon afterwards you realise, too, that had you tried to take this same corner at the same speed in any previous generation of 911, you'd have been buried deep in the undergrowth right now, wondering what on earth you'd being trying to attempt. The new 911, you rapidly conclude, truly is quite a piece of work.

And it doesn't stop there. A little later, having driven for an hour or two down the M4, the quality of refinement becomes ever more apparent. Okay, there's a fair bit of tyre roar from the fat Michelins (there always is on Porsches), but the sense of relaxation you experience is so strong you almost ignore the white noise emanating from the tyre treads. The seats are so well shaped, the Bose stereo of such high quality and the suspension so well resolved you can't help but climb out amazed by this car's character after a day behind the wheel. Never before – and I mean never – has a machine so successfully combined so many attributes under one roof. It is pure sports car, relaxing GT car and everything you can think of in between.

## 'NEVER BEFORE HAS A MACHINE SO SUCCESSFULLY COMBINED SO MANY ATTRIBUTES UNDER ONE ROOF'

At this point you should know that this is not the much-talked-about S model; this is your regular bread-and-butter 321bhp/273lb ft 911 Carrera on 18in wheels and standard suspension. The only options it has are the Bose stereo and ceramic brakes – the same as those fitted to the 996 Turbo and yours in this instance for a wincing £5349. Basic price £58,380. On-the-road price £64,497 with options.

So does all this mean that the new 911 – better to drive, not to mention faster, more thoroughly built, much more refined and hugely more comfortable over any UK road – represents incredible value in 2004? Or has it, in fact, begun to get ideas above its station? Sixty-five big ones will, after all, buy you a very fast TVR *and* a Peugeot 407 for the other 364 days of the year. Or it would buy you an extremely refined Jaguar XJ and a Renault Clio Renaultsport 182. Alternatively, you could have a Range Rover and change for the mother and father of all holidays. And a Daewoo Lacetti.

To judge the new 911 by such humble standards, however, would be to judge it badly, because what it is is a stand-alone enigma. Always has been, always will be. In reality it's far closer to being a cut-price Ferrari rival than a pricey alternative to a TVR. And the real killer (for Ferrari) is that it goes damn near as well, has almost as much brand cachet yet costs approximately half the price of the new F430.

But in the end such comparisons are largely meaningless because, as ever, the 911 has no obvious set of rivals. Imitators, yes, but true competition, no. And what's most important is that in every way but one it represents another major improvement over its ancestors. In many ways it is the finest 911 so far.

Yet it's also difficult not to wonder just how affected the 997 will be in the long run by its styling, which to these eyes is not what it could be. To these eyes it is what the 996 always should have been, and even today, when the shape is as fresh as it'll ever be, it looks too samey to what's gone before. In two years' time it's hard to see how that will have changed for the better.

I hope I'm wrong. And a part of me hopes Porsche continues to make better and better 911s until the end of time. But maybe, just maybe, it could be time to call it a day; to move on and design something genuinely new which carries a different number from the one we know and love. Otherwise someone, somewhere, might just accuse Porsche of running out of good ideas.

# SPECIFICATIONS 911 CARRERA

## DIMENSIONS

| | |
|---|---|
| Length | 4427mm |
| Width | 1808mm |
| Height | 1310mm |
| Wheelbase | 2350mm |
| Weight | 1395kg |
| Fuel tank | 64 litres |

## ENGINE

| | |
|---|---|
| Layout | Flat six, 3596cc |
| Max power | 321bhp at 6800rpm |
| Max torque | 273lb ft at 4250rpm |
| Power to weight | 230bhp per tonne |
| Installation | Rear, longitudinal, 4WD |
| Bore/stroke | 96.0/82.8mm |
| Compression ratio | 11.3:1 |
| Management | Motronic ME 7.8 |

## STEERING

**Type** Rack and pinion, variable-ratio, power assisted
**Turns lock-to-lock** 2.6

## GEARBOX

**Type** 6-speed manual

## SUSPENSION

**Front/rear** MacPherson struts, anti-roll bar/multi-link, coil springs, anti-roll bar

## BRAKES

**Front and rear** 330mm ventilated discs

## TYRES

**Tyres** 8.0J × 18in 235/40 ZR18 (f), 10.0J × 18in 265/40 ZR18 (r), Michelin Pilot Sport

# 911 CARRERA S

The arrival of a new 911 is always a special occasion for motoring enthusiasts, but is the old magic still there or has Porsche dumbed-down the experience?

Cars don't come any more iconic than Porsche's evergreen 911. A maverick design that has defied not only its critics but also its maker's attempts to pension it off, the 911 still clings to the basic rear-engined 2+2 concept of the original car, yet thoughtful evolution means it's as relevant today as it was 41 years ago.

It remains the benchmark performance coupé for enthusiasts and car makers alike, and thanks to compact dimensions and a decent dose of practicality it's one of the most usable sports cars on sale. It's also something of a bargain. Codenamed 997 (the last car was 996, its predecessor 993) but still known as the 911, the sixth incarnation is finally here on British soil. Two versions are available, the £58,380 Carrera and the £65,000 S tested here. *Autocar* expects, but does Porsche deliver?

### DESIGN & ENGINEERING ★★★★
**Evolutionary skin, cutting-edge technology**

If the styling suggests this is merely a facelift (its round lights and more pronounced hips clearly echo the much-lauded 993 of the mid '90s) the engineers tell a different story. Eighty per cent of the 997's parts are new, from the aluminium bonnet to the six-speed gearbox and the radically revised cabin.

Though the 2350mm wheelbase is carried over, the new car is 3mm shorter and 38mm wider than the old one, while track width is up 21mm at the sharp end and 11mm out back. Careful wind tunnel work has knocked a point off the 996's 0.30 Cd figure.

Motive power for the standard £58,380 Carrera comes from a development of the 996's 3.6-litre flat six, again slung way out beyond the rear axle but this time producing 321bhp (up from 315bhp thanks to ECU tweaks) at 6800rpm and the same 273lb ft of torque at 4250rpm. But S versions have an extra 200cc, boosting output to an almost GT3-rivalling 350bhp at 6600rpm and a solid 295lb ft of torque, albeit developed higher up the rev range than in the standard car at 4600rpm.

Weight has crept up, too – the base Carrera by 25kg to 1395kg, giving a power-to-weight ratio of 230bhp per tonne and 246bhp for the 1420kg S, compared with 234bhp for the last of the 996s. Both cars get a new six-speed manual gearbox, although the familiar five-speed Tiptronic auto remains an option, at least until the PDK dual-clutch DSG-style 'box arrives sometime within the next two years.

For now, the most intriguing changes are both chassis related: variable-ratio steering replaces the existing linear-ratio rack on both models, while optional on Carrera but standard on S models is Porsche Active Suspension Management, the first outing for an adaptive damping system on a 911. Developed with Bilstein, the dampers react to information about vertical, lateral and longitudinal body movements. This occurs in both normal and sport settings, these being selected via a button on the centre console.

There are no brash spoilers to let the world know your car is an S rather than a standard

## QUICK FACTS

| | |
|---|---|
| **Model tested** | 911 Carrera S |
| **List price** | £65,000 |
| **Top speed** | 182mph |
| **30–70mph** | 4.1sec |
| **0–60mph** | 4.6sec |
| **70–0mph** | 44.0m |
| **MPG combined** | 20.9mpg |
| **For** | Greater refinement and quality, brilliant chassis |
| **Against** | Wider body, duller steering |

# ROAD TEST

## 5 OCTOBER 2004

Volume 242

No 1 | 5608

Carrera, but the clues are there. S cars tote four (not two) exhaust pipes, a discreet script on their rumps and roll on chunky new 19-inch alloys rather than the 18s fitted to the base model.

## PERFORMANCE/BRAKES ★★★★★
**One of the great engines; excellent brakes**

Why five stars when the raw numbers are no better than its predecessor's? Because performance is about much more than bald figures and this 3.8-litre flat six ranks as one of the finest engines on sale anywhere. Lusty, tuneful and with a chameleon-like character that enables it to play the docile obedient puppy in town or a snarling Rottweiler away from it, you'd never tire of that distinctive metallic yowl as the rev needle sweeps around for another assault on the 7300rpm limiter. It'll pull happily from under 1000rpm but the real action starts with the crank spinning at three times that speed. There's another lunge forward at 5500rpm and yet another at 6500rpm before the final trip to the red line.

And this is one mightily quick car: 60mph flashes by in the same 4.6sec we recorded for the 996 and 100mph in 10.8sec, up from 10.1sec, but drive one and you'd never feel short-changed.

**RIGHT** 130-litre boot surprisingly useful; Brakes give huge stopping power.

**OPPOSITE** Ample head- and legroom up front; quality of cabin plastics improved; rear seats best suited for children.

**BELOW** Handling even better than excellent 996's and ride quality and refinement have been transformed.

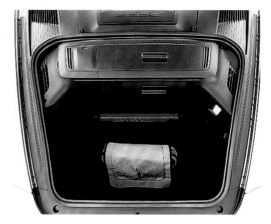

# ROAD TEST 911 CARRERA S

## MAXIMUM SPEEDS

| | | | |
|---|---|---|---|
| 6th | 182mph/7300rpm | 5th | 152/7300 |
| 4th | 123/7300 | 3rd | 99/7300 |
| 2nd | 71/7300 | 1st | 42/7300 |

## ACCELERATION FROM REST

| True mph | seconds | speedo mph |
|---|---|---|
| 30 | 1.8 | 31 |
| 40 | 2.4 | 42 |
| 50 | 3.6 | 52 |
| 60 | 4.6 | 62 |
| 70 | 5.9 | 73 |
| 80 | 7.4 | 83 |
| 90 | 8.8 | 93 |
| 100 | 10.8 | 104 |
| 110 | 12.9 | 114 |
| 120 | 15.2 | 124 |
| 130 | 18.7 | 135 |
| 140 | 22.2 | 145 |
| 150 | 27.7 | 155 |

Standing qtr mile 13.0sec/111mph
Standing km 23.4sec/143mph
30–70mph through gears 4.1sec
30–70mph in 4th 8.1sec

## ACCELERATION IN GEAR

| MPH | 6th | 5th | 4th | 3rd | 2nd |
|---|---|---|---|---|---|
| 20–40 | 7.9 | 6.7 | 4.5 | 3.4 | 2.2 |
| 30–50 | 7.2 | 5.4 | 4.3 | 3.2 | 2.1 |
| 40–60 | 7.0 | 5.4 | 4.1 | 2.9 | 2.0 |
| 50–70 | 7.3 | 5.2 | 3.8 | 2.9 | 2.5 |
| 60–80 | 7.2 | 4.8 | 3.7 | 3.0 | – |
| 70–90 | 6.7 | 4.8 | 3.8 | 3.0 | – |
| 80–100 | 6.8 | 4.8 | 4.0 | 3.3 | – |
| 90–110 | 7.0 | 5.1 | 4.1 | – | – |
| 100–120 | 7.2 | 5.6 | 4.4 | – | – |
| 110–130 | – | 5.9 | – | – | – |
| 120–140 | – | 6.6 | – | – | – |
| 130–150 | – | – | – | – | – |

## FUEL CONSUMPTION

Average/best/worst/touring
20.9/25.3/9.5/25.3mpg

| | |
|---|---|
| Urban/combined | 16.5/24.6mpg |
| Tank capacity | 64 litres |
| Theoretical range | 356 miles |
| Real-world range | 294 miles |

## BRAKES

| | |
|---|---|
| 30/50/70mph | 8.5/22.6/44.0 metres |
| 60–0mph | 2.9sec |

Pedal feel poor/fair/**good**/excellent
Fade poor/fair/**good**/excellent

## HANDLING AND RIDE

**Normal driving**
Balance understeer/oversteer/**neutral**
Steering feel poor/fair/**good**/excellent
Body control poor/fair/good/**excellent**
Ride quality poor/fair/**good**/excellent
Grip poor/fair/good/**excellent**

**Hard driving**
Balance understeer/oversteer/**neutral**
Steering feel poor/fair/**good**/excellent
Body control poor/fair/good/**excellent**
Ride quality poor/fair/**good**/excellent
Grip poor/fair/**good**/excellent

**Test notes** Meaty steering now slower off-centre, but works well with firm chassis and good damping to give outstanding agility. Ride disappointing on Sports damper setting, characterised by excess vertical motion.

## NOISE

**Idle/max revs** in 3rd 49/78dbA
**30/50/70mph** 60/67/71dbA
**Sound quality** poor/fair/good/**excellent**

## HEADLIGHTS

Dipped beam poor/fair/good/**excellent**
Full beam poor/fair/**good**/excellent
**Test notes** Standard bi-xenon headlamps offer great illumination but seem to irritate other drivers.

## TESTER'S NOTES

We know the new car has taken some stick for its derivative styling, but in the metal it has a presence sorely lacking in the old 996 and not fully realised on non-S Carreras.

---

Zealously honest, Porsche claims the S will hit 182mph just shy of the 7300rpm limiter in sixth, something we weren't able to verify. On an unpleasantly gusty day at the Millbrook proving ground, and with the Vbox digital speed readout registering 170mph and climbing, the inherent instability of the rear-engined layout in crosswinds revealed itself, ushering the car up the banking towards the Armco before we decided circumspection was the order of the day.

Thankfully the brakes (standard steel rather than ceramic discs on the test car) proved more reassuring, offering plenty of feel through a solid pedal and hauling the 911 up from 70mph in just 44m.

## HANDLING AND RIDE ★★★★
**Steering takes a step back, handling improved**

---

If, as is likely, you've already digested *Autocar*'s thoughts on this new 911 in other features, you'll know that just one highly contentious issue threatens to sour proceedings. We like to think of the steering column as a mechanical umbilical chord, a crucial

# SPECIFICATIONS 911 CARRERA S

## DIMENSIONS

Min/max front legroom 860/1110mm  Min/max front headroom 870/970mm
Min/max rear legroom 460/780mm  Rear headroom 800mm  Kerb weight 1420kg
Max boot width 700mm  Boot height 590mm  Boot volume 135 litres/dm³
Front/rear tracks 1486/1516mm  Width (with/without mirrors) 1900/1808mm

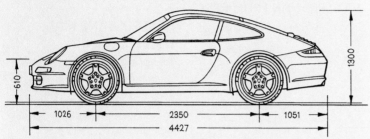

1300
610
1026  2350  1051
4427

## ENGINE

| | |
|---|---|
| Layout | Flat 6 cyls, 3824cc |
| Power | 350bhp at 6600rpm |
| Torque | 295lb ft at 4600rpm |
| Max engine speed | 7300rpm |
| Specific output | 92bhp per litre |
| Power to weight | 246bhp per tonne |
| Torque to weight | 208lb ft per tonne |
| Installation | Longitudinal, rear, rear-wheel drive |
| Construction | Alloy head & block |
| Bore/stroke | 84.0/75.0mm |
| Valve gear | 4 per cyl, dohc |
| Compression ratio | 11.8:1 |
| Management | Motronic ME 7.8 |

## TRANSMISSION

| | |
|---|---|
| Gearbox | 6-speed manual |
| Ratios/mph per 1000rpm | |
| Final drive ratio | 3.44 |

| | | | |
|---|---|---|---|
| 1st 3.91/5.7 | 2nd 2.32/9.7 | | |
| 3rd 1.66/13.5 | 4th 1.28/17.5 | | |
| 5th 1.08/20.8 | 6th 0.88/25.5 | | |

## CHASSIS AND BODY

| | |
|---|---|
| Body | Two-door coupé, steel/aluminium unibody construction Cd 0.29 |
| Wheels | 8.0J x 19in (f), 11.0J x 19in (r) |
| Tyres | 235/35 ZR19 (f), 295/30 ZR19 (r) Michelin Pilot Sport N1 |
| Safety | Driver, passenger, side and head airbags, seatbelt pretensioners, PSM (Porsche Stability Management) |

## STEERING

**Type** Rack and pinion, hydraulic power assistance
**Turns lock-to-lock** 2.6
**Turning circle** 10.9m

## SUSPENSION

**Front** MacPherson struts, coil springs, anti-roll bar
**Rear** Multi-link, coil springs, anti-roll bar

## BRAKES

**Front** 330mm drilled/ventilated discs
**Rear** 330mm drilled/ventilated discs
**Anti-lock** Standard, with EBD brakeforce distribution and EBA brake assist

---

lifeline to the road and a means of communication that has benefits not only in pure enjoyment terms, but in safety, too.

Without that dialogue you're deprived of information that – for the enthusiast – is vital to the driving experience. It's acceptable, if not desirable, on a city runabout; unforgivable on a high-performance coupé.

Fortunately, the 911's is still a great helm: beautifully weighted, crisp on turn-in and fearsomely accurate. But subjectively some of the life seems to have been squeezed out of the system. No longer does it writhe gently in your hands at even modest speeds, and only when traversing more challenging roads does the wheel come alive, gently tugging at your wrists and streaming details back through your fingertips.

Worse, the new steering wheel seems to have been designed with style rather than ergonomics in mind. Hand positions vary from driver to driver of course, but the fact that two testers felt cause to mention discomfort – something we've never heard levied at the old car's wheel – validates our concern.

What the slightly muted feel does, is create a far more relaxed environment for those occasions (or perhaps just those drivers) when you'd prefer to saunter home with the least fuss possible. That's a theme that seems to pervade throughout. The 911 still flows wonderfully over longer undulations, but no recent version has ridden smaller bumps with such ease.

But there's a caveat. We're referring to the car's behaviour with the PASM adaptable dampers set to normal. Switch to sport on British roads and though body roll diminishes and the eagerness to change tack improves, the ride falls apart. It's best reserved for track use when you can fully exploit the delicious handling balance.

On public roads traction is staggering, even in the wet with the standard PSM stability system switched off. In the dry only the truly committed will set the tail wagging, understeer being the predominant handling characteristic.

## COMFORT AND SAFETY ★★★★★
**Better built, more comfortable, more kit**

---

If any area of the 996 needed massaging it was the cabin. The new dash is functional, and unarguably ergonomically superior to its predecessor's. Echoing the 993-aping exterior details, the new dash takes

**Gearbox even more precise than before.**

**Steering crisp but wheel uncomfortable.**

**Digital speedo now sits beneath rev counter.**

**LEFT** Column stalks much better quality; Cup holders glide out from dash.

cues from past 911s, mixing subtle retro influences with the edgier architecture and latest Porsche switchgear first seen on the Cayenne SUV.

It's a fundamentally clean design but there's a slight fussiness to the plethora of small buttons surrounding the console-mounted central screen, while the buttons to manually raise the rear spoiler, switch settings on the PASM adaptive dampers and disengage the PSM stability system are tucked away behind the gearlever where they're difficult to reach.

Not so the major controls. Already close to perfect, the driving position is now even better for a broader range of drivers thanks to a 20mm lower seat and a steering wheel that adjusts not just for reach, but rake, too.

Treat the 997 as a two-seater, as most owners will

## WHAT IT COSTS

### PORSCHE 911 CARRERA S

| | |
|---|---|
| **On-the-road price** | £65,000 |
| **Price as tested** | £69,689 |
| **CO$_2$** | 277g/km |
| **Tax at 22/40% pcm** | £417/758 |
| **Cost per mile** | na |
| **Contract hire/month** | na |

### INSURANCE

Insurance/typical quote    20/£808.90

### WARRANTY

24 months/unlimited miles

### EQUIPMENT CHECKLIST

| | |
|---|---|
| Climate control | ■ |
| **CD autochanger** | **£248** |
| Xenon headlamps | ■ |
| **Metallic paint** | **£543** |
| **Electrically adjustable seats** | **£1006** |
| Leather interior | ■ |
| 19-inch alloys | ■ |
| **Satellite navigation** | **£1260** |
| Multifunction steering wheel | £329 |

Options in **bold** fitted to test car
■ = Standard  na = not available

# THE CLASS

## PORSHE 911 CARRERA S £65,000 ★★★★★

Capacity 3824cc
Power 350bhp
Torque 295lb ft
0–60mph 4.6sec
Max speed 182mph
$CO_2$ 277g/km

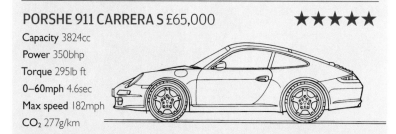

Sixth installment in the 911 saga the most refined yet. Hottest of two non-turbo cars available packs 350bhp from 3.8-litre six. Variable-ratio steering not as feelsome as we'd hope, but this is still the coupé to beat.

## BMW 645i £50,450 ★★★★

Capacity 4398cc
Power 333bhp
Torque 332lb ft
0–60mph 5.4sec
Max speed 155mph
$CO_2$ 279g/km

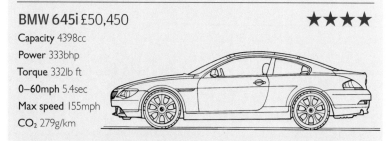

BMW's take on the performance coupé makes a welcome return after a decade away. Brimming with innovative details like active steering, it's the most relaxing and practical coupé here but slightly short on soul.

## HONDA NSX £60,100 ★★★★

Capacity 3179cc
Power 276bhp
Torque 224lb ft
0–60mph 4.8sec
Max speed 172mph
$CO_2$ 291g/km

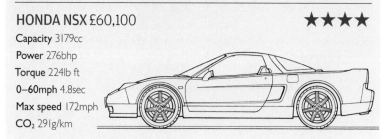

Thirteen years on and Honda's mid-engined supercar still manages to impress. With a fabulous V6 wail, rewarding handling and a surprisingly user-friendly cabin – shame the Type-R is no longer UK-bound.

## JAGUAR XKR £58,120 ★★★

Capacity 4196cc
Power 400bhp
Torque 408lb ft
0–60mph 5.2sec
Max speed 155mph
$CO_2$ 304g/km

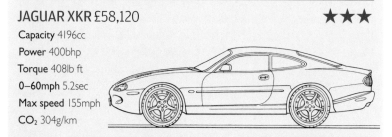

Recent refresh wallpapered over the cracks in this ageing design but they're still there. Engine strong but tuneless and the cabin is surprisingly cramped for such a big car. New car due 2006 will have its work cut out.

do, and it's surprisingly practical. Leg- and headroom are plentiful and though the front-mounted boot offers just 130 litres of storage, some creative packing enables much to be stashed away. And the rear seats (one of the few items to be carried over to the new car) still fold down to create an additional luggage area. But travelling four up isn't out of the question: small children should find the rear seats reasonably comfortable and even adults can be squeezed in there for very short journeys.

Road noise has long been a 911 bugbear and, while still the S's fat rear tyres do generate a fair degree of hum, there's a greater air of refinement to the way the new car tackles coarse motorway surfaces which makes it a quieter long-distance companion.

Porsche Stability Management, previously available at extra cost, is now standard on both Carrera and S models while front occupants now get two-stage airbags up front and two airbags mounted in their seats, rather than the previous one.

There's still plenty to choose from the options list, though: a sports exhaust (£1160), a dash-top-mounted lap timer (£507) and Porsche's excellent PCCB carbon-ceramic brakes (£5349) being just a few of the highlights.

Restyle subtle; headlights back to traditional round shape; only roof panel remains from previous car.

## RUNNING COSTS ★★★★
### As sensible as performance cars get

The 911's famed usability comes not just from its relative practicality but also the near-guarantee of pain-free ownership. The 996's residual values (70 per cent retained after three years) were among the best in the business and we'd expect the 997 to at least match that performance. And, unlike some more exotic rivals, you can use the car every day safe in the knowledge that, even if you have driven more than 3000 miles in the past year, you won't be offered a silly trade-in price.

Porsche has worked hard to reduce other running costs, extending the intervals between oil services from 12,000 to 18,000 miles, while a major service isn't now needed until 36,000 miles, up from 24,000.

Company car drivers will still be taxed at the maximum 35 per cent, but the fuel consumption seems entirely reasonable given the performance. Our 25.3mpg touring figure is impressive enough but we wouldn't be surprised to see parsimonious owners getting nearer 30mpg. The fuel tank holds the same 64 litres as before which should allow the 911 to easily pass the 300-mile barrier between fills on longer trips.

**ABOVE** Steering not as feelsome as previous model's but makes this 911 the most relaxing and easiest to drive of all.

**LEFT** New centre console too fussy.

## AUTOCAR VERDICT

There were bound to be grumbles at the unveiling of a new 911; there always are. But despite the moans from purists that accompanied the 964's switch to power steering or the 996's adoption of water cooling, those cars were fundamentally better than those they replaced. Better suited to the wants and needs of the people that matter most, not excitable motoring journalists or armchair critics, but the Porsche-buying public.

The 997 has its problems, too: having grown wider it's in danger of losing the compactness that has long been one of the car's greatest assets, the styling isn't perhaps the advance we'd hoped for and the slightly anaesthetised steering is probably the single biggest disappointment, especially so in a car with such a strong driver-focused tradition.

But those are minor gripes, and even the slightly duller helm is forgivable because in every other respect this 911 represents a step forward. And not just thanks to the welcome refinement boost that makes this the most usable iteration of the 911 yet. Few cars offer drivers such an invigorating or involving experience and those that do usually have six-figure prices or prove unusable every day.

Forty-one years on, the 911 remains the yardstick by which all other coupés are measured. If there's a better way to spend £65,000 on a sports car we've yet to find it. Still the coupé to beat.

### Still the coupé to beat

# OPEN TO QUESTION

**911 CARRERA S CABRIOLET** The new Porsche 911 Carrera S cabrio has just landed in the UK. But can it seduce Steve Cropley on the same roads where he drove his first 911?

It used to be fashionable, whenever anyone mentioned the Porsche 911, to talk at length about the odd place Professor Porsche had chosen to mount his flat-six engine. The idea of slinging your car's heaviest component outside its wheelbase at the rear, thereby concentrating two-thirds of its mass at the rear – the wrong end for stability – struck many as distinctly ill-advised. Even 911 experts talked of 'knife-edge' oversteer and 'tail-happy' handling.

Elsewhere, the rear-engine layout (vehemently condemned by US safety campaigner Ralph Nader) was the death of quite a few rear-engined cars: the Chevrolet Corvair, the Renault R8 and R10, the Simca 1100, the Skoda Estelle and, eventually, the huge-selling VW Beetle. The on-limit handling of rear-engined cars was unsafe, critics insisted. A rear-end breakaway could never be recovered. The reality was never so dramatic, but it all smacked of the heroic test pilot going into a flat spin for the last time.

This campaign nearly killed the 911, too. There was a point in the late '70s when company bosses at Zuffenhausen accepted that their rear-engined sports car (already diminished and uglified by crash and pollution legislation in the US) was going to have to die. So they quickly conceived the 928 and 924 as replacements, and began talking up a brave new Porsche world filled with front-engined sports cars.

Then came the revolution. Buyers insisted that they didn't want Porsches with front engines. Ford made cars like that. They demanded a continuance of the 911's unique balance of qualities – compactness, agility, timeless styling and that fantastic engine – and any fool could see these were directly attributable to its unique layout. They kept right on ordering 911s, and those orders saved the car. Porsche started refining away the car's famous drawbacks with renewed vigour, a process which continues to this day. A great car was saved by its own authenticity.

About a decade later, the same desires motivated me when I set out to buy a 911. I'd enjoyed owning a Ferrari for a few years, but had been unable to live with its impracticalities. My ideal was a machine with equal breeding and performance, but more durable and useful – in other words, a Porsche 911. With the help of a car-trader friend, I hawked myself in *The Sunday Times* as a cash buyer, and finished up with 10 cars to choose from. The best was a 1988, 18,000-mile, 3.2-litre Carrera coupé in gunmetal grey.

For two reasons, I'll never forget the day I took delivery. First, it was the first day of the 1991 Gulf War, and as I wrote the cheque I remember wondering what this would do to Porsche prices (answer: nothing significant). Second, to celebrate my ownership I set off on one of the great drives of my life, a long looping solo strop from home in Gloucestershire to the welcoming roads and fantastic scenery around Crickhowell on the edge of the Brecon Beacons. And 14 years on, it's where we *Autocaristes* still take cars when we want to enjoy them. There was certainly no better place to choose when, recently, a new Porsche 911 Carrera S cabrio came my way.

So much has changed about the 911 since I owned one. Everything, you could say, but the spirit. This became apparent for the first time as I drove out of London on the M4 and discovered that the motorway speed you can reliably get away with in a 911 – 87mph indicated, 84mph actual – still corresponds precisely to 3400rpm in this 3.8-litre, 350bhp car's top gear (sixth),

## QUICK FACTS

| | |
|---|---|
| **Model tested** | 911 Carrera S Cabriolet |
| **Price** | £72,830 |
| **Top speed** | 182mph |
| **0–60mph** | 4.6sec |
| **MPG combined** | 24.1mpg |
| **CO₂ emissions** | 283g/km |
| **Insurance group** | 20 |
| **Engine** | Flat-six, 3824cc |
| **Power** | 350bhp at 6600rpm |
| **Torque** | 295lb ft at 4600rpm |

# FIRST DRIVE

## 17 MAY 2005

Volume 244

No 7 | 5639

JAPAN'S JAG New Lexus GS meets (and beats) real thing

AUTOCAR

1000-MILE SHOOTOUT

3500 quality cars for sale INSIDE

NEW EVO

Sub £30k heroes... A to B just got quicker

For the 9th and final time

FASTEST-EVER ASTON
Full test of astonishing Vanquish S

AUDI'S BABY LIMO
Top-secret luxury city car revealed

just as it did in my old 3.2-litre, 231bhp five-speeder 14 years ago. In fact, looking at the new car's tacho needle, I could instantly recall my old F-plater's rev counter graduations, and see precisely the same angle on its needle. It was eerie, and wonderful. But then Porsche has always traded hugely on continuity. You can quibble about weights and dimensional changes and engine capacities and model nomenclature. Hell, there have been four root-and-branch revisions of the 911 since my old car was the thing to own. But the seminal stuff, the things that make the Porsche 911 unique, are exactly the same. These are the things that rise above the rest – the brilliant packaging and the almost unearthly precision of the controls.

On packaging, start with the driving position. The 997 cabrio places you perfectly in the car, backside an inch off the floor, equidistant from front and rear contact patches. You're in unfettered cabin space, supported everywhere between knees and shoulder blades by the most perfectly designed leather bucket seat ever to grace a sports car. Your seat is uncompromised either by an engine bulkhead pressing from behind (mid-engined supercar) or a huge, wide, centre console/engine cover (front-engined GT). The steering wheel, a bent-arm's

**BELOW** The 911 flows beautifully over these roads, where you can see for miles.

distance away, is set high and nearly vertical. Perfect. The pedals exactly meet the balls of your feet. And if you close your eyes and reach with your left hand to the spot that seems natural, it'll close over the gearlever.

You're closer to the fascia than in most supercars, which helps ergonomics. You're also not far from the windscreen, which is set more upright than most so you continue to see well in rain and don't get confused by instrument reflections at night. The 911's unique mechanical layout also allows the car a shortish wheelbase and a body no wider than a normal car's (rare in a supercar). This and good visibility mean the 911 feels agile and easy to commit on narrow roads and in town. Yet despite the compactness there's still enough cabin space for a pair of occasional seats, which owners will tell you are a boon, the difference between owning the car or not. Finally, your 911's smaller size (coupled with Porsche's stern efforts to cut engine mass) mean less overall bulk. Zuffenhausen's honest-to-a-fault technical specs reveal a 1550kg kerb weight for this car, 150-200kg less than rivals.

Now for the controls. Nobody ever wrote a poem about a clutch pedal, which is no surprise given that it's buried out of sight in a dusty footwell. But in this Porsche, it's a precision instrument. Even with the car static, you can sense from the subtly varying efforts along its stroke exactly where the take-up point is. On the move, it's strong and accurate, the kingpin in a system which delivers brilliant sequences of perfectly timed gearchanges, whether you're plying village streets or snapping between ratios at 7200rpm on one of those superb 10-mile sprints still possible in Wales, where you can see the next three apexes coming, one after another. The time needed to dip the clutch harmonises exactly with the fall or rise of revs between ratios, which in turn matches the speed of your hand, smoothly snicking the next ratio.

The best expression of this all-round excellence is the third to second downchange, a quick dog-leg movement which often has to be pulled off with accompanying subtle throttle control, when you're braking, or near obstacles, with some pretty accurate steering to be done at the same time. In the 911, you always seem to hit it perfectly. You can congratulate yourself on your expertise if you want, but it's really Porsche's achievement in honing its controls to be the most predictable and the most accurate in the business.

No surprise, of course, that the 3.8-litre mill is magnificent. For decades, this flat six and its ancestors

have been among the world's finest engines and this one has only grown in smoothness and response. But if you concentrate on performance figures alone (182mph, 0-60mph in 4.6sec) you'll miss this Porsche's point. There's nothing explosive about its acceleration; that implies a lack of ultimate control, whereas this is one of the most controllable ultra-fast cars you can buy. Even blipping the accelerator is an exercise in precision: after a bit of practice you'll be adding engine revs to smooth downchanges the way a fiddle player chooses notes for a violin solo.

Don't mention the tail-happy thing. It's no longer a relevant property in a road-going 911. Wet or dry, this car's huge tyres, wide tracks and several levels of slide-taming electronics keep nose and tail pretty much in line, no matter what. Powerslides are possible as a curiosity, but only with the hands of a more skilled and committed driver than me on the wheel, and with the Porsche Stability Management well and truly switched off. The steering set-up is as close to perfect as any: it's beautifully weighted, perfectly geared, accurate and lightly damped against tramlining or kickback.

The controversial bit, to my mind, is the car's frequent lack of ride composure, a result of its rear-heavy layout. Despite clever adaptive damping and several selectable ride levels (including one which practically eliminates suspension altogether) the 911 has a tendency to bob about uncomfortably at the nose on uneven surfaces, especially when a light fuel load stresses its imbalance. You feel the effect in conditions which simply don't bother mid-engined and front-engined cars, and it's no wonder, given that the 911 (like nearly every car on the road) is stiffer at the rear than the front. The mass behind the rear axle causes the rear wheels to act as a fulcrum and the nose to bob about over bumps on its relatively softer front suspension.

Even with the roof missing, it's lovely on reasonably smooth stuff, and the effect on rougher roads is not new; it has been implicit in the rear-engined Porsche for over 40 years. But I reckon it's now more intrusive (well, noticeable) than ever, simply because the car is so good in every other area. Does the buyer care? The enduring demand for the 911 says he does – in spades. Would I care, if I found the money? Not at all. But I'll be surprised if Porsche's exacting engineers can tolerate such a fundamental flaw for long. I'd like to know what's in their minds, even now, to refine it out of sight.

**ABOVE** Driving position is a work of art, and the seats offer incredibly precise support.

# RACING CERTAINTY

**911 CUP** Forget that this is a 911 racer: underneath the wings and spoilers lies the new GT3. And Chris Harris has driven it

Remove the stickers, fit a slightly less-obnoxious rear wing, find some carpet, slot in a wireless and the car you're looking at is nearly the new Porsche 911 GT3. Very nearly.

Looks pretty neat, doesn't it? Most people suspected that the latest-generation 911 would lend itself to the go-faster treatment a touch more successfully than the previous model did, and that is surely the case. And before you switch off because this is just another track test, remember that Porsche has always ensured that its Supercup and Carrera Cup race cars are closely based on the road versions, and it hasn't changed that philosophy with the new 911.

So how much can we read in to the specification of this car? Well, we know that the new GT3 will have the final iteration of the GT1-based 3.6-litre flat-six engine, and the fact that this racer is fitted with a version rated at 400bhp would indicate that the road car will have something close to that figure. The sequential gearbox won't make it onto the road car and beheaded pedestrians aren't a pretty sight, so the rear wing will be smaller. Otherwise, it's not far off.

It has to be said, though, that this 911 Cup car is a few steps closer to being a bespoke racing car than its predecessor was. The sequential 'box is a factor in this, but so is the special interior and Motec digital dash display. Even so, the Cup is still made from a regular 911 shell without any special seam-welding and the front bodywork looks suspiciously production-ready. Including the carbonfibre air intake just in front of the bonnet shut line. In fact, both this and the front splitter bear more than a passing resemblance to the front end of the old 996 GT2. Don't pay too much attention to the centre exit exhaust, though: these are race cans.

And they make a gorgeous noise as the car sits idling in the pit lane. Sitting inside, the tune is even better. There is no sound-deadening material and minimal exhaust baffling: pinch the aluminium organ pedal of a throttle and even wearing a helmet you

# FEATURE

## 23 AUGUST 2005

Volume 245

No 8 | 5653

**ABOVE** New 911 Cup racer much easier to drive quickly than old one – bodes well for road version.

don't just hear the noise, you feel it tracing through the shell and fizzing under your feet and backside.

With 400bhp and just 1140kg to lump about, this is a respectably fast racing car and feels very quick by road-car standards. The engine management has been mapped to give good torque in the mid-range and to keep going to the 8200rpm limiter. And even though peak power comes at 7300rpm, the final 900rpm still make quite a difference. It's a remarkable engine, and even though it feels and sounds very similar to the current version, that isn't a problem because it remains one of the finest motors ever made.

Making a connection between the way the Cup handles on the track and the way the road car might behave is a dangerous exercise because this car is set-up so differently to anything you'd ever drive on the road. But there are some valid conclusions to be drawn. First, the basic geometry of the suspension will be very similar, and that is a big improvement on the old GT3's. What you tended to find with the previous Cup car was that its handling characteristics were an exaggerated reflection of the road car's behaviour, and most of that centred around a rear axle that often felt unsettled.

The 997 is far better in this respect. It tracks

## DIAL 911 FOR FUN 36 YEARS OF LIGHTWEIGHT 911S

### 1969
**911R**

First ever lightweight 911

### 1971
**911 S/T**

2.5 litres, 190bhp

### 1973
**911 2.7RS**

The most celebrated

### 1974
**911 3.0RS**

270bhp, G-series look

### 1981
**911 SC RS**

Rally special 911

straight where the 996 wandered alarmingly – even if you concentrated on keeping it in line – and the rear suspension copes with all kinds of bumps and camber changes far more serenely. The steering is almost inert, though: slick tyres have a habit of doing that. This car also has electric power assistance which adds to the numbness and, if it makes the production version, could prove to be the biggest surprise on the specification sheet.

Whereas the 996 Cup car was one of the few one-make racers to keep anti-lock brakes, it has been ditched on this car. From a racing perspective, that's a good thing. Getting the best from the anti-lock on the 996 was a bit of a dark art, but the system still allowed the odd klutz to post faster lap times than they perhaps deserved.

The brakes themselves are 380mm steel discs up front with 350mm discs behind, and they have you hanging into the harness belts. The Supercup cars that run at European GP meetings – and are identical to this version in every other mechanical area – use a new evolution of the PCCB ceramic discs, but it has been decided that they are too expensive for the national championship cars, so this steel rotor has been developed instead.

Porsche's motorsport department has had some fun with the interior. The attention to detail is delightful, with a bank of toggle switches sitting where the centre console should be. It just feels so much more finished than most racing cars, to the extent that you rather curse the section at the end of the accompanying specification document that states: "The vehicle cannot be registered for public road use." It feels like all it needs is a set of number plates. And, in essence, you have to conclude that the road-going GT3 will be just that.

It's curious that Porsche has only seen fit to increase power by 10bhp over the 2004 996 GT3 Cup, and given that the road car had 375bhp, we wouldn't be surprised if the 997 GT3 doesn't have either a few more ponies than the racer or weigh slightly less than its predecessor. But if the suspension improvements from 996 Cup to this car are any indication, then the road car will be something very special indeed and well worth the wait. Having said that, if patience isn't listed among your core assets, you could give Porsche GB a ring and give them a cheque for £108,452 – race entries are included in the price – and spend a season racing one in 2006.

**BELOW** The sonorous flat-six out back makes 400bhp and revs to 8200rpm; lovely toggle switches, but the electric power steering feels numb.

## 1991
**911 (964) RS**

First modern RS

## 1995
**911 (993) RS**

Still one of the best

## 1996
**911 (993) RS**

430bhp turbo

## 2000
**911 (996) GT3**

Not light, but 360bhp

## 2002
**911 (996) GT2**

The 'widow-maker'

## 2004
**911 (996) GT3 RS**

Trick, lightweight GT3

# BLOW OUT

The iconic 996-series Porsche 911 Turbo bows out this year, to be replaced a new 997 Turbo. Chris Harris takes a final drive in the greatest of them all, the 444bhp S

We were told to collect the car from Zuffenhausen at about midday. The hand-over process for press cars at the Porsche factory isn't always the well-oiled perfection you'd expect, but this time there was no mistaking which car slightly younger versions of myself and Steve Sutcliffe would be leaving with. The booking sheet said 911 Turbo, and only one was visible among the Boxsters, 911 convertibles and motley collection of old-timers waiting for restoration. It was brilliant white and to this day is the best-looking 996-series 911 I have ever seen.

We drove that car for four days around southern Germany. Drove it to meet a Ferrari 360 Modena for a twin test, which it duly won. Drove it as fast as the law would allow, which meant mostly travelling at two miles a minute, but very often somewhere beyond three. We agreed to drive it until we became less bewildered by what this staggering car was capable of over any section of the German road network. But the order to return it came long before we came close to achieving that goal. This was our first taste of the new Turbo, and on the plane home I remember concluding that this would surely represent the pinnacle of sports car achievement before legislation made any sort of fun illegal.

I haven't driven a new (997-series) 911 Turbo yet and until I do, six years after driving that white 996, there is currently no reason to alter the decision that was reached on that plane. Over its lifespan, the 996 Turbo was joined by countless other rivals. All had more exotic badges, most boasted extra power and far greater exclusivity, but none has matched what the 911 Turbo offers to a particular type of customer. And that is the person who intends to use their car on a regular basis and, crucially, values the way it goes down a road above the effect it has on pedestrians in central London.

'All-round supercar' is a phrase liberally applied to most exotics these days, purely on the basis that they seem less prone to mechanical failure. But from the moment it was launched in 2000, to the day the last one rolled off the production line in the summer of 2005, the 996 Turbo was the only car that could support the title.

## TURBO WITH THAT LITTLE EXTRA

As is customary at the end of a Turbo's life-span, in 2005 Porsche added a letter S below the retractable spoiler of the 911. This was a run-out special with the X50 Powerkit fitted as standard, PCCB ceramic brakes and some choice hunks of carbonfibre in the cabin. I had one for a week last year. It went to Tesco twice (dog food, groceries, charcoal briquettes), the Nürburgring once (23 laps, 168mph on the approach to Schwedenkreuz, climate control set to 19C), carried the driver plus one or two passengers and left all those who benefited from experiencing it with the same feeling I'd felt all those years ago – that it was a superior being.

But, of course, the 911 Turbo wasn't unbeatable in these pages. In March 2004 the Lamborghini Gallardo and Aston Martin DB9 were launched and we ended up with all three together on some of Europe's best roads. Someone called Chris Harris wrote that test and gave both newcomers the nod over the Porsche. Driving the S made me question that verdict, but having re-read the story I stand by everything I wrote.

The 911 Turbo isn't a car of universal appeal. Those who love it and can't conceive of driving anything whose performance isn't as accessible as their Turbo's will never understand this, and the older I get the more I find myself in their camp. But I would like one aspect of that test to be known. I have never driven

'POWER SWELLS THROUGH THE MID-RANGE AND MANAGES A CRESCENDO JUST BEFORE THE 6750RPM LIMITER'

# FEATURE

## 14 FEBRUARY 2006

Volume 247

No 7 | 5677

**ABOVE** Secret of 911 Turbo's appeal is its usability: it's so easy to drive very fast, yet equally happy cruising or around town; 'Powerkit' means 444bhp and 457lb ft, even if rear-mounted six doesn't look that special; S gets carbonfibre trim, otherwise it's a black cabin with a fabulous driving position.

a DB9 that felt as supple or capable as that original launch car, but every one of the dozen different Turbos I have driven were consistent in the way they accelerated, steered and handled. And the Gallardo? As I wrote that piece I was a Gallardo owner, and despite its obvious brilliance in so many areas, there's just no way something so impractical could substitute a 911 Turbo as an everyday car. But the fact remains that as static object and juke-box, both had the Porsche well beaten. They also ran it close enough on the road for me to feel less overawed by the Porsche's cross-country powers than I had before. I have no doubt that had that group test been a shrunken version of the gruelling week I spent in the 911 Turbo S, the Porsche would have won.

## DRIVABILITY, NOT POWER

At the core of the 911 Turbo was the knowledge that it was so much more than a standard Carrera run through the tuning shop. Porsche engineers are unfailingly consistent in their response to the what's-your-favourite interrogation. But when I'd gone to collect a 911 GT3 in the summer of 1999, I'd asked one of them what he thought about that car. He brushed over it in unemotional language before excitedly saying that the forthcoming 911 Turbo would blow our minds.

When the first press releases seeped out, the numbers actually did quite the opposite. From what was effectively a twin-turbo, low-compression version of the GT3's 3.6-litre flat six, the figures were 414bhp and 413lb ft. Okay, this was just before the German saloon power orgy was born, a time when anything beginning with a four made you pay attention, but even so there were those who remembered driving the run-out 993-series Turbo S from 1997 and could quote its 430bhp output from experience.

So 414bhp didn't sound like much of an improvement. That was until you drove the car. Of course it was foolish to assume that Porsche would

'THIS IS STILL THE FASTEST CAR YOU CAN BUY. NOT IN A STRAIGHT LINE, BUT FOR DOING WHAT MOST OF US DO WITH OUR CARS'

not have moved the game on significantly, and it had done just that through drivability rather than crowing about numbers. There were many innovations that made the 996 Turbo's engine superior: thanks to those large front radiator apertures, air could flow through at more than 100 cubic feet per second at the Turbo's 190mph top speed. It also used the revolutionary Variocam Plus variable valve timing technology to improve flexibility, but most of all it had an unbelievably high compression ratio for a turbo Porsche. Whereas the 993 could handle just 8.0:1, on the 996 it was raised to 9.4:1.

This meant, and still means, that the 996 Turbo has the best-judged turbocharger installation ever developed for people who love driving. Higher compression gives better throttle response: this is an engine that just doesn't feel like it's turbocharged. It pulls from idle, power swells through the mid-range and manages a crescendo just before the 6750rpm limiter. And, of course, the S benefits from what is known colloquially as the Powerkit. This brings 444bhp and 457lb ft – very useful gains over the standard outputs.

## LOTUS-LIKE

Driving the Turbo S now in the knowledge that the replacement Turbo has 473bhp as standard – with talk of over 500bhp for the replacement S version – is quite odd. Day-in, day-out, this is still the fastest car money can buy in the UK. Not in a straight line or above 175mph, but for doing what most of us do with our cars.

If the engine ticks the boxes, then the chassis and steering are arguably even more impressive. This is one of those cars you're certain must have benefited from some development time in the UK to cope with our road network. But it never did. It is one of the only Porsches to feel genuinely Lotus-like. It feels softly sprung, but firmly damped and it has impressive wheel travel. This means it does its fair amount of pitching, yawing and general rolling about, allowing it to better telegraph its behaviour and the nature of the road to the driver. People often wonder why the Turbo is so much easier to drive fast on the road than a GT3, and this is partly why. Four-wheel drive and hefty mid-range grunt naturally play a part, too.

I've always found the GT3 versus Turbo debate highly entertaining, not least because to outsiders it's like arguing over the facial beauty of Christie Turlington and Cindy Crawford, and then labelling the loser a moose. One is ostensibly a track car, the other a road car. But use them in their non-specialist fields – the Turbo on a track and the GT3 on the road – and the Turbo's phenomenal skill base shines through. I will always agree that someone who knows what they're doing and is a committed track-day enthusiast is far better off in a GT3. But the way the Turbo sauntered over to the Nürburgring, was only overtaken once during an entire weekend (by a Noble M400 on shaved rubber) and then mooched home with the Queens of the Stone Age shaking the cabin thanks to the optional Bose hi-fi was, to put it mildly, spooky. It's even a good car on tighter UK tracks. I once duped Porsche into letting me borrow 911 HUL (always the reg number of the current press Turbo in the UK) and took it to an *Autocar* evening track event. It changed a few people's opinion of the relationship between four-wheel drive and oversteer.

Perhaps it's fitting that the last photo shoot *Autocar* will ever commission on the 996 Turbo was taken not at the 'Ring, or semi-airborne over a crest in deserted mid-Wales, but in town at night. A car for all occasions and all seasons. A car all of us at *Autocar* will miss. Auf wiedersehen; thanks for the torque, the traction and the memories.

**BELOW** Want supercar pace mixed with everyday civility? This is the car that delivers it best.

# THE BLOWDOWN

`911 TURBO` Meet the new 911 Turbo: all 473bhp and 451lb ft of it. And, as our exclusive back-to-front guide reveals, a new type of turbo is only half of the story. *By Keith Howard*

For 32 years the Porsche 911 Turbo has battled it out with Ferraris and Lamborghinis, often leaving us blown away with the depth and breadth of its talents. This summer, it gets even better: the sixth generation of Turbo goes on sale in the UK on 24 June, sharing little but its general layout with the first 911 Turbo of 1974. Across those three decades, power output alone has leapt 85 per cent.

But the new 473bhp Turbo delivers more than stunning performance. For its new-found handling stability and all-weather speed and security, it owes a debt of gratitude to the Cayenne. Porsche's winter testing in Scandinavia had shown that, on the slipperiest surfaces, the big 4x4 outshone Porsche's sports cars, even four-wheel-drive models such as the outgoing Turbo. This made it inevitable that some of the Cayenne's 4wd technology would be transferred to the new Turbo.

As well as putting its power down more effectively, the new blown 911 has significantly more to put down. It also has a much wider torque band, due to the fitment – for the first time in a petrol-engined car – of a variable-geometry turbocharger. This combines the low-rev boost and quick response of a small turbo with the high-rev power of a larger blower.

Combined with the advanced 4wd transmission, this increased engine output makes the new Turbo significantly more accelerative than the old model. From a standing start it reaches 62mph in under 4.0sec (compared to 4.2sec) whether fitted with the manual or Tiptronic auto gearbox, and it can achieve this almost regardless of road conditions.

## DESIGN AND ENGINEERING

To deploy this level of performance safely, the new Turbo is fitted with three electronic control systems which interact to enhance traction and handling. These are Porsche Traction Management (PTM), which controls torque split between the front and rear wheels; Porsche Active Suspension Management (PASM), which adjusts the continuously variable Bilstein dampers according to inputs from various sensors around the car; and Porsche Stability Management (PSM), a stability control system that intervenes to control under- or oversteer in extremis. PASM offers the choice of normal or Sport modes so the driver can elect to favour ride comfort over handling or vice-versa.

Porsche's legendary brakes have, of course, been upgraded to match the improved performance. Diameters of the standard cast-iron discs have increased to 350mm front and rear, and the front calipers now have six pistons and larger front brake pads with 42 per cent greater friction area. PCCB ceramic composite discs are an option, in which case front disc diameter increases to 380mm and the overall weight of the car is lowered by 17kg.

Given the target of not increasing weight over the outgoing Turbo, Porsche's engineers actually went a little better. Kerb weight has been reduced by 5kg through the use of lightweight materials at key points on the car. One example is the doors, which now have a diecast aluminium frame and aluminium skin. As well as saving 7.2kg (41 per cent) per door, this construction also reduces the number of major assembly components from 15 to five.

Porsche's aerodynamicists are proud of the fact that, despite the extra cooling demands of the new engine and the addition of cooling ducts for the rear brakes, the outgoing car's 0.31 drag coefficient has been retained. Meanwhile Porsche's internal measure of aerodynamic quality – the ratio of rear axle lift to

'THE NEW PORSCHE TRACTION MANAGEMENT APPEARS TO DELIVER ALMOST FOOLPROOF ON-LIMIT HANDLING'

# FEATURE

22 MARCH 2006

Volume 248

No 12 | 5682

The original car magazine

AUTOCAR

PORSCHE'S NEW HEROES

THEIR SECRETS UNCOVERED

They're making a Freelander! And we're out joking yet p33

Full road guide: 200mph Turbo. Meet just another mega-coupé

PLUS New 928 ■ 'Green' Cayenne ■ New 4dr ■ Cayman RS and more...

INSIDE THIS WEEK

FIRST DRIVE

New Golf CC v Astra TwinTop→

New RAV4 tested

Tuscan 2! Sutcliffe slides TVR's latest →

Malaysian GP

ALL-NEW PEUGEOT 207 At last: baby Pugs are fun again

turbo

S · GO 13

D

drag coefficient – has been improved by achieving greater rear downforce. Because the rear-mounted flat-six engine prevents the use of a rear underbody diffuser, this is achieved by fitting a much larger flat undertray and by refinements to the engine cover-mounted wing, which deploys at 75mph and retracts at 37mph.

As a result, rear axle lift coefficient has been reduced to -0.03, equivalent to a modest 17kg of downforce at 150mph. Front axle lift coefficient is just positive (0.01), so the car generates a small amount of front lift (equivalent to 6kg) at the same speed. There is a mild increase in understeer as the car travels faster.

A new design of 19-inch forged aluminium wheel is fitted, with standard rubber from Bridgestone or Michelin. Specially developed Michelin sports tyres are also available, which have reduced tread depth (5mm) and increased tread area, particularly on the outer shoulders. Cornering and braking grip are enhanced on dry surfaces, the trade-off being reduced aquaplaning resistance in standing water.

Around Germany's Nürburgring track in the dry, the car's lap time is 7min 49sec on standard tyres (8min flat for the outgoing model) and 7min 42sec on the sports tyres.

### ENGINE
Despite capacity remaining the same at 3.6 litres, the new turbocharged flat six achieves significantly higher outputs than its predecessor. Peak power is up by 14 per cent from to 414 to 473bhp, while maximum torque increases by almost 11 per cent from 413 to 457lb ft. Just as important, the rev range over which this maximum torque is available has widened. In the outgoing engine peak torque was developed between 2600 and 4800rpm; in the new engine it can be had from 1950 to 5000rpm. At 2000rpm the new engine has a massive 89lb ft (24 per cent) more torque on tap, which gives it an effortless flexibility more typical of diesel engines than a blown petrol unit developing over 130bhp per litre. Maximum engine speed is a modest 6750rpm.

**BELOW** Sixth-generation Turbo's 3.6 flat six can produce 502lb ft with optional overboost; manual hits 62mph in 3.9sec; auto takes 3.7sec.

**ABOVE** Rear spoiler raises at 75mph; new 19in wheels cover huge 350mm discs.

Even more torque is available – albeit for short periods and over a narrower rev range – if the optional Sports Chrono overboost is specified. Peak torque leaps a further 10 per cent to 502lb ft from 2100 to 4000rpm, and can be exploited for a maximum of 10 seconds.

Porsche quotes a 192mph top speed, 2mph faster than before, but that figure is probably conservative. Calculated from the power increase, it should be nearer to 198mph.

Key to this has been the fitment of a new BorgWarner variable-geometry turbocharger for each bank of three cylinders. A total of 11 tilting vanes surround the exhaust turbine and control both the direction and flow rate of the exhaust gas. At high engine speed/load the vanes are turned inwards to maximise flow to the turbine; at low engine speed/load they turn outwards to constrict and so speed up the flow, like pinching the end of a garden hose. The vanes are operated by an electric stepper motor under command from the engine management system, and can be opened or closed in 100 milliseconds (0.1sec).

Turbochargers of this type have been used on diesels for years, but this is the first application on a petrol engine because of problems posed by higher exhaust gas temperatures. Whereas turbodiesels operate at a maximum temperature of around 800C, in this application the turbo has to cope with as much as 1000C, at which temperature its housing glows white hot.

The variable-geometry blower also aids fuel consumption, which is quoted as 22.1mpg overall for the manual transmission and 20.8mpg for the Tiptronic S auto – figures which are significantly superior to the competition, says Porsche, particularly in relation to the Turbo's acceleration performance.

Quoted sprint times from rest to 62mph are 3.9sec for the manual and 3.7sec for the Tiptronic – the first time that an auto Porsche has been faster. The advantage continues at higher speeds, with 50-75mph dispatched in 3.5sec with the Tiptronic 'box as opposed to 3.8sec with the manual.

### TRANSMISSION

At the heart of the Porsche Traction Management system is a compact, fast-acting multi-plate clutch that, under electronic control, varies the amount of torque directed to the front axle. Unlike a viscous coupling, PTM can distribute torque regardless of relative wheel slip front and rear, and does so in response to sensors that measure road speed, steering angle, lateral acceleration, throttle position and other factors.

**ABOVE** Lashings of leather plus top-end stereo and sat-nav standard.

Because of this, PTM doesn't just enhance traction – it is also used to adjust the car's handling balance. If the control system senses that the car is understeering, torque to the front axle is reduced to allow the tyres to generate more cornering force. Likewise, if the car is oversteering, less torque is directed rearwards.

From the passenger seat, PTM appears to deliver almost foolproof on-limit handling. Demonstrating the system at Porsche's R&D centre in Weissach, Germany, the test driver deliberately induced oversteer during maximum-effort cornering on a hairpin, and with the stability control system turned off, the car recovered without his intervention. A limited-slip rear differential is an option, while new Fast-Off and Fast-Back functions prevent the auto 'box upshifting prematurely when the driver lifts off on winding roads and allow quicker downshifts under braking. Porsche won't offer an automated manual transmission because it says they are not refined enough. But the company invented the dual-clutch transmission and sees this as the superior option once it can be developed to handle sufficiently high levels of torque.

## CABIN

Subject of an extensive redesign, the new Turbo's interior also provides a high standard of passive safety with the fitment of six airbags. There are airbags for the driver and front passenger, two window sill-mounted airbags to protect occupants' heads in a side impact and two thorax 'bags in the front seat backrests.

Leather upholstery and trim are standard, as are DVD-based sat-nav, Porsche's Communication Management system, a seven-channel surround sound system, auto-dipping rear-view mirror and an enhanced anti-theft system.

## SELLING IT

The new 911 Turbo goes on sale in the UK on 24 June for £97,840. No price has yet been announced for the optional Sports Chrono package, but it will probably cost only another £500.

Porsche plans to manufacture around 4000 Turbos a year, probably a little more than that during the first 12 months of production. The number of cars allocated to the UK has not been revealed, but will comprise about 10 per cent of total production – or 400 very lucky people each year.

# X-RAY SPECS

### AIRFLOW

Triple front radiators provide the increased cooling demanded by the hike in engine power. At 186mph, airflow through the three cores totals 4000 litres per second. Outlet air from the central radiator is ducted out through the undertray; the two side radiators exhaust into the front wheel wells.

### FOUR-WHEEL DRIVE

New four-wheel-drive transmission now incorporates PTM (Porsche Traction Management), a clutch-based system which apportions torque between the front and rear axles, regardless of wheel slip. As well as aiding traction, PTM enhances handling by redirecting torque to quell under- or oversteer.

### GEARBOX

Still no dual-clutch gearbox from Porsche: the new Turbo can be had with either a six-speed manual or Tiptronic S auto. For the first time the auto 'box offers quicker acceleration to the stick shift, trimming 0.2sec off the 0-62mph time and 0.3sec from 50-75mph. It is less fuel efficient, however.

### COOLING

Cooling air for the turbos' intercoolers is ducted from inlets in the widened rear wheel arches, immediately aft of the doors. There is also a new ventilation system for the rear brake discs, which draws cooling air from beneath the car via ducts in the undertray.

### LIGHTWEIGHT TECH

Use of lightweight materials throughout the car has reversed the weight spiral – the new Turbo actually weighs 5kg less than the old car. The doors are now skinned in aluminium, like the bonnet, and have a diecast aluminium frame that reduces the number of components and saves weight.

### TURBO ENGINE

Revised twin-turbo flat six develops 14 per cent more power and 11 per cent more torque over a wider rev range, despite no increase in engine capacity. New variable-geometry turbochargers combine the low-end response of a small turbo with the high-end power of a larger unit.

# BALLISTIC, BRILLIANT

**911 GT3** The new Porsche 911 GT3 combines huge power with enormous ability in one sensational package

This is frustrating. First drive of the new 911 GT3 and it's pouring down. The autostrada between Verona and Venice is a river; standing water licks up the wheel arches as we surge alongside a rusty barrier. Hardly the weather for a car with 409bhp, no stability control and what amount to cut racing slicks.

But who's complaining? This latest 911 is sensational. Demonically fast. Viciously raw. Incredibly involving. Bellowingly loud. And, boy, does it grab attention. It's not just the yellow paint or towering rear wing that has our fellow motorists in a spin – the whole car generates anticipation.

The GT3 started life as a limited-edition special in 1999, but it has become part of Porsche's line-up. Like its predecessor, this second-generation model is aimed at track-day enthusiasts, and it's offered with an optional Clubsport package including a roll cage, lightweight carbonfibre-backed seats, six-point harnesses, fire resistant trim and an extinguisher.

Engineered by Porsche Motorsport – the outfit responsible for the Carrera GT – it is a vastly different beast to your average 911. The styling changes – developed for racing homologation – are all about aerodynamics or cooling: there's a deeper front bumper incorporating a splitter and an air vent ahead of the bonnet to draw heat away from

the trio of front mounted radiators. At the rear, the extended bumper includes horizontal air ducts to expunge air from catalysts in the wheel arches. There's also a new centrally mounted exhaust that's claimed to reduce turbulence, and 235/35 ZR19 (front) and 305/30 ZR19 (rear) tyres on 19-inch alloys.

The 3.6 flat six is a development of the 1998 Le Mans-winning GT1's powerplant. The four-valve-per-cylinder engine has been completely overhauled; the crankcase is the only carry-over from the old GT3. Highlights include titanium conrods, forged aluminium pistons, variable valve timing, a variable length manifold and dry sump lubrication.

The engine produces 409bhp at 7600rpm – 34bhp more than the last GT3 and a whopping 113.6bhp per litre (a standard Carrera packs a lowlier 90.4bhp per litre). At 1395kg, it weighs exactly the same as a standard 911 and 18kg more than the old model. This is down to the decision to base the GT3 around the Carrera 4's structure, which includes added stiffening in the front. The torsional rigidity of the bodyshell is claimed to be eight per cent better, while the heavily upgraded suspension is lowered by 30mm over the standard 911 Carrera and now comes with Porsche Active Suspension Management (PASM), which automatically varies the damping. Other changes include firmer springs, larger diameter roll bars (adjustable for track use) and tougher bushes.

From the moment you turn the key and hear the engine momentarily strain before firing in earnest, you are keenly aware just how much of a difference the lightweight engine components make. High-lift camshafts provide for a rather lumpy idle, but revs are the vital ingredient here. The GT3 gains and loses them with the friction-free abandon of a proper racing car. Keep your right foot buried and it gets pretty frenetic – at least on public roads. Acceleration in the first four gears is savage. It is only when you slide the gearlever up and across to the right to engage fifth that the intensity really

## QUICK FACTS

| | |
|---|---|
| **Model** | 911 GT3 |
| **Price** | £75,000 (est) |
| **0–62mph** | 4.3sec |
| **Top speed** | 193mph |
| **Power** | 409bhp at 7600rpm |
| **Torque** | 298lb ft at 5500rpm |
| **Power to weight** | 293bhp per tonne |
| **Torque to weight** | 214bhp per tonne |
| **MPG combined** | 21.7mpg |
| **Emissions ($CO_2$)** | 312g/km |

# FIRST DRIVE

## 29 MARCH 2006

Volume 248

No 13 | 5683

**ABOVE** On a dry track GT3 is simply awesome, with all the grip and speed you could ask for; 0–62mph in 4.3sec, 0–100mph 8.7sec

## GO WITH THE FLOW

The adjustable rear wing towers over two Gurney flaps incorporated into the top of the engine cover. Together, they generate 25kg of downforce at 186mph according to project manager Andreas Preuninger. With an almost flat underbody smoothing airflow, the drag co-efficient remains the same as the standard 911 Carrera's at 0.29 – a remarkable figure given all the ducting and cooling addenda the new GT3 carries.

begins to wane, by which time you're well on the high side of 150mph.

The challenge is in extracting the performance. Getting the best out of the GT3 requires a fiercely single-minded approach – if you're not nailing it up to the 8200rpm limiter, you're nowhere near its limits. Yet for all that the GT3 is surprisingly tractable: although peak torque doesn't arrive until 5500rpm, it will pull from 1500rpm in sixth gear without any unruly driveline antics.

The gearbox is a superbly precise six-speed manual. Porsche has also fitted the GT3 with traction control for the first time, alongside a diff lock with a 28 per cent ratio under power and 40 per cent on the overrun.

With a claimed 0-62mph time of 4.3sec, the new GT3 eclipses its predecessor by 0.2sec. The really telling figure, however, is the 0-100mph time: it drops by 0.7sec to just 8.7sec. Top speed is only up a fraction, from 191mph to 193mph. With lift – the bane of the earlier GT3 – now greatly reduced, stability has improved markedly at high speed.

There's a rabid enthusiasm to turn-in, although

# SPECIFICATIONS 911 GT3

## DIMENSIONS

| | |
|---|---|
| Length | 4427mm |
| Width | 1808mm |
| Height | 1280mm |
| Wheelbase | 2355mm |
| Weight | 1395kg |
| Boot | 135 litres |
| Fuel tank | 90 litres |

## ENGINE

| | |
|---|---|
| Layout | 6 cyls horizontally opposed, 3600cc |
| Max power | 409bhp at 7600rpm |
| Max torque | 298bhp at 5500rpm |
| Specific output | 113.6bhp per litre |
| Installation | Rear, longitudinal, rwd |
| Bore/stroke | 100mm/76.4mm |
| Compression ratio | 12.0:1 |

## STEERING

**Type** Variable rate, power assisted rack and pinion
**Turns lock-to-lock** 2.5

## GEARBOX

**Type** 6-speed manual
**Ratios/mph per 1000rpm**
**Final drive ratio** 3.44:1

| | | | |
|---|---|---|---|
| 1st 3.82/5.9 | | 2nd 2.26/10.0 | |
| 3rd 1.64/13.8 | | 4th 1.29/17.6 | |
| 5th 10.6/21.4 | | 6th 0.92/24.6 | |

## SUSPENSION

**Front** MacPherson struts, coil springs, anti-roll bar
**Rear** Multi-links, coil springs, anti-roll bar

## BRAKES

**Front and rear** 350mm, ventilated, drilled

## WHEELS AND TYRES

**Wheels** 8.5Jx19 (f), 12Jx19 (r)
**Tyres** 235/35 ZR19 (f)
305/30 ZR19 (r)

---

Porsche says there have been no significant changes to the steering. The firm suspension, coupled with a larger footprint, heightens feel and feedback from the rack-and-pinion system; the weight and precision is wonderful, and with the variable-rate ratio you use less lock than in the old car.

Dry grip limits are massively high – too high to safely explore on public roads. Unfortunately, rain limited our track time and on standard Michelin Pilot Sport Cup tyres, we aquaplaned around with little reference to real-world handling. Traction is superb, however: with 62 per cent of its weight at the back, even in blinding downpours the traction control light wasn't blinking.

On smooth roads, its inherent tautness gives the GT3 incredible immediacy and whip-crack responses. On rough bitumen, however, you're fighting to point it in the intended direction. Thumb the PASM switch into Sport mode and it deteriorates further; you drive around surface imperfections rather than crashing and banging over them, and there's plenty of tramlining under braking.

No concerns about the brakes themselves, though.

The ventilated and cross-drilled discs are 350mm in diameter and gripped by six- and four-pot calipers front and rear. Ceramic units are an option.

Inside, it's sumptuous, with lots of Alcantara and shiny aluminium-look highlights. Electric windows, central locking, airbags and remote boot release all remain, but the seats hug your body tight and are mounted lower than the standard items; the rear seats have been ditched to save weight. The options list is plentiful, including the Porsche Communication Management system that combines CD, sat-nav and telephone functions.

But no amount of optional equipment can make the GT3 seem anything other than raw. The new car might only be marginally quicker, but its all-round ability has taken a huge step forward. Now, if only Porsche would consider placing this engine and associated chassis tweaks in a lighter Cayman, we'd see some real cut-price fireworks.

**FIRST VERDICT ★★★★★**
**The purest, most desirable 911 available. Not for the fainthearted.**

**ABOVE LEFT** Optional carbonfibre-backed race buckets are same as those in the Carrera GT. They are massively supportive. Three-point belts are standard, harnesses optional; vent in front of bonnet draws air away from three radiators.

# PORSCHE 911 TURBO

With the all-new 997 Turbo, Porsche has tried to marry thundering power and performance, genuine everyday practicality and huge sophistication. But is it the best 911 Turbo yet?

You can almost plot the evolution of mankind over the last 30 years by looking at the Porsche 911 Turbo. In the beginning (1974, to be exact) the fastest 911 was ragged, rugged, very fast and not especially responsible. And throughout the '80s it was more of the same, only wilder.

Then in the late 1990s Porsche realised that there should be more to the 911 Turbo than pure excess. As the world was getting richer and more sophisticated, so did the Turbo, reaching its zenith in Y2K. By replacing the fast but still furious 993 Turbo with the altogether more rounded and, yes, faster-still 996 Turbo, Porsche produced what was arguably its best road car up to that point – and not surprisingly it sold in way bigger numbers than any previous Turbo had.

Which brings us to this car, the all-new 997 Turbo. The message is nothing if not clear. This time Porsche has tried to marry all the elements that have contributed to the 911 Turbo's enduring success under one roof: thundering power and performance, genuine everyday practicality and huge technical sophistication. It's the fastest, most advanced, most civilised and, in Porsche's view, best Turbo yet. It's also the most expensive at £97,840.

## QUICK FACTS

| | |
|---|---|
| **Model** | 911 Turbo, manual |
| **Price** | £97,840 |
| **Top speed** | 193mph |
| **0–60mph** | 3.6sec |
| **30–70mph** | 5.4sec |
| **MPG** | 17.2mpg |
| **Emissions** | 307g/km $CO_2$ |
| **70–0mph** | 44.4m |
| **Skidpan** | 1.02g |
| **For** | Huge performance/braking ability, grip, usability, comfort |
| **Against** | Steering lacks feel for a 911, tyre noise, poor range |

MASSIVE DOUBLE ISSUE
AUTOCAR
MOTOR
SHOW
FULL STAND-BY-STAND GUIDE

12 WORLD FIRSTS
A must read
whether you're
going or not

The great British motor show is back

NEW 911 TURBO
Just how fast is it?
Full road test inside

CLIO 197 v FOCUS ST
v ASTRA VXR
Giant killing, anyone?

# ROAD TEST

## 19 JULY 2006

Volume 249

No 3 | 5699

# ROAD TEST PORSCHE 911 TURBO

**ACCELERATION** Standing qtr mile 11.3sec/120.0mph **Standing km** 21.5sec/154.2mph **30–70mph** 3.6sec

| 30mph | 40 | 50 | 60 | 70 | 80 | 90 | 100 | 110 | 120 | 130 | 140 | 150 | 160 |
|---|---|---|---|---|---|---|---|---|---|---|---|---|---|
| 1.3s | 2.2s | 2.9s | 3.6s | 4.9s | 5.9s | 6.9s | 8.0s | 9.6s | 11.4s | 14.1s | 16.8s | 19.6s | 25.5s |

0 — 5s — 10s — 15s — 20s — 25s

## DRY/WET BRAKING

| 30mph-0 | 30mph-0 | Dry 50mph-0 | Wet 50mph-0 | 70mph-0 | 70mph-0 |
|---|---|---|---|---|---|
| 8.4m | 9.7m | 23.0m | 27.3m | 44.4m | 64.2m |

0 — 10s — 20s — 30s — 40s — 50s — 60s

## ACCELERATION IN GEAR

| MPH | 2nd | 3rd | 4th | 5th | 6th |
|---|---|---|---|---|---|
| 20–40 | 2.0 | 3.3 | 4.5 | 6.3 | |
| 30–50 | 1.5 | 2.6 | 3.4 | 4.8 | 7.2 |
| 40–60 | 1.4 | 2.1 | 2.6 | 3.6 | 5.7 |
| 50–70 | 1.7 | 1.8 | 2.2 | 3.0 | 4.5 |
| 60–80 | | 1.8 | 2.2 | 2.9 | 4.0 |
| 70–90 | | 2.0 | 2.4 | 2.9 | 4.0 |
| 80–100 | | 2.3 | 2.7 | 3.1 | 4.2 |
| 90–110 | | | 2.9 | 3.3 | 4.5 |
| 100–120 | | | 3.2 | 3.5 | 4.8 |
| 110–130 | | | | 4.0 | 5.0 |
| 120–140 | | | | 4.5 | 5.4 |
| 130–150 | | | | 5.0 | 6.1 |

## MAX SPEED IN GEAR

| 42mph | 108mph | 164mph |
|---|---|---|
| 6800rpm | 6800rpm | 6800rpm |

(1) (3) (5)

(2) (4) (6)

| 74mph | 125mph | 198mph |
|---|---|---|
| 6800rpm | 6800rpm | 6700rpm |

## ECONOMY

| | TEST | | CLAIMED |
|---|---|---|---|
| Average | 17.2mpg | Urban | 15.0mpg |
| Touring | 26.2mpg | Ex-urb | 29.7mpg |
| Track | 7.6mpg | Comb | 22.1mpg |
| Tank size | 67 litres | Test range | 254 miles |

## CABIN NOISE

Idle 53dbA **Max revs in 3rd** 83dbA **30mph** 68dbA
**50mph** 69dbA **70mph** 72dbA

## HEADLIGHTS

**Dipped beam** Good **Full beam** Excellent

**Test notes** With a car this fast, you need very powerful lights to sustain the pace at night. The Turbo has exactly that.

## WIPERS

Fine – as per usual 911.

## TESTER'S NOTES

So far nothing has pounded the *Autocar* dry circuit into submission like the 997 Turbo. The acceleration out of corners leaves you gasping and braking power is extraordinary yet amazingly resilient. The peak speed on the long curve after T3 starts to feel, frankly, rather uncomfortable, given the surroundings. Why such a slow wet time? The Turbo's wide, ultra-low-profile tyres don't suit the narrow, heavily wetted track. There's still fabulous power out of bends, and a delicate chassis balance that allows either clean lines or wild oversteer, but it's a struggle to brake hard without a 'moment' for T1. The Turbo weaves through puddles, wriggles under braking and you end up turning in gingerly for T1.

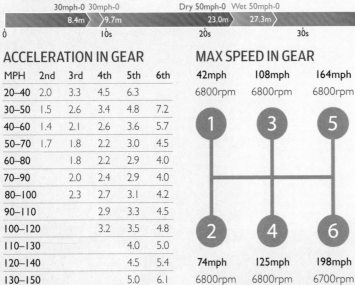

**DRY CIRCUIT**

Start
Peak Speed 114.3mph
Peak G 1.02g
Min Speed 23.9mph
T7 T1 T6 T2 T4 T5 T3

### 911 TURBO v BENCHMARKS

| Porsche 911 Turbo | Lap time 1:14.45 dry, cloudy, 23C |
|---|---|
| Porsche 911 Carrera S | Lap time 1:16.80 dry, cloudy, 9C |
| Aston Martin V8 Vantage | Lap time 1:18.00 dry, cloudy, 9C |

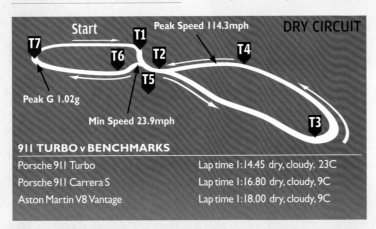

**WET CIRCUIT**

T2 T3 T1 T4 T5
Entry Speed 65.9mph
Apex Speed 46.4mph
Min Speed 29.85mph
Peak Speed 86.6mph
Start
T6 T8 T7

### 911 TURBO v BENCHMARKS

| Porsche 911 Turbo | Lap time 1:11.54 |
|---|---|
| Porsche 911 Carrera S | Lap time 1:09.20 |
| Aston Martin V8 Vantage | Lap time 1:08.78 |

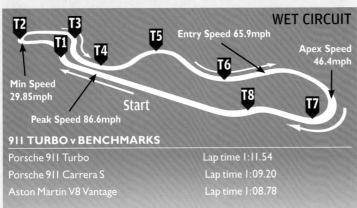

## LATERAL G

| | Dry | Wet |
|---|---|---|
| | 1.02 | 0.73g |

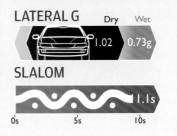

## SLALOM

1.1s

0s — 5s — 10s

Very grippy in the wet or dry; quick and agile through the slalom

## DESIGN & ENGINEERING

Central to the technical advances Porsche has made with this car over its predecessor is the development and evolution of the Cayenne. When developing their Range Rover rival, Porsche's engineers realised just how beneficial a cutting-edge four-wheel drive system can be when trying to deploy large amounts of power and torque. As a result, the new Turbo features much of the all-wheel drive technology pioneered on the Cayenne.

It has three electronic control systems that interact to maximize the Turbo's traction, handling and stability, and unlike the previous model they actively react to what the car is doing on the road. These are Porsche Traction Management (PTM), which controls torque split between front and rear axles; Porsche Active Suspension Management (PASM), which adjusts the electronic Bilstein dampers accordingly, and Porsche Stability Management (PSM), which uses the brakes, throttle and rear diff to control understeer and oversteer. The driver can also select sport mode, which firms up the dampers, pulls back the PSM and ABS thresholds and raises the rev limit.

Of course, none of this would be necessary were the 911 Turbo not equipped with a monstrous amount of power and torque from its twin-turbo flat six engine. Capacity remains at 3.6 litres but, thanks largely to the development of a new Borg Warner variable-geometry turbocharger for each bank of three cylinders (a first for a petrol engine), power jumps from 414 to 473bhp at 6000rpm, while torque rises from 413 to 457lb ft. More important still, this torque peak is delivered all the way from 1950rpm to 5000rpm, endowing the 911 with a phenomenal amount of flexibility.

If that's not enough, yet more torque is available

**ABOVE** Turbo gets biplane wing and extra intakes/vents.

**BELOW** It takes quite a bit of provocation to make the rear end break loose, but it's very controlled when it happens.

**Gearchange – quick but easy, this car had the optional quick shift that makes changing gears simply a determined flick of the wrist.**

**Nothing wrong with the power of the climate control in operation, but some of the switchgear is a little awkward to use.**

**Typical Porsche layout to dials. Now has digital boost gauge below rev counter.**

**ABOVE** Optional 'adaptive' seats are more comfortable than they look. Driving position more upright than most supercars and visibility is excellent.

**OPPOSITE** Dampers are adjustable, as is the degree of stability control; carbon-ceramic brake discs are expensive (£5349) but fabulous.

if a customer specifies the optional Sports Chrono pack for an extra £1015. This in effect provides an overboost period that allows torque to swell under full throttle to 502lb ft between 2100 and 4000rpm – for all of 10sec. Our test car was specified as such.

Two transmissions are available: six-speed manual or Tiptronic. Porsche's official figures suggest the Tiptronic car is quicker – slightly – than the manual under acceleration. But it's the manual we test here. A 911 Turbo wouldn't be a 911 Turbo without a monumental set of brakes, and the new car is no exception. Standard stoppers are 350mm cast iron ventilated discs front and rear, with six-piston calipers at the front. Specify the PCCB ceramic composite discs (a whopping £5349 extra) and the disc sizes rise to 380mm all round while the kerb weight (normally 1585kg) drops by a significant 17kg. We measured the test car at 1557kg.

Visually, the Turbo can be distinguished from lesser 911s by its bespoke 19in wheels, its deeper front valance featuring numerous new cooling ducts, and by its bigger twin-wing rear spoiler, the upper section of which deploys at 75mph and lowers at 37mph.

Porsche has also worked hard on aerodynamics. The drag factor is the same as before at 0.31, despite

the many new cooling channels required by the more powerful engine, but it now produces a small amount of downforce at the rear (17kg at 150mph) while generating a tiny degree of lift at the front (+6kg at 150mph). Both of these are improvements over the old car.

Tyre sizes have risen fractionally at the front to 235/35 ZR19, with significantly wider 305/30 ZR19s at the rear, supplied by Michelin or Bridgestone. Michelin has also developed special covers that boost grip in the dry but have slightly less resistance to aquaplaning.

## PERFORMANCE AND BRAKES

To get a clear idea of just how rapid the new 911 Turbo is, imagine yourself trundling along in a queue of traffic at 40mph. In front there is a long line of cars and a straight piece of road with nothing coming the other way and no side turnings anywhere in sight. And you wonder how many cars it would be possible to pick off in one hit: three, four, six or all eight?

In sixth gear you'd probably have enough acceleration to pass at least the first two, because the Turbo takes just 5.7sec to get from 40–60mph in top. Drop to fifth and you'll cover the same ground in 3.6sec. So say three cars, maybe four.

Select fourth and you'll nail 40–60 in 2.6sec, which is when your spine starts to bend the back of the seat and when the entire queue no longer presents much of a problem. Hook third and both you and the rest of the traffic in that queue will begin to feel a distinct sense of unease as the Turbo blows its way from 40–60mph in a faintly ridiculous 2.1sec. And if you're feeling really unsociable you could drop to second – in which case you'll do it in 1.4sec. That's the point at which your mind has to focus hard to stay in control – and when you leave just about everything this side of a Bugatti Veyron trailing in your wake.

And that's to say nothing of the 911 Turbo's party trick, which is what it does when you dump the clutch at 6000rpm from a standstill and go. Instantly the back of your head thumps the seat, hard, as the Turbo spins its back wheels momentarily. But there's not even a hint of a delay as it does so. The sense of acceleration is absolute and immediate.

Seemingly within less than a heartbeat you're travelling at 30mph (in fact, it takes 1.3sec), at which point a gearchange is already needed. Nail the short throw from first to second (not difficult considering how fast and slick the manual gearbox is) and

# SPECIFICATIONS 911 TURBO

## DIMENSIONS

**Front track** 1490mm  **Rear track** 1548mm  **Width inc mirrors** 1960mm
**Width excluding mirrors** 1852mm  **Front interior width** 1350mm

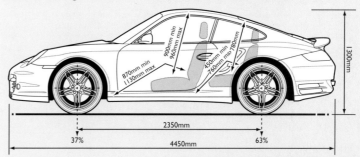

## ENGINE

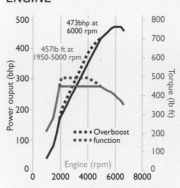

| | |
|---|---|
| Red line | 6750rpm |
| Power | 473bhp at 6000rpm |
| Torque | 457lb ft at 1950–5000rpm |
| (with overboost 502lb ft at 2100–4000rpm) | |
| Type/fuel | Flat 6cyls, 3600cc, petrol |
| Made of/Installation | Alloy/rear, longitudinal, 4wd |
| Power to weight | 298bhp per tonne |
| Torque to weight | 288lb ft per tonne |
| Specific output | 131bhp per litre |
| Compression ratio | 9.01:1 |
| Bore/stroke | 100.0/76.4mm |
| Valve gear | 4 per cyl, quad OHC |

## GEARBOX

**Type** 6-speed manual
**Ratios/mph per 1000rpm**
**Final drive ratio** 3.33:1

| | |
|---|---|
| 1st 3.82/6.1 | 2nd 2.14/10.9 |
| 3rd 1.48/15.8 | 4th 1.18/19.8 |
| 5th 0.97/24.1 | 6th 0.79/29.6 |

## CHASSIS AND BODY

| | |
|---|---|
| **Construction** | Steel unibody |
| **Weight/as tested** | 1585kg/1557kg |
| **Drag coefficient** | 0.31Cd |
| **Wheels** | Alloy (f) 8.5Jx19, (r) 11Jx19 |
| **Tyres** | 235/35 R19, 305/30 R19 Michelin Pilot Sport |
| **Spare** | Mousse |

## SUSPENSION

**Front** MacPherson struts, coil springs, anti-roll bar
**Rear** Five-link, coil springs, anti-roll bar

## STEERING

**Type** Hydraulically variable-rate rack and pinion
**Turns lock-to-lock** 2.55
**Turning circle** 10.9m

## BRAKES

**Front** 350mm ventilated discs (380mm ceramic optional)
**Rear** 350mm ventilated discs (350mm ceramic optional)
**Anti-lock** Standard

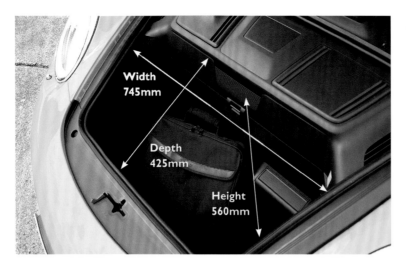

Width 745mm

Depth 425mm

Height 560mm

**ABOVE** Decent space for luggage up front. Gets even better if you treat the tiny rear seats as additional storage space.

**OPPOSITE** One variable-vane turbo for each bank of cylinders. Result: no lag.

after 3.6sec you're doing 60mph. Yes, we're aware Porsche claims 3.9sec to 62mph, but we logged this car at 3.60sec to 60mph, simple as that.

After 60mph flashes up it becomes less frantic, slightly. Just before 70mph you change from second to third, again noting how sharp the shift feels (the test car was fitted with the £380 short-shift gearchange). Then just before 100mph you grab fourth. Getting to three figures takes just 8.0sec; for

the record, that's just 0.1sec slower than £403,000 worth of Jaguar XJ220 managed when we tested it way back when.

One-fifty arrives 19.6sec after you set off, and that's seriously impressive. By comparison, an Aston Martin DB9 takes 26.9sec to reach the same speed and a Ferrari F430 21.5sec.

Just for good measure, the Turbo will officially do 193mph flat out. Unofficially, the Turbo will run to 198mph before nudging gently against its rev limiter in sixth.

So it's fast with a capital F, yes, but what really distinguishes the Turbo's performance is its flexibility. Which is something else again. Hard though it may be to imagine considering the outputs, there's no turbo lag to speak of. Instead, you put your foot down at, say, 1800rpm in fifth gear and it goes.

There's a definite swell in the rate of acceleration as the revs reach 2000-2500rpm, but below that there's still bags of response, seemingly in any gear. And yes, it'll still do the trick of pulling cleanly from below 1000rpm in top gear; every 911 since the dawn of time has been able to do that.

No, the only debatable side to the performance

## HOW THEY COMPARE

| MAKE | PORSCHE | FERRARI | LAMBORGHINI | NOBLE |
|---|---|---|---|---|
| **Model** | **911 Turbo** | **F430 F1** | **Gallardo** | **M15** |
| Price | £97,840 | £129,800 | £121,000 | £74,950 |
| Power | 473bhp at 6000rpm | 483bhp at 8500rpm | 520bhp at 7800rpm | 455bhp at 6800rpm |
| Torque | 457lb ft at 1950-5000rpm | 343lb ft at 5250rpm | 376lb ft at 4500rpm | 455lb ft at 4800rpm |
| 0–60mph | 3.6sec | 4.4sec (tested) | 4.1sec (tested) | 3.3sec (prototype test) |
| Top speed | 193mph (claimed) | 196mph (claimed) | 197mph (claimed) | 185mph (estimated) |
| Fuel consumption | 22.1mpg (combined) | 15.4mpg (combined) | 14.5mpg (combined) | 17.0mpg (estimated) |
| Kerb weight | 1585kg (claimed) | 1480kg (claimed) | 1570kg (claimed) | 1250kg (claimed) |
| Boot space | 105 litres | 250 litres | na | na |
| $CO_2$/tax band | 307g/km/35 per cent | 420g/km/35 per cent | 400g/km/35 per cent | na/35 per cent |
| We think | Still the all-weather supercar benchmark. Astounding pace and ability mated to daily usability. | Beautiful to behold, fabulous to sit in and exquisite to drive. More willowy and delicate in feel than brutal 911 Turbo. | Italy meets Germany, with the looks and sound of an Italian classic, plus genuine integrity and purpose. | If the prototype we've driven is anything to go by, M15 will easily hold its own on pace & entertainment. |
| **VERDICT** | ★★★★☆ | ★★★★☆ | ★★★★☆ | TBC |

is the fact that it feels little stronger at 6000rpm than it does at 2000rpm, which is a strange sensation. The shove between these two points is huge and relentless, but it's also eerily consistent right across the rev range once you pass 2000rpm and full boost (0.8bar) has registered. There's no sense of a crescendo to the performance over the last 2000rpm, as there is in an F430, for instance. Nor is the throttle response as crisp between 4000 and 6500rpm as it was in the previous Turbo. Blame the 997's slightly lower compression ratio for that, as well as its greater spread of torque beneath that point.

The Turbo's braking ability is predictably immense, especially when fitted with the PCCB option, as the test car was. It takes just 2.5sec to stop from 60mph and covers just 44.4m in getting from 70-0mph. These are phenomenally good results. But, as ever, it's the level of feel through the pedal and the total absence of fade that most impress. If anything, it stops even better than it goes.

## HANDLING AND RIDE

Porsche's intention with this car is clear: despite its monumental performance, the 911 Turbo is meant to be a car you can drive and live with every day, largely without compromising ride comfort and long-distance refinement.

And in the main it hits the bull's eye on all counts. First thing you notice is how amazingly calm and sophisticated the ride is. Encounter a speed hump and the crash you're expecting to reverberate through the chassis never arrives; instead, the springs and electronic Bilstein dampers soak up most road scars as if they didn't exist.

That's the first surprise. Second is how well damped the steering is, to the extent that there is virtually no kickback through the rim, even when you run over relatively large potholes. Overall this is both a good and bad thing. Good because it means the Turbo is an amazingly refined and civilised car to drive, seemingly irrespective of the conditions underfoot. Bad because, like all 997s with variable-rate assistance, the seam of communication between car, driver and road surface has unquestionably faded a little. Instead of providing a delicious stream of feedback, the steering reacts to and erases any inconsistencies in road surface before they are relayed to the wheel, which is great if you merely want to sit back and go as fast as possible, but less welcome if you relish the sort of steering interaction a 996 Turbo used to deliver.

## WHAT IT COSTS

### PORSCHE 911 TURBO

| | | | |
|---|---|---|---|
| **On-the-road price** | £97,840 | Adaptive sports seats | £674 |
| **Price as tested** | £107,263 | Heated seats | £269 |
| **Retained value 3yrs** | na | Sports seats | NCO |
| **Typical PCP pcm** | na | Climate control | ■ |
| **Contract hire pcm** | na | Airbags front/side | ■/■ |
| **Cost per mile** | na | Park assist | £325 |
| **CO$_2$** | 307g/km | PSM and traction control | ■ |
| **Tax at 22/40% pcm** | £513/£933 | Bi-xenon lights | £705 |
| **Insurance/typical quote** | 20/£809 | **Embossed seats** | **£126** |
| | | **Telephone module** | **£523** |

### EQUIPMENT CHECKLIST

| | | | |
|---|---|---|---|
| Tiptronic auto 'box | £1961 | **Carbon interior trim** | **£492** |
| **Sports shortshift** | **£380** | **CD autochanger** | **£348** |
| Locking rear differential | £753 | Electronic logbook | £385 |
| Cruise control | £294 | Tracking system | ■ |
| Stainless tailpipes | £175 | **Sports Chrono package** | **£1015** |
| Rear wiper | NCO | **Ceramic brakes** | **£5349** |
| Parking sensors | £325 | Factory collection | £960 |
| 19in alloy wheels | ■ | **Electric sunroof** | **£864** |
| Steering height/reach adj | ■ | | |

Options in **bold** fitted to test car
■ = Standard  na = not available

# TEST SCORECARD

## ENGINE ★★★★★
Quite simply one of the best road car engines there is. Absence of turbo lag is almost as extraordinary as the raw performance. Almost…

## TRANSMISSION ★★★★★
Much improved over the 996 Turbo's. Clutch is impressively light, too. All in all a great manual gearbox, and the Tiptronic is even faster

## STEERING ★★★
Impressively free from kickback but also lacking in genuine feel. It does the job, no more; in a 911 Turbo you expect a bit more than that

## BRAKES ★★★★★
Awesome. Tons of feel through the pedal, huge resistance to fade, and very strong. PCCB option is expensive, but probably worth it overall

## HANDLING ★★★★★
Hard to think of a car that generates more grip, or which has better body control at high speed. Fabulously well balanced, too, once you get used to the amount of movement there is on turn-in

## RIDE ★★★★
Real surprise, this, because you just don't expect a 911 Turbo to ride especially well. This one does, however

## ECONOMY ★★★
Not too bad at all in terms of basic consumption, but 67-litre fuel tank means real-world range is pretty pathetic at no more than 220 miles

## DRIVING POSITION ★★★★
There are no other 195mph cars out of which you can see this well. Driving position is pretty much perfect, too

## CONTROLS ★★★★
Electric window switches aside, cabin is compact, logical and very well ordered, if a little plain in design considering the price

## EQUIPMENT ★★★★
All the basics that you'd expect are present, including DVD sat-nav, leather and full climate control

## LIVEABILITY ★★★★
Amazingly civilised for a 195mph car generally, but tyre roar lets its down, especially on coarse surfaces

## QUALITY ★★★★
Notably better made than previous 996 Turbo, and therefore very well made indeed. No real sense of luxury to the cabin; it feels functional

## VALUE ★★★★
On the one hand, 97 grand sounds like an awful lot considering it's a 911. On the other, no car at the money is faster…

## SAFETY ★★★★
Full complement of airbags, traction and stability devices – and then there's the inherent benefits of AWD. Pretty damn good, then

## TRACK WORK ★★★★★½
Blistering power, grip and traction. Not as deft as a a GT3, though

## DESIRABILITY ★★★★
Doesn't possess the same aching sense of occasion as an Aston or Ferrari F430, but the attractions are more subtle than that. To some it's the only car worth having, and it's not difficult to see why

## NOISE ★★★★
Doesn't make a ripping noise like a Ferrari F430 but in its way it sounds great

Everything else about the Turbo's chassis is so close to perfection, however, that you don't miss the absence of steering feel as much as you'd think. From the way it's damped and so controlled at speed (which is genuinely extraordinary) to the way it clings to the road seemingly oblivious of weather conditions, it's hard to think of a car that can cover ground more quickly or in such security.

Although there's some movement of the body when you really lean on it in a quick corner, this rarely develops into anything more than just that: a controlled and very slight movement. And although the tail will eventually let go if you back away from the throttle sharply into a tightening bend, it never just snaps away as of old. There's always a sense of balance to the chassis, even if you provoke it into a slide. And in any case, that's only if you switch all the stability and traction control systems off.

What isn't so impressive is the amount of tyre roar it generates, especially from the rear over coarse surfaces above 60mph – in other words, on motorways. This is no doubt the result of those bigger 305-section rear covers, although perhaps the fact that the test car wore Michelin's upgraded pseudo-competition rubber didn't help. Either way, it's a shame because it's one of the few things that spoils the Turbo's credentials as a mile-eater.

## LIVING WITH IT

What also does it no favours as a continent-crusher is its measly 67-litre fuel tank. Even driven gently, the Turbo will rarely achieve better than 20mpg, and if driven hard it does about 12mpg. Our test average was a creditable 17.2mpg and at that rate you have to stop for fuel every 200 miles before the warning light appears. Which makes long-distance cruising little more than a series of fuel stops.

This and the tyre roar issue aside, the Turbo is a quite extraordinarily civilised device, considering how fast it is. Space in the rear is the same as it ever was: just about okay for kids, otherwise the space acts merely as a useful extention of the surprisingly roomy boot in the nose.

Admittedly there isn't the same sense of occasion or luxury inside the Turbo as there is in the DB9 or F430; instead it feels deliberately more functional than that. Truth is, you'll either love the cabin for its compact dimensions and its simplicity, or you'll think it pretty disappointing considering it costs 97 grand.

Not that there can be many complaints about the driving position (just about perfect) or the basic goodie count, which includes full leather and DVD sat-nav. The test car also came with an electric sunroof (£864), carbon trim (£492), more supportive 'adaptive' front seats (£674) and headrests embossed with a Porsche logo (£126).

Assuming Porsche doesn't stray from its traditional policy of keeping demand well above the rate of supply, the Turbo will be one of the more secure methods of keeping depreciation at bay over the next few years. The waiting list is already 18 months. And only now, after six years, have 996 Turbo values started to fall to below 50 per cent of the original £86k asking price.

**ABOVE** 911 Turbo has presence from almost any angle. Extra intakes and vents help to cool 473bhp twin-turbo flat six.

**OPPOSITE** Top plane of rear wing rises at 75mph and drops back at 37mph.

## AUTOCAR VERDICT

Why not a perfect five, you're no doubt wondering? Three things: the lack of steering feel, the amount of tyre roar it generates on motorways, and the size of the fuel tank. Other than that, it's hard to think of ways in which the latest 911 Turbo could be improved. Not only is it one of the fastest cars we've ever tested, but it's also the best 911 Turbo yet, no question.

**Faster and more complete than ever**

# PORSCHE 911 GT3

We put Weissach's hardcore track day hero through its paces
to give it the full road test treatment. The best 911 of the lot?

The evolution of the Porsche 911 has given
us some of our most cherished enthusiast icons:
the delicate but angry 1970 ST and '73 Carrera RS,
the storming sequence of Turbo 911s, the mighty
964 and 993 RS, and in 1999 the GT3. Named after
and conceived for the FIA sporting category of the
time, the GT3 was less about shedding kilos and
more about speed, technology and driver-focused
dynamics. At its core was a much more exotic
and stronger flat six. This powerplant, originally
designed in turbocharged form for the fearsome
GT1 racing car, evolved with the spikier 381bhp Mk2
GT3 in 2003. Now, with countless race victories
in international competition worldwide and a
stranglehold on the wealthy end of the track day
market born from a typical Porsche mix of durability
and speed, the 997 GT3 has arrived.

## DESIGN & ENGINEERING

The more you delve into the reams of information
emanating from Stuttgart, the more you realise the
dedication that has gone into creating this GT3. The
essential 'body in white' structure is from the Carrera
4 to allow the fitment of a larger fuel tank, but the

## QUICK FACTS

| | |
|---|---|
| **Model** | 911 GT3 |
| **Price** | £79,540 |
| **Top speed** | 190mph (claimed) |
| **0–60mph** | 4.2sec |
| **MPG** | 17.0 mpg |
| **Emissions** | 307g/km $CO_2$ |
| **70–0mph** | 47.3m |
| **Skidpan** | 1.13g |
| **For** | Sensational engine, performance, soundtrack, chassis |
| **Against** | Gear ratios long for UK roads, hard work in traffic |

# ROAD TEST

## 7 FEBRUARY 2007

Volume 251

No 6 | 5727

# ROAD TEST 911 GT3

## ACCELERATION
**Standing qtr mile** 12.8sec/116.2mphh **Standing km** 22.6sec/153.0mphh **30–70mph** 3.4sec

| 30mph | 40 | 50 | 60 | 70 | 80 | 90 | 100 | 110 | 120 | 130 | 140 | 150 |
|---|---|---|---|---|---|---|---|---|---|---|---|---|
| 1.7s | 2.3s | 3.4s | 4.2s | 5.1s | 6.1s | 7.8s | 9.2s | 10.8s | 13.1s | 15.2s | 18.2s | 22.0s |

## DRY/WET BRAKING

| Dry 30mph-0 | Wet 30mph-0 | Dry 50mph-0 | Wet 50mph-0 | Dry 70mph-0 | 70mph-0 |
|---|---|---|---|---|---|
| 8.6m | 10.0m | 23.8m | 29.2m | 47.3m | 65.9m |

## ACCELERATION IN GEAR

| MPH | 2nd | 3rd | 4th | 5th | 6th |
|---|---|---|---|---|---|
| 20–40 | 2.2 | 3.9 | 4.2 | | - |
| 30–50 | 2.0 | 3.7 | 4.0 | 5.1 | 6.4 |
| 40–60 | 1.9 | 3.5 | 3.9 | 5.1 | 6.2 |
| 50–70 | 1.8 | 3.4 | 3.8 | 5.1 | 6.4 |
| 60–80 | 2.0 | 3.2 | 3.8 | 5.0 | 6.5 |
| 70–90 | | 3.3 | 3.6 | 5.1 | 6.5 |
| 80–100 | | 3.5 | 3.5 | 5.2 | 6.8 |
| 90–110 | | | 3.6 | 4.9 | 7.3 |
| 100–120 | | | 3.7 | 4.9 | 7.2 |
| 110–130 | | | 4.0 | 5.2 | 7.0 |
| 120–140 | | | 4.7 | 5.6 | |
| 130–150 | | | | 6.3 | |

## MAX SPEED IN GEAR

| 50mph | 116mph | 180mph |
|---|---|---|
| 8400rpm | 8400rpm | 8400rpm |

1 — 3 — 5

2 — 4 — 6

| 84mph | 149mph | 192mph |
|---|---|---|
| 8400rpm | 8400rpm | 7790rpm |

## ECONOMY

| | TEST | | CLAIMED | |
|---|---|---|---|---|
| Average | 17.0mpg | Urban | 14.3mpg |
| Touring | 26.6mpg | Ex-urb | 31.7mpg |
| Track | 8.9mpg | Comb | 22.1mpg |
| Tank size | 90 litres | Test range | 340 miles |

## CABIN NOISE

**Idle** 58dbA **Max revs in 3rd** 86dbA **30mph** 69dbA **50mph** 71dbA **70mph** 74dbA

## HEADLIGHTS

**Dipped beam** Good **Full beam** Excellent. **Test notes** Dipped good but sharp cut-off, main absolutely superb.

## WIPERS

Good wipers with economical wash.

## TESTER'S NOTES

A sensational track performance from the GT3, destroying our dry circuit lap record by two seconds. Obviously, the Cup tyres make a big difference, pulling over 1.1g around the final corner (T7) and providing superb grip through the S bend of T2 – usually a rapid and repeated direction change that doesn't suit a 911. And the superb brakes pull the car down for T1 with awesome power.

The GT3 is sensational for entirely different reasons on the wet circuit. To be fair, the tread was slightly worn on the Cup tyres, but even so it struggled to put any power down, proving hopelessly slow on the main straight. What it did allow was fabulous drifts through most of the corners, although this required serious throttle and steering control.

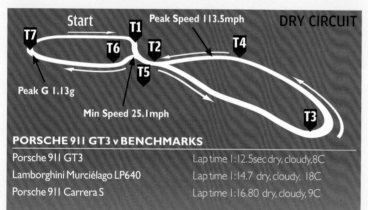

### DRY CIRCUIT

Start · Peak Speed 113.5mph · T7 · T1 · T6 · T2 · T4 · T5 · Peak G 1.13g · Min Speed 25.1mph · T3

**PORSCHE 911 GT3 v BENCHMARKS**

| | |
|---|---|
| Porsche 911 GT3 | Lap time 1:12.5sec dry, cloudy, 8C |
| Lamborghini Murciélago LP640 | Lap time 1:14.7 dry, cloudy, 18C |
| Porsche 911 Carrera S | Lap time 1:16.80 dry, cloudy, 9C |

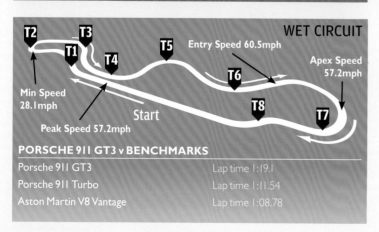

### WET CIRCUIT

T2 · T3 · T1 · T4 · T5 · Entry Speed 60.5mph · Apex Speed 57.2mph · Min Speed 28.1mph · T6 · Start · Peak Speed 57.2mph · T8 · T7

**PORSCHE 911 GT3 v BENCHMARKS**

| | |
|---|---|
| Porsche 911 GT3 | Lap time 1:19.1 |
| Porsche 911 Turbo | Lap time 1:11.54 |
| Aston Martin V8 Vantage | Lap time 1:08.78 |

## LATERAL G

| Dry | Wet |
|---|---|
| 1.13g | 0.66g |

exterior panelling is from the narrow-hipped Carrera 2 (only the GT3 RS variant gets the wider arches) with an aluminium bonnet and ultra-light plastic doors and engine cover.

Although the GT3 is still essentially a 911, and as such its appeal will always be compromised for some by its ubiquity, this is one of the more dramatic derivatives. It sits squat and purposeful (30mm lower from ground to roof than a Carrera), and despite the aggressive air intakes the Cd is a svelte 0.29. At the rear, the imposing wing is much bigger than before and can be adjusted by six degrees.

The heart and soul of this new GT3, however, is still very much its flat six engine. With a capacity of 3600cc and no sign of any forced induction beyond the ram air dome forcing the slipstream into the airbox, the development theme has been to reduce the mass of the engine's internals, allowing higher rotational speeds. For example, the forged pistons have been redesigned with a 1mm narrower shape, saving 30g, the titanium connecting rods have been lengthened but similarly trimmed and weigh just 418g each, and the main bearing crank has lost 600g.

Once the air is inside, it passes through a new, larger butterfly valve and down a variable intake

manifold with two precision-made alloy flaps that create the most favourable resonance in the charge depending on engine speed. There's Variocam variable valve timing on the intake side of the engine, plus new polished cylinder head ports, double valve springs and hollow camshafts, while the compression ratio has been raised over the old GT3's 11.7:1 to 12.0:1.

The end result is an astonishing 114bhp per litre (higher even than a Ferrari F430) and a peak output of 409bhp at 7600rpm, with the limiter not arriving until 8400rpm. Torque is rated at 298lb ft at a relatively high 5500rpm, but on paper at least the graph's curve looks usefully flat.

The expulsion of spent gases is as efficient as their combustion, thanks to a new exhaust system that not only weighs 8.5kg less and has eight per cent less back pressure but which, when the Sport button is engaged, also emits a delicious throb from the twin centrally mounted tailpipes even at idle.

The GT3's bespoke gearbox has also been revised, with ratios two to six brought closer together and a 15 per cent reduction in shift movement between gears.

Perhaps the most significant change with this GT3 is the adoption of the electronically controlled

**Gearchange – Very direct, with grippy Alcantara gear knob.**

**Steering wheel – Alcantara-covered rim is a good size and feels great in the hands. Reach and rake adjustment.**

**Instrumentation – Yellow font inspired by Carrera GT. Very clear, with all the info you want, but some minor switchgear looks and feels a bit ordinary.**

## WHAT IT COSTS

### PORSCHE 911 GT3

| | |
|---|---|
| **On-the-road price** | £79,540 |
| **Price as tested** | £88,346 |

### EQUIPMENT CHECKLIST

| | | | | |
|---|---|---|---|---|
| **Ceramic brakes** | **£5800** | Heated seats | £269 | |
| Limited-slip differential | ■ | Adaptive seats | £1423 | |
| PASM suspension | ■ | Lightweight bucket seats | £3130 | |
| Sports exhaust | ■ | (Leather to all, add | £1648) | |
| Metallic paint | £570 | ISOFIX passenger seat | ■ | |
| Special paint | £1522 | Coloured seat belts | £163 | |
| Paint to sample | £2180 | Electric sunroof | £864 | |
| Exterior-coloured wheels | £705 | **PCM inc. sat nav** | **£1921** | |
| CD player | ■ | Phone module | £523 | |
| Leather dashboard | £1109 | **Chrono package** | **£380** | |
| Carbon interior package | £1624 | Cruise control | £294 | |
| Climate control | ■ | Fire extinguisher | £98 | |
| Clubsport pack + buckets | No cost | **Xenon headlights** | **£705** | |
| | | Auto-dip mirror/rain sensor | £353 | |
| | | Factory collection | £960 | |

Options in **bold** fitted to test car

■ = Standard   na = not available

damping found in most current 911s (PASM in Porsche-speak) and the mandatory variable-ratio steering rack. The steering gear itself is left unchanged from the Carrera, which means the ratio is slower at high speed but changes for a faster one once some lock has been applied in a corner.

As for the chassis, it's a typical case of strengthening, upgrading and tweaking, with firmer springs and dampers and thicker anti-roll bars. The PASM dampers have two settings: a normal mode for road use and coyly recommended by Porsche for the north circuit of the Nürburgring, and a sport setting purely for "very smooth racetracks".

That's not all enthusiasts get. With adjustable spring platforms front and rear allowing various ride heights, two basic camber settings for either road tyres or competition slicks with fine adjustment from the track control arms, and five anti-roll bar settings up front and three at the rear, ruining your GT3's set-up in the garage should take mere hours.

Naturally a limited-slip differential is fitted, and

unlike previous iterations there's also a traction control system tied into the car's main electronics, but still no ESP: Porsche expects you to use your hands and feet to sort out such issues.

Although a mighty set of 350mm cast iron brakes discs are fitted as standard – with six-pot calipers up front and four-pots at the rear – another £5800 will give you Porsche's PCCB carbon-ceramic brake discs. They bring 380mm discs and alloy brake covers that save 900g; a PCCB-equipped car weighs a remarkable 20kg less.

Ordering the Clubsport specification at no extra cost gives you the deep bucket seats, the rear half of a roll cage and preparation for a battery master switch, fire extinguisher and harness.

## PERFORMANCE AND BRAKES

Once inside the GT3, you're faced with a classic line-up of analogue instrumentation, the yellow font inspired by the Carrera GT's.

The hardcore bucket seats of this Clubsport sit you virtually on the floor and their deep bolsters clamp you in place so it's hard to move.

The flat six jars into life with an angry clatter and you soon realise that a change of gear requires a bit of bicep work. The trade-off is the pure, satisfying sensation of gear teeth meshing with each other and a tremendously quick overall shift time. At low revs there's a familiar mix of 911-esque whining, but as the revs rise above 3000rpm a mighty induction roar reverberates around the cabin, leaving you in no doubt about this car's potential.

Off the line on cold and slightly greasy asphalt, our GT3 leaped to 60mph in a scant 4.2sec, reached 100mph slightly behind the claimed figure at 9.2sec and topped 150mph in 22sec, just 0.5sec behind our time for an F430. Once into its stride the GT3 is even more impressive, as our Bruntingthorpe test shows. With its slim-hipped aerodynamics, it passed the set point at 183mph – just 3mph behind the 550bhp Ford GT and a staggering 4mph faster than its much more powerful Turbo sibling.

On the road, the effect of this performance is predictably tremendous. This is a very quick car, dispatching the 50-70mph increment in second gear in just 1.8sec, only a tenth down on a Murciélago LP640.

If we do have a criticism, it's that the gear ratios are set too long; second takes you to over 80mph and third to nearly 120mph, which isn't terribly useful for driving in the UK. An F430 is notably faster at the top of each gear. Shorter ratios would improve the

# SPECIFICATIONS 911 GT3

## DIMENSIONS

Front track 1497mm   Rear track 1524mm   Width inc mirrors 1960mm
Width excluding mirrors 1808mm   Front interior width 1350mm

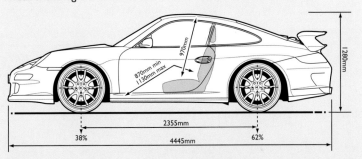

## ENGINE

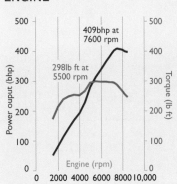

409bhp at 7600 rpm
298lb ft at 5500 rpm

| | |
|---|---|
| Red line | 8400rpm |
| Power | 409bhp at 7600rpm |
| Torque | 298lb ft at 5500rpm |
| Type/fuel | Flat 6cyls, 3600cc, petrol |
| Made of/Installation | Alloy/rear, longitudinal, rwd |
| Power to weight | 293bhp per tonne |
| Torque to weight | 214lb ft per tonne |
| Specific output | 114bhp per litre |
| Compression ratio | 12.0:1 |
| Bore/stroke | 100.0/76.4mm |
| Valve gear | 4 per cyl, quad OHC |

## GEARBOX

**Type** 6-speed manual
**Ratios/mph per 1000rpm**
**Final drive ratio** 3.44:1

| | |
|---|---|
| 1st 3.82/5.9 | 2nd 2.26/10.0 |
| 3rd 1.64/13.8 | 4th 1.29/17.6 |
| 5th 10.6/21.4 | 6th 0.92/24.6 |

## CHASSIS AND BODY

| | |
|---|---|
| Construction | Steel unitary |
| Weight/as tested | 1395kg/1443kg |
| Wheels | Alloy (f) 8.5Jx19, (r) 12Jx19 |
| Tyres | 235/35 ZR19, 305/30 ZR19 Michelin Pilot Sport Cup |
| Spare | Mousse |

## SUSPENSION

**Front** MacPherson struts, coil springs, anti-roll bar
**Rear** Multi-link, coil springs, anti-roll bar

## STEERING

**Type** Hydraulically variable-rate rack and pinion
**Turns lock-to-lock** 2.6
**Turning circle** 10.9m

## BRAKES

**Front** 380mm ceramic (optional)
**Rear** 340mm ventilated discs
**Anti-lock** Standard
**Parking brake** Hand operated

# TEST SCORECARD

**ENGINE ★★★★★**

Weight-saving efforts mean the flat six unleashes an incredible 114bhp per litre and spins to 8400rpm. Utterly, utterly wonderful.

**BRAKES ★★★★★**

Optional ceramic discs are close to perfection: strong, feelsome and highly resistant to fade. They also save 20kg.

**TRANSMISSION ★★★★☆**

A superbly tight gearchange with a pure, mechanical feel, but ratios are a bit long for UK driving. Clutch is heavy in traffic.

**STEERING ★★★★**

Ideal for weight and accuracy, although it doesn't have as much feel as that of the 996 GT3.

**HANDLING ★★★★☆**

Usual 911 rules apply on cornering technique, but immense grip levels and adjustability for the experienced driver.

**RIDE ★★★★**

Considering the operating brief, remarkably comfortable. Sport setting is for billiard table-smooth racetracks.

**ECONOMY ★★★☆**

One of the better supercars, which is to say it likes a drink, but can be surprisingly frugal when cruising.

**DRIVING POSITION ★★★★★**

Superb sporting driving position as you're sat very low in the car. Typically excellent 911 visibility all round.

**EQUIPMENT ★★★☆**

Reasonably equipped, but add extras (all too easy to do) and the price soon starts to escalate.

**CONTROLS ★★★★**

Well laid out with everything you need, but minor switchgear looks and feels ordinary. Roll cage restricts rear space but looks the business.

**LIVEABILITY ★★★**

You could use it every day, but the question is more whether you'd actually want to. Fairly practical, but a rich experience perhaps best savoured on the right occasion.

**QUALITY ★★★★★**

Feels immensely solid, both structurally and mechanically. This is a car you could enjoy for 20 years or more, no doubt.

**VALUE ★★★★**

Save the options list, the basic price is somewhat of a bargain considering the cross-country pace and performance on offer.

**SAFETY ★★★★**

Six airbags (four with bucket seats) but no ESP, only traction control. Immense brakes help.

**TRACK WORK ★★★★★**

In its element here; smashed our dry circuit lap record with ease. Heroic brakes, grippy Cup tyres and plenty of power.

**DESIRABILITY ★★★★☆**

To those in the know, this is about as good as it gets. To others, it's just another 911…

**NOISE ★★★★★**

Awesome –especially with sports exhaust open –from a deep rumble to an ecstatic howl. Pedestrians will hear it long before they see it.

GT3's acceleration. Indeed, shorter gear sets are available to order, at a cost naturally.

Nevertheless, this is a magical engine to work hard, with a wall of screaming noise as it revs ever higher and a 'crack' from the gearchange mechanism as a flash of hand grabs the next gear.

Porsche has a reputation for great brakes, and with the ceramic option fitted our car didn't disappoint. They are as close to faultless as we've ever experienced, with brilliant resistance to fade, lovely pedal feel and immense power. In the dry it pulled it up from 60mph to zero in just 2.6sec, and on a wet road its stability was superb, with 50-0mph requiring only 29m.

## HANDLING AND RIDE

Any concerns about the GT3's electronic dampers are quickly dispelled once you're on the road. In essence, this is a car that doesn't feel much more uncomfortable than a Carrera S, so although at times it is unyielding – exactly telegraphing the surface you are passing over – because it deals with bumps and ridges in such a decisive manner you're inclined to relax and let it do its thing.

At speed, body control is terrific over all but the bumpiest of road surfaces. With Michelin Pilot Sport Cups – a lightly treaded road-legal slick – it is necessary to re-calibrate the brain as to what will stick and what won't.

But it's on a circuit that the GT3 is in its absolute element, with prodigious levels of grip adding to the package of power and braking ability. You can see for yourself by the way it destroyed our previous dry lap record at MIRA by over two seconds, and yet this is a car that also gives real pleasure on the road. Although the variable-ratio steering isn't as alive as before, there is plenty of feel through the thin, hard, Alcantara-clad wheel and absolute precision.

That sums up the whole driving experience really: precision. Whether at turn-in, balancing the throttle or applying power, the GT3 makes exacting demands on the driver, and in extremis displays the typical handling characteristics of any 911 (that's to say, faster out of a corner than into it, although it resists understeer strongly, certainly on dry roads).

It doesn't suffer fools gladly and reacts instantly to changes in the grip threshold, expecting and requiring the appropriate throttle control and steering input to stay on target. But while this character makes it an intimidating car for less experienced drivers – if still a wildly exciting one – it makes for a supremely

rewarding device for those with the necessary skills. Such is the balance and communication of the chassis that the GT3 can be cornered extremely quickly or drifted at will once the nose is nailed into the corner.

One caveat for potential GT3 buyers, though: beware very wet days. The Cup tyres work well on averagely wet roads, but simply don't have the necessary tread to shift deep standing water, and the consequent drama isn't always pleasant.

## LIVING WITH IT

Those PASM dampers mean the ride is adequately comfortable for commuting, but the GT3 is still hard work in traffic because of the gearshift and a heavy clutch.

The rear cage in our Clubsport model restricts the ability to load bags into the rear seat area (all GT3s are strictly two-seaters for racing homologation purposes), but there's always the surprisingly spacious boot in the nose. Just don't go expecting many thrills in the cabin. It's brilliantly laid out, but there's little more to distinguish it over a regular 911 — that's to say, well made with good materials, but lacking entirely the exclusive style you'll find in an Aston Martin Vantage.

As for fuel consumption, taking it steady allows for a touring figure in the low to mid-20s, but of course that figure plummets with spirited use of engine revs.

At £79,540, the GT3 actually seems something of a bargain considering its performance and general ability, but the addition of ceramic brakes and a smattering of the toys from the Porsche cupboard can cause the price to rise rapidly. But the bottom line is this: the GT3 is a car that will lap the Nürburgring all day long at fantastic speeds and then provide you with an air-conditioned, CD-fed cruise home in relative comfort. And yes, you could use it every day, with dedication.

**ABOVE** Drivers now get traction control, but no ESP means your hands and feet will be kept busy.

## AUTOCAR VERDICT

The 997 GT3 is a beautiful example of a car fulfilling its design brief. Outstandingly rapid on a circuit, blisteringly fast and yet beguilingly usable, it builds on the merits of the old car and then some. Whether you drive it flat out or slowly, it's full of drama, character and involvement, and it's the most enjoyable all-round performance car currently on sale.

### The drivers' car of choice ★★★★★

# BRILLIANCE TO SPARE

**911 GT3 RS** ...but can the UK handle it? Porsche's latest extreme 911 can hit 114mph in third gear, leaving Chris Harris to wonder if our humble road network has finally met its match

Select third gear and the new 997 GT3 RS has performance to spare. With 415bhp pushing 1375kg, its driver can be assured that he or she is steering one of the most accelerative cars on the road. There is no forced induction to bolster the mid-range, the gearing is little different from that of a normal 911, and still the ease with which it will dispose of other supposedly fast cars using its third ratio alone is disarming.

But if third gear in this latest Renn Sport product is a macro cause for performance fetishists everywhere to party in the streets, it also serves to undermine its road-going credentials. You see, should you use all of third gear in the 997 RS – should you watch the yellow needle swing beyond the vertical, then listen as the trick induction system does its best to impersonate a leopard undergoing root canal treatment with a poorly administered anaesthetic – then you will be travelling at 114mph. After which there are three more gears to use until the engine's electronic limiter calls time.

Porsche claims 192mph; I gave up at an indicated 196mph. Back in Germany, naturally. Because as we all know, these numbers do not sit comfortably with current speeding legislation.

Driving the GT3 RS in the UK flips any assessment procedure such as this one through 180 degrees and leaves you in a strange situation. One in which the talents of the car are so obvious (because this is one of the very best cars the company has ever produced) that anything other than hyperbolic praise seems the wrong response. It's not the car under scrutiny here; it's the road network on which it should ideally be used. We know it has brilliance to spare, but can the UK handle it?

Certain areas of the Cotswolds cannot handle its greenness. Children whoop with amazement, parents sneer at the ostentatiousness of it. I am rather affected by the styling and colour of this car. I think it looks sensational, and being a lifelong viper green fan I can only thank the factory for reintroducing this famous 1970s colour.

It's a wide beastie, though. The RS uses a Carrera 4 shell, meaning it is 44mm wider around the hips. Those few centimetres have quite an effect on three aspects of the car, only one of which is evident when stationary. By chance, I had a standard GT3 on hand at the same time. Admiring its muscular frame, then seeing the green creation, is no different from being impressed by how ripped Daniel Craig was in *Casino Royale,* only to then watch something involving Arnie in his mid-1980s pomp. One is lean, the other is distended.

That girth has both a positive and a negative effect on the RS as a road car. Lest we should forget, the car doesn't just serve as a means of hoicking a further £14,740 from unsuspecting customers bent on owning the lairiest production 911. It is the homologation model produced to legitimise the 997 RSR race car, and therefore the rear suspension's split lower arms give further scope for adjustment and result in a marginally longer wheelbase.

With these changes come quite different kinematics. The RS responds to steering inputs in a subtly different manner to its cheaper relative. As befits its stance on the road, it feels squarer, squatter and more immediate. Recalibrated electronic damper settings mean it rolls slightly less, but the key

## QUICK FACTS

| | |
|---|---|
| **Model** | 911 GT3 RS |
| | (911 GT3) |
| **Price** | £94,280 (£79,540) |
| **0–62mph** | 4.2sec (4.3sec) |
| **Power** | 409bhp at 7600rpm |
| **Torque** | 298lb ft at 5500rpm |
| **Power to weight** | 298bhp per tonne |
| | (293bhp per tonne) |
| **Emissions (CO$_2$)** | 307g/km |
| **Combined** | 22.1mpg |

# FEATURE

9 MAY 2007

Volume 252

No 6 | 5470

**ABOVE** Subtle it ain't: despite devastating peformance, the RS's colour was one of the biggest obstacles to its acceptance as a usable road car. Regular shades cost £3500.

**ABOVE RIGHT**
Interior can contain plenty of creature comforts; engine produces same power as in GT3, but lighter flywheel improves response.

difference is at the rear axle. The standard 997 has done more to eradicate inherent 911 handling flaws than most modern Porsches, but the RS goes further.

Mid-corner, the standard GT3 still takes the odd squirm over bumps and camber changes – never enough to unsettle it on the road, but more than enough to remind drivers where the centre of mass lies. The RS does none of this. You turn, you add throttle and it scoots through, free from shimmy.

But if extra track width brings added stability, it also consumes road space. The sheer girth of this car's backside is a problem on B-roads. I currently own a 993 RS and it feels like a scale model of this version. For me, on-road 911 performance has always been defined by its net accessibility; not only were the cars fast on paper, but they could also translate those numbers into real-world performance through traction and exterior dimensions. The 997 GT3 RS goes like a supercar but also leaves its driver worried by a potential HGV side-swiping in the way something broad and Italian does.

I have no answer to the gearing. We're talking about a road car that will hit 100mph around the mid-nine-second mark, despite long intermediate ratios. If there was any suspicion that those ratios

were in any way hampering the car's straight-line potential, then I would second a call for different gear clusters, but the simple fact is this car's powertrain comes as close to perfection as anything on sale.

It may not claim any numerical advantage over the standard GT3 (the same 409bhp at 7600rpm and 298lb ft of torque at 5500rpm) but the single-mass flywheel allows it to spin faster and respond more urgently. It will pull from 1700rpm, begins to stroll at 3500rpm and from then on provides so much thrust and volume – especially with the 'Sport' button switched on to release more noise and a smidge more torque – that you wonder why anyone would want to own a different supercar.

And there are still subtleties to this car's lower-speed performance that most people would never credit. It is comfortable, and the damping in the softer of the two modes leaves occupants' heads bobbing about no more severely than they would in a standard Carrera. This is helped by the optional ceramic brakes, which save an astonishing 22kg from the car's unsprung mass.

You can specify it with sat-nav and a telephone, both of which will be seen as heresy by the old guard, but given that they add a huge 250g to the overall weight I see no reason why they shouldn't be available.

This is a car with a quite specific role. It is a car optimised on the circuit – hence the standard Michelin Cup rubber – but also tuned to work on the street. It is a car to drive in comfort to European track events, lap heavily for a few days, then return similarly cosseted afterwards.

You might think that only a committed lunatic would use it every day, but after scratching around for a few days trying to uncover barriers between it and daily driving, the best I could find was a problem dealing with the bright paint job. The RS colour schemes are garish, but for £3500 Porsche will paint it in any one of its regular 911 colours. How generous.

Restraint is the key to enjoying the RS. Time and self-preservation quickly teach you that only a small percentage of its performance is available for road use, and that's why it is imperative that every owner makes several diary commitments for track days this year. It's only then, as a track-day genius that happens to be pretty special on the road too, that the RS not only makes sense but also ceases to be a machine whose third-gear performance seems wildly out of kilter with the modern world. Deploy its abilities on a circuit and you will then be purged of the need to expose your licence on the public highway. You will be set free to acknowledge that Porsche finally has a decent sat-nav system in its cars, that the optional digital hi-fi pack brings decent sounds and that the front boot will accommodate four swollen Waitrose bags. Therein lies the true brilliance of the 997 RS. Making a fast track car is no great achievement; making one that works at low speed, on the road, is borderline alchemy.

It isn't perfect: the gearshift is too abrupt and short, and while the front splitter might provide some front axle downforce at obscure points on the Nordschleife, it also ploughed much of Gloucestershire's minor roads. And then there's the price: as a road car the base GT3 is undoubtedly better value and many people will prefer the subtler styling and narrower hips.

The lightweight claims are being pushed to the limits of credibility, too. Despite various chunks of carbonfibre and a Perspex rear screen, this car is only a small child lighter than the standard version. All of the airbags have to remain, and they're heavy.

However, be in no doubt that this is some of Porsche's best work to date: directly related to a racing car, staggering on the circuit, but also quite at home on the road. So long as you take it easy in third gear.

# SPECIFICATIONS 911 GT3 RS

## DIMENSIONS

| | |
|---|---|
| Length | 4460mm (4445mm) |
| Width | 1852mm (1808mm) |
| Height | 1280mm |
| Wheelbase | 2880mm (2360mm) |
| Front track | 1497mm |
| Rear track | 1558mm (1524mm) |
| Weight/as tested | 1375kg (1395kg) |
| Fuel tank | 90 litres |
| Boot | 105 litres |

## ENGINE

| | |
|---|---|
| Layout | Flat 6 cyls, 3600cc |
| Max power | 409bhp at 7600rpm |
| Max torque | 298lb ft at 5500rpm |
| Specific output | 113.6bhp per litre |
| Power to weight | 298bhp per tonne (293bhp per tonne) |
| Installation | Longitudinal, rear, rwd |
| Bore/stroke | 100.0/76.4m |
| Compression ratio | 12.0:1 |

## GEARBOX

Type 6-speed manual
Final drive ratio 3.44:1

| Ratios | 1st 3.82 | 2nd 2.26 |
|---|---|---|
| | 3rd 1.64 | 4th 1.29 |
| | 5th 10.6 | 6th 0.92 |

## SUSPENSION

**Front** MacPherson struts, coil springs, anti-roll bar
**Rear** Multi-link, coil springs, anti-roll bar

## BRAKES

**Front** 350mm ventilated discs
**Rear** 340mm ventilated discs
**Anti-lock** Standard

## WHEELS AND TYRES

**Size** 8.5Jx19in (f), 12Jx19in (r)
**Tyres** 235/35 ZR19 (f), 305/30 ZR19 (r)

Increased width is probably the RS's biggest flaw as an everyday road car.

# 911 TURBO CABRIO

**911 TURBO CABRIOLET** At £106,180, is Porsche's latest Turbo drop-top a worthy addition to the 200mph cabrio club, or does taking the roof off ruin it? We find out

Imagine the sort of noise that would result from pouring a sack of gravel into the intake of a jet engine and you've got a fairly good idea of the sort of aural assault the occupants of a 911 Turbo cabriolet will experience with the combination of roof down and full throttle.

It's not a particularly harmonic noise, but the startling sound of the full-taps induction roar is definitely the defining characteristic of this car.

More so because in other regards it's a bit of a 473bhp pussycat, about the most effortless way yet of combining very rapid progress with serious sunburn.

By sticking with a fabric hood, the Turbo cabrio weighs just 70kg more than its coupé equivalent. Not the sort of difference to stand in the way of the twin-turbocharged 3.6-litre motor's fat power and torque curves; an overboost function allows the normal peak of 457lb ft to swell to 501lb ft for brief periods.

The net result is one of the quickest open-top cars in the world, and probably the only one of the near-200mph club that anyone other than a multi-millionaire could feasibly run on an everyday basis. Porsche's claimed 4.0sec 0-62mph time (for the manual version) is just 0.1sec behind the coupé's time for the same benchmark.

## SO GOOD

- Massive performance, especially the deep-lunged grunt of the mid-range.
- Very easy to drive quickly – and impressively refined at speed with roof down.
- Cheaper to buy and run than its obvious rivals.

## NO GOOD

- Engine roar takes some getting used to.
- Fiddly switches are a pain to use when trying to lower the rear side windows.

# FIRST DRIVE

## 27 JUNE 2007

Volume 252

No 13 | 5747

Optional contrasting stitching won't be for most; more sombre finishes are available.

## NEW TECH – ACTIVE AERODYNAMICS

High-performance cabriolets present engineers with all kinds of aerodynamic problems, the biggest being that of making sure the car works equally well with the roof up or down.

The 911 Turbo cabriolet's active rear wing moves up 65mm at speeds above 75mph (30mm more than in the coupé), allowing it to work in clearer airflow. The net result is 27kg of downforce on the rear axle at the official 192mph top speed. Porsche claims this aero masterstroke makes the 997 the only production cabrio in the world with genuine downforce (rather than just a reduction in lift) at the rear.

The cabriolet has been Turbo'd with the addition of the same 19-inch alloys and active rear spoiler as the coupé, the wing looking a bit stuck on and (whisper it) aftermarket when the top is down. Fortunately it serves more than aesthetic purposes, delivering genuine aero downforce at speed.

Velocity, of course, is something the Turbo cabrio delivers with almost effortless disdain. Even with 320km/h (199mph) showing on a quiet stretch of autobahn it felt like there was more to come. But more impressive is the sort of refinement the Turbo delivers for roof-down cruising around the 90-100mph mark; the pop-up aero screen keeps the cabin calm enough to allow conversation in a normal voice.

The rest of the dynamic package is equally impressive. The Turbo's firmer suspension brings out very occasional evidence of less-than-absolute body rigidity, usually manifested as steering column vibration. But otherwise it drives with the same taut assurance as the coupé, even with the electronically controlled dampers in their firmest position. The four-wheel drive system delivers near-perfect traction.

# FACTFILE

| | |
|---|---|
| **Model** | 911 Turbo Cabriolet |
| **Price** | £106,180 |
| **On sale** | Now |
| **Top speed** | 193mph |
| **0–62mph** | 4.0sec |
| **Economy** | 21.9mpg |
| **CO$_2$** | 309g/km |
| **Kerb weight** | 1655kg |
| **Engine** | Flat six, 3600cc, twin turbo |
| **Installation** | Rear, longitudinal, 4wd |
| **Power** | 473bhp at 6,000rpm |
| **Torque** | 457lb ft at 1850rpm |
| **Gearbox** | 6-spd manual |
| **Fuel tank** | 67 litres |
| **Boot** | 105 litres |
| **Wheels** | 8.5J x 19in (f), 11J x 19in (r) |
| **Tyres** | 235/35 ZR19 (f), 305/30 ZR20 (r) |

The Turbo cabrio's £106,180 price marks a new high for the 997, but the £8340 supplement is pretty reasonable by the standards of such things. And it's substantially cheaper than the Lamborghini Gallardo Spyder, Ferrari F430 Spider and Bentley GTC, while being a genuine alternative to any of them.

**ABOVE** 911 is a worthy addition to 200mph cabrio club.

## FIRST VERDICT ★★★★☆

**The 997 Turbo's powertrain has created one of the fastest cabriolets in the world**

473bhp flat six delivers jaw-dropping performance for any car, let alone a drop-top. Shame it doesn't sound better.

# WHAT A WAY TO GO

**911 GT2** Supercars will have to change, so the Ferrari 430 Scuderia and Porsche 911 GT2 could be the best and last of the breed. Chris Harris drives Porsche's loveable thug

And so there I was, all ready to admonish the new GT2 for having the same inconveniently short gear ratios as the Turbo. We drove the car away from the factory gates at 9.30am and by 9.45am I was whingeing about gear ratios. Why did the GT2 need to have such short legs? Why had Porsche chosen to keep the same gear set for a car that weighs 100kg less and has an extra 50bhp? Under full acceleration, the need to change gear so frequently was irritating: I just couldn't see why the GT3's longer intermediate ratios hadn't been used.

Then the speedometer revealed some worrying information. A quick glance down as a yellow triangle glowed to suggest (another) gearchange indicated that we were travelling at 112mph. Being socially deficient, I knew that a Turbo would run to only 104mph in third gear and therefore had cause to rescind the objection.

You see, the GT2 is silly fast. Its overall gearing *is* longer than the Turbo's and yet you seem to have to chuck even more gears at it than you do the regular turbocharged Porsche. Then again, this isn't an ordinary car. The GT2 is living proof of just how far the fast car business has progressed even in the past few years. The £131,070 Porsche wants for one may seem silly in light of the mechanically similar £99,920 Turbo, but then that doesn't take into account the fact that in straight-line performance and most other conventional measures of performance, the new GT2 is as fast as a Carrera GT. And that was well over £300k.

The GT2 formula is much like the BMW M3 formula, in that both were homologation exercises that proved successful enough to persuade their makers to launch subsequent versions as series production cars. The 1995 993 GT2 remains one of the most extraordinary road cars ever built, but the 996 that followed five years later was roundly kicked for being too similar to the regular Turbo, lacking that motorsport sparkle and being in possession of more understeer than a lawn tractor. This car needs to right those wrongs, accepting that most of the handling

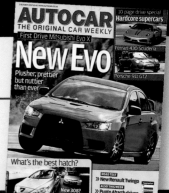

# FEATURE

## 3 OCTOBER 2007

Volume 254

No 1 | 5761

gripes of the 996 were fixable with some simple geometry alterations and decent rubber.

The 997 GT2 is based on the Turbo. It shares the same bodyshell and the 3600cc motor has identical internals. But thereafter this car is quite different. In the GT2 tradition, it is rear-wheel drive with a limited-slip differential. But to extract the extra 50bhp it produces over the Turbo (now 523bhp at 6500rpm), Porsche concentrated on two specific areas: the turbochargers themselves and the intake manifold. Those rear air intakes provide a ram air effect to feed a pair of uprated variable-vane blowers with larger compressor wheels and flow-optimised turbines. Boost has been raised to 1.4bar, 0.4bar more than the standard car.

Peak torque is now a hedge-threatening 501lb ft, but clever types will already have noticed that a Turbo fitted with the Sport Chrono pack offers the same thump by way of its overboost facility. Fear not, future GT2 owners. In the Turbo

that figure is available only in short bursts; in the GT2 it is a permanent, threatening presence from 2200–4500rpm. Ouch. Porsche is at pains to describe the technology that has allowed it to feed cooler air into the intake system of the GT2, but we haven't the time here. It effectively uses expanding rather than compressed air to create a more efficient burn – although the only burn most drivers will recognise is that of melted tyre and cindered brake (380mm ceramics up front and 350mm at the back, now you ask). The performance figures are startling: 0–60mph in 3.7sec, 0–100mph in 7.4sec and 204mph, given enough space.

This isn't a limited-edition Porsche, but then neither is it a regular series production car. It was developed by the motorsport department, the same bunch that gave us the stunning GT3. The chassis is a combination of Turbo and GT3 with some specific modifications. Spring and damper rates are bespoke because it weighs a full 100kg less than the Turbo by ditching the

## 'THERE WILL BE THOSE WHO WANT IT TO PRODUCE MORE THAN 530BHP, BUT I WOULDN'T BE AMONG THEM'

**ABOVE** Inevitable turbo lag means you have to plan ahead for corners.

**LEFT** Not just a great track weapon; rival Ferrari 430 Scuderia is a gem on the road too.

front drivetrain and using carbon buckets and ceramic brakes. The rear axle subframe is aluminium instead of the Turbo's steel item and the rear suspension is rose-jointed. This car shares the large amount of suspension adjustment available on the GT3 and adds moveable spring plates. So what we're saying is that if you don't like it out of the box, there's a strong chance you'll be able to tweak it to suit.

And there will doubtless be those who want it to produce more than the 530bhp it does as standard, but I wouldn't be among them. The 997 GT2 is now fast enough to warrant the fitment of some kind of DSG 'box or F1-style transmission; it consumes gears like Bill Werbeniuk did lager.

Noise isn't its strong point. The turbos deny it any sharp induction noises, although the titanium exhausts make up for this. It's clear that Porsche has tried as much as possible to make this car a turbocharged version of the GT3, but therein lie a couple of problems. The first is that regardless of how much Porsche has done to eradicate turbo lag – and the GT2 is now so responsive that it doesn't really feel turbocharged – there's still a slight pause between throttle action and acceleration. Which means that pointing it at an apex is a less accurate exercise than it

## A DYING BREED?

The world is unlikely to see another GT2 in five years' time. The pace of environmental politics makes even this crazed 911's 0–100mph time of 7.4sec seem quite ordinary.

The only way for vehicles like the Porsche and new 430 Scuderia to survive is by forging a new direction formed around low emissions – in particular, low mass and cleaner engines. Both cars make concessions to overall mass in being lighter than the cars on which they are based, but then in their current forms, both produce $CO_2$ in quantities that will doubtless soon be unacceptable.

So this is a celebration of what the super-sports car has become in late 2007: outrageously fast and supremely competent. But it could also become an epitaph for a way of making high-performance cars that will soon end.

# THE LIGHTER SIDE OF LIFE

| MAKE | FERRARI | PORSCHE |
|---|---|---|
| **Model** | **430 SCUDERIA** | **911 GT2** |
| Price in UK | £172,500 | £131,070 |
| 0–60mph | 3.6sec | 3.7sec |
| Top speed | 198mph | 204mph |
| Power | 503bhp at 8500rpm | 523bhp at 6500rpm |
| Torque | 347lb ft at 5250rpm | 502lb ft at 2200rpm |
| Power to weight | 373bhp per tonne | 363bhp per tonne |
| Torque to weight | 256lb ft per tonne | 349lb ft per tonne |
| Emissions ($CO_2$) | 360g/km | 306g/km |
| | | |
| Economy | 18.0mpg (combined) | 22.6mpg (combined) |
| Range | 376 miles | 333 miles |
| | | |
| Length | 4512mm | 4450mm |
| Width | 1923mm | 1852mm |
| Height | 1199mm | 1300mm |
| Wheelbase | 2600mm | 2350mm |
| Kerb weight | 1350kg | 1440kg |
| Fuel tank | 95 litres | 67 litres |
| Boot (max) | 250 litres | 105 litres |
| | | |
| Engine layout | V8, 4308cc, petrol | Flat six, 3600cc, turbo, petrol |
| Installation | Mid, longitudinal, rwd | Rear, longitudinal, rwd |
| Specific output | 117bhp per litre | 145bhp per litre |
| Compression ratio | 11.88:1 | 9.0:1 |
| Gearbox | 6-speed sequential manual | 6-speed manual |
| | | |
| Front suspension | Double wishbones, coil springs, adjustable dampers, anti-roll bar | MacPherson struts, coil springs, anti-roll bar |
| Rear suspension | Double wishbones, coil springs, adjustable dampers, anti-roll bar | Multi-link, coil springs, anti-roll bar |
| Brakes | Carbon ceramic, 398mm ventilated discs (f), 350mm ventilated discs (r) | Carbon ceramic, 380mm ventilated discs (f), 350mm ventilated discs (r) |
| Wheels | 19in magnesium alloy | 19in magnesium alloy |
| Tyres | 235/35 R19 (f), 285/35 R19 (r) | 235/35 ZR19 (f), 325/30 ZR19 (r) |

It costs £30k more than a Turbo. Is it worth it? In many ways, yes.

is in a normally aspirated car. You have to anticipate, hang the throttle slightly and make sure everything's in order before opening the taps.

This is the first GT2 to have any form of electronic traction or stability device, and the car's appeal will be all the broader because of it. You can drive it hard on damp surfaces, relying on subtle intervention to keep it pointing where you intended. It also has launch control, which is less subtle but will provide access to that 3.7sec sprint whenever necessary.

Traction in the dry is excellent – although it's still possible to fizzle the 325-section rear tyres on bone-dry asphalt – and the bespoke Michelin Pilot Sport Cups are miles better than the ropey old Pilots supplied with the 996 version. The new carbon buckets, which fold forwards to allow luggage to sit behind the seats, are excellent too.

On most levels the 997 GT2 is a resounding success: faster, more sorted and far more usable than the previous version. But despite its supreme speed, or perhaps because of it, it remains less accessible than the cheaper GT3 – more difficult to build a bond with, more remote, because extracting what it has to offer

requires more skill and more space.

For some, the thrust will be addictive, and we'll need to try one on a circuit to form a definitive opinion; test driver Walter Röhrl has already clocked 7min 32sec at the 'Ring. And even though the price looks steep, it's still £40k less than a 430 Scuderia, and likely to be a rarer sight on British roads.

**OPPOSITE** Familiar 911 interior gets a pair of carbon bucket seats; carbon, carbon everywhere in Ferrari and… oh dear, they forgot the carpet.

## AUTOCAR VERDICT

Forza Scuderia. There can be no doubt that of these two new arrivals, it's the Ferrari that has you reaching more frequently for hyperbole. That's as much to do with the sheer enthusiasm it draws from any driver as the fact that I think it's the best road car the company currently sells. The GT2 is blunter, less affable – more a brooding presence that occasionally shocks you with bouts of barely contained velocity.

The Scuderia also sits more easily with that future framework. It is lighter and it has a transmission that the GT2 would certainly benefit from.

For driver enjoyment, a GT3 RS does a better job than the GT2 because there are so few roads on which it is possible to use the performance, and when you do find a circuit the chances are the car will still feel too quick. Think of it as a loveable thug. Whereas the Ferrari is plain wonderful.